META~PHYSICALL Y SPEAKING

D1081928

By: William douglas owens jr.

BOOK 1

~ KNOW THY SELF ~

Copyright © 2020
Cover Designed By: Dakiah Atiya ALi
Editing & Formatting By: Quadama Fareed Azzam ALi
ISBN# 978-1-63625-120-2

DEDICATION

I, with much honor and respect, do dedicate this book to my father & mother, The Reverend William Douglas Owens Sr. & Cora Lee Golden-Perry-Owens. And to just a few of the men & women that made far more than just a ripple in my life; Odel Fisher, Shelby Leon Porter, Conrad McKnight, Phyllis Gray, Judy Hemphill, LaLee, Adrienne Turner, Carole D. Rose, my twin flame, and Cynthia Jeweline Johnson, my Soul-Mate, and the re-incarnation of Mama Cora.

CONTENTS

MISSIVES   PAGES

INTRODUCTION...14

1 18
   SURRENDER & ACCEPTANCE OF… 18

2 20
   AS A WOMB-MAN THINKETH! 20

3 24
   "UNCONDITIONAL LOVE" 24

4 26
   THE FREQUENCY OF UNCONDITIONAL LOVE.....................26

5 28
   "FEAR & UNCONDITIONAL LOVE" 28

6 30
   RECALIBRATE YOUR LIFE 30

7 32
   EVIL IS A SUBJECTIVE EXPERIENCE! 32

8 35
   HOW & WHY DUALITY EXIST...35

9 37
   YOU ARE ALL DIVINE TRANSCENDENT BEINGS 37

10 48
   THE RISKS OF LIFE! 48

11 49
   THE PERVERSION OF IMAGERY! 49

12 51
   RELIGION?..51

13 53
   R U THE CREATOR OF YOUR REALITY OR A VICTIM IN IT....53

14 55
   IT IS JUST A 'GAME' 55

15 58
   R WE ALONE? 58

16 60
   CREATOR & CREATION 60

17 62
   'MY' SPIRIT' 62

18 64
   HINDRANCES TO AWAKENING 64

19 66
   "EXISTENCE" 66

20 68
   DOES NON-EXISTENCE EXIST! 68

21 70
   NON – EXISTENCE 70

22 72
   SO! YOU WANT TO IMPROVE YOUR LIFE 72

23 76
   THE UNIVERSAL LAW OF ALLOWING 76

24 82
   CREATION VS CREATOR 82

25 84
   FORGIVENESS & UNCONDITIONAL LOVE 84

26 86
   WHAT IF? 86

27 90
   STAYING FOCUSED AS A MULTI-DIMENSIONAL BEING 90

28 92
   LIFE IS JUST A RIDE! 92

29 94
   PART 1, LIFE IS JUST A RIDE 94

30 97
   PART 2, LIFE IS JUST A RIDE 97

31 100
   SO YOU THINK YOU UNDERSTAND WHAT IS TRUTH 100

32 102
   WHAT ARE YOU FOCUSING ON?.................................102

33 104
   THE 'SPELLING' OF WORDS AND DEFINITIONS! 104

34 106
   THE REFLECTIONS OF LIFE.....................................106

35 108
   THE ESOTERIC NATURE OF META-PHYSICAL THOUGHT...108

36 110
   MOST PEOPLE HAVE NEVER QUESTIONED! 110

37 112
   U R A UNIQUE EXPRESSION OF 'ALL THAT IS' 112

38 113
   NATURAL SELF HYPNOSIS 113

39 115
   THE PERVERSION OF IMAGERY 115

40 117
   NEVER DISCREDIT, REGRET, NOR INVALIDATE 117

41 119
   EVERY MOMENT...119

42 121
   SYNCHRONICITY 121

43 123
   STOP LOOKING BACK...123

44 125
   AT THE BASIS OF: IS THE EGO… 125

45 128
   THERE IS ONLY ONE SOURCE OF FLOWING ENERGY 128

46 130
   IT REALLY DOESN'T MATTER 130

47 132
   EVERYTHING IS SACRED & VALID 132

48 134
   NO THING CREATED – EXIST 134

49 137
   ENERGY FLOW 'LIFE SOURCE' 137

50 141
   BETTER OR WORST BELIEF SYSTEMS 141

51 143
   PREFERENTIAL CONTRADICTION 143

52 146
   THE VARIABILITY OF FREQUENCY 146

53 148
   GAME 148

54 151
   GAME! (POEM) 151

55 153
   ISN'T YOUR GOD, GOD? 153

56 154
   THE ESSENCE OF PEACE 154

57 156
   A CREATOR NEVER HAS VICTORY 156

58 158
   YOUR MOTIVATIONAL MECHANISM 158

59 160
   ULTIMATE SELF-EMPOWERMENT! 160

60 165
   ALL EXPERIENCES ARE VALID 165

61 168
   THAT PERSON USE TO BE ME… 168

62 170
   LIFE HAS NO INNATE MEANING, ...170

63 172
   I CREATE MY REALITY 172

64 174
   YOUR PERSONAL REALITY 174

65 179
   FEAR, HATE & LOVE ARE ALL THE SAME ENERGY 179

66 181
   ENERGY ALIGNMENT 181

67 182
   SEE A SERMON 182

68 184
   DIMENSIONAL VESICA PISCIS 184

69 186
   ENERGY WAS CREATED 186

70 188
   THERE ARE NO ACCIDENTS 188

71 190
   THE CORE OF EVERY THING 190

72 192
   SELF-RESPECT 192

73 194
   ALL THINGS ARE ALL OTHER THINGS!… 194

74 197
   'THE ONE' IS NOT SELF – AWARE! 197

75 199
   YOUR LIFE IS… SELF IMPOSED! 199

76 200
   EVERY WAKING MOMENT 200

77 202
   SEXUALLY TRANSMITTED DEMONS 202

78 206
   R U MORE CONCERNED WITH HAVING THAN BEING?........206

79 208
   YOUR THOUGHTS ARE NOT YOUR THOUGHTS!..................208

80 211
   WITH WHO, WHAT, WHEN, WHERE 211

81 213
   THIS IS NOT YOUR EXPERIENCE 213

82 214
   OMNISTANDING!...214

83 216
   HIGHER SELF! HUMAN BRAIN! HUMAN MIND! 216

84 220
   WHOSE THOUGHTS ARE YOU THINKING?..........................220

85 224
   WHAT IS AILING YOU? 224

86 227
   DIS-EASE!...227

87 229
   ASCENSION SYMPTOMS… 229

88 231
   WHEN LIFE NO LONGER REFLECTS.....................................231

89 235
   YES, I SAID 'NO'!...235

90 240
   WHATEVER YOU BELIEVE IS TRUE 240

91 242
   HEALING OR PREFERENTIAL SHIFTING...............................242

92 245
   SHOULD OF, COULD OF, WOULD OF!....................................245

93 247
   REGRETS OF LIFE..247

94 251
   KEYS TO GREATER CONSCIOUS AWARENESS 251

95 254
   GLOBAL EARTH VS. FLAT EARTH 254

96 256
   REALITIES... SUPERIMPOSED 256

97 260
   MENTAL BELIEF LENSES 260

98 263
   THE LAW OF ATTRACTION & MANIFESTATION 263

99 266
   SELF EMPOWERMENT! 266

100 271
   PAST – PRESENT – FUTURE 271

101 272
   DISCONNECT... DETACH... DISENTANGLE... 272

102 277
   ALLOW... PERMIT... ACCEPT... 277

103 280
   WHAT YOU BELIEVE, YOU FEEL 280

104 282
   A SINGLE REALITY 282

105 286
   U R CHANNELED BEINGS 286

106 293
   NEUTRINOS 293

107 296
   A WISE ADMONISHMENT ATTENTION! 296

108 299
   NOW IS THE TIME 299

109 302
   I COULD CARE LESS! 302

110 304
   NO SUBSTANCE 304

111 306
   NO THING IS REALLY SOME THING 306

112 310
   JUDGMENT! 310

113 314
   INFINITE THINKING 314

114 317
   VICTIMHOOD 317

115 319
   I AM RESPONSIBLE TO YOU 319

116 321
   LIFE IS A VERSION OF YOUR CREATED BELIEFS ... 321

117 323
   A GREATER OMNISTANDING OF LOVE 323

118 334
   EVERYTHING STAYS AS-IS 334

119 337
   THE DIVISIBILITY OF ONE'S PHOTON SELF 337

120 340
   TRANSCENDENCE OF DUALITY 340

121 349
   – DEFINITIONS – 349

122 352
   CONTROL YOUR ANGER 352

123 355
   LOOKING BACK 355

124 359
   INSTRUCTION MANUAL 359

125 361
   ABOUT THE AUTHOR 361

126 394
ABOUT THE AUTHOR'S FAMILY LIFE 394

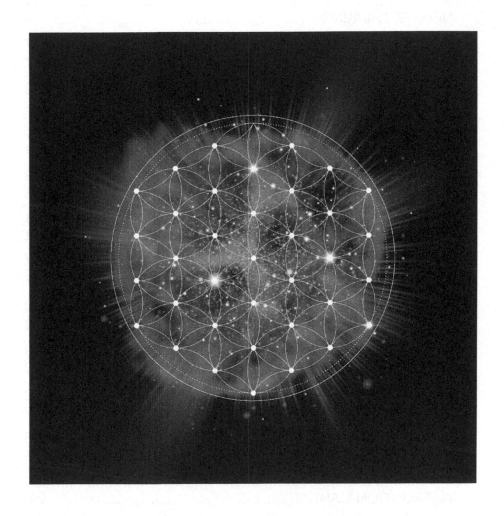

"What you say to yourself is one-hundred times more personally effective than anything that anyone could ever say to you, in your life!"

By: Dr. ALi

INTRODUCTION

Now, this is very, very important, so we need you to pay close attention. This book is channeled explicitly for the 'Awakened'! The consciously aware! This book is not religious material, nor is it for the religious-minded! Although you will find some scripture references included. It is not meant to be read straight through nor with casual intent. The purpose of this book is to help open your mind towards higher vibrational concepts; to act as a type of study guide or reference manual. The study guide itself is within the book for you to discover. Glance at the content and find the missive that particularly resonates with your vibration and present life experience. There you will find the appropriate information needed to assist you with your current moment. This book was written in a manner to help one while on their spiritual earth adventure. It covers fifth-dimensional principles that deal with most of the challenging situations you may come to experience while on your third-dimensional hero's journey. Meta-Physically Speaking, Book 1, will help raise your vibratory resonance by cognizing higher thought-provoking concepts.

The syllabus for this book is to find the sympathetic resonance with the seemingly impossible thoughts; Segregate and cognize the probable thoughts; Investigate the seemingly infinite but possible thoughts;

Then, whatever rational or reasonable thoughts remain, no matter how challengingly improbable, we will accept as our perspective! The thoughts in this book do not have to make third-dimensional sense! This thought, along with many other enlightening treasures you will find hidden, not deliberately, on these pages. Enclosed are essential keys! Thoughts that will help to free you from the mental prison of your mind. The views are deep, yes, but all you need is an earnest & sincere desire to discover them. And you will!

These missives were channeled mainly for the previously stated purpose. And maybe to give you a few laughs along the way. One missive may be studied for months, and still, there would be more depth of thought to discover, greater enlightenment to perceive, and an infinite amount of satisfaction of joy to gleam! This book is not meant to be politically correct in language format, so-called proper English, nor to meet your customary societal norm.

If you are looking for grammatical inconsistencies, you can bet they are here! You may also find a few small inaccurate wording or even odd and unusual sentencing phrases. Some thoughts may have been a little... 'Lost in translation,' because, on your level of limited verbal expression, there are no adequate words to express some higher dimensional concepts or ideals. If you focus on this book's correctness of print, you will miss its original beneficial intent!

Like we have previously stated, this book is not grammatically correct! It was not meant nor intended to be. Within these pages is a vast amount of profound knowledge which may offend many. Example: Jesus was an African Prophet. There is much here to help you strengthen your self-will, create greater self-empowerment, raise your frequency, and help hold your vibration at an even, balanced, consistent, and steady tone! Still, this spirit/mind/body complex did its best with what it had to work with. In this book, you will find some missives with only a title and a blank page. These pages are there for you to write your personal channeled missive. Do not be overly critical of what you write. Just let it flow and write the thoughts as they come into your mind. Remember, there is no right or wrong missive. You cannot make a mistake.

If you are reading this and do not believe that you have awakened and or are waking up! If you do not 'FEEL' a personal vibrational connection...Then please, once again, we express... DO NOT PURCHASE THIS BOOK! IT WAS NOT MEANT FOR YOU! This book is compiled of the missives Ephraim channeled to help William Douglas Owens jr., while on his spiritual journey! He was permitted to offer these same writings to you. They are not meant to persuade, convince, or prove that what has been stated is right or true! These writings are simply... 'A different perspective.'

Now, let's get the obvious stuff out of the way. Dr. ALi is not human. It's tough to get any more obvious than that. If I had to guess, I would say he is another version of 'YOU'? Alright, so far, so good! But if that is true, that would make him a part of your reality; another kind or expression of Prime Creator! Should I keep going? Yes, go ahead. I suppose the most obvious question is, 'How can I trust or believe what I am about to read in this book'? **BINGO!** It is a pickle, no doubt about it. The negative news is, there is no way for you to know whether this book will benefit you or not. So it is really all up to you. You just have to make up your own damn mind, whether to accept the missives you are soon to read in this book or reject them. **CANDY?**

Now, after purchasing this book and you cannot understand nor do not like this book, just remember one crucial thing; WE TOLD YOU NOT TO BUY IT! Are you listening to the words that are coming out of this book?

P.S. Well, my friend, it is my hope that you enjoyed this intro. Get ready! You are about to go down the 'Rabbit Hole'! Please remember, it is all just a Ride! Nothing more, and Nothing less! NAMASTE!

P.S. John 16:12
By: Dr. Quadama Fareed Azzam ALi

1
SURRENDER & ACCEPTANCE OF

Surrender and Acceptance of whatsoever are manifested in your now moment allow the powerful flow of Divine Love to handle any circumstance. You will be kept centered, aligned, and at perfect peace! You must be honest and sincere with yourself against every judgment, belief, and opinion. Immediately acknowledging and expelling any emotion, feeling, or thought that even appears out of harmony with your vibrational tone of 'Surrender & Acceptance! You must let go of all 'Negative Beliefs,' which create 'Negative Judgments' that create 'Negative Opinions' that create 'Guilt – Fear'! Which is the seemingly opposite of love.

Now by opposite, what we intend is the most diminished form of expression of love. Love naturally has no opposite. Why? The One is All, and The All is One! Every expression is of love! Remember, there is only one thing, and that is Love! It is logical to conclude that whatsoever it may be that you choose to believe will reveal a clear, harmonic, pure, or deformed, distorted, polluted concept of Love. You are free to explore all possibilities.

It is through your eyes or lenses of 'Belief' that you conceive, create everything! You are neither Right nor Wrong as you create! It is all a spiritual experience.

And whatsoever you choose to believe; the universe will create a 'Self-Perpetuating,' 'Self-Sustaining' system of evidence to validate and support that belief. Therefore, everyone's chosen belief holds validity! All possess the cosmic freedom to believe as they freely choose! This is why one should never argue.

So then, choose your beliefs wisely. Your life will reflect the very essence of that choice, and you will live that experience. What you put out is what you get back.

Of course, this is only my perspective: Nothing more and nothing less!

06/12/2014
By: Dr. ALi

2
AS A WOMB-MAN THINKETH!

You are the architect of your own life: it is yours to make or to mar. By the power of 'Belief,' you are Constructive or Destructive. Which are you? The power of belief/thought is a spiritual power. It is the most incredible power that womb-man has at their disposal. The world today is in its present state only as a result of womb-man's collective thinking. Each nation is in its current state of evolvement, enjoying peace and prosperity or trouble and poverty; fellowship and unity or murder and anarchy; merely as a result of its thinking as a nation. Each individual is who they are, and their life is what it is, and their circumstances what they are, only by the results of their thoughts/beliefs. What one thinks, they become; what one thinks is the mainspring of all their beliefs and becomes the reason for all of their actions. What an individual believes they attract to themselves circumstances and the environment they experience. What one believes determines what type of friends and companions will gather around them. What one believes decides whether they shall be happy or miserable, successful or unsuccessful, healthy or unhealthy, prosperous or poverty-stricken, hated, or loved. What we come to believe has and will always attract those things to us.

Your life is evidence of your prior beliefs. What one believes either builds up your character or tears it down. What one believes can overcome fate and strengthen your beliefs. It can align one with a glorious destiny, or make them an outcast and a wanderer in desert places. Indeed, there is no limit to the power of 'Belief' because it is a spiritual, divine & immeasurable power. It is the power that distinguishes humans from the brute; it is the power by which one can mount up with its source. It is the power by which can make the unsuccessful successful in the battle of life. It is the power by which can make the loftiest achievement possible. It is the power by which difficulties can be overcome, disadvantages become simple challenges, and a life of disappointments become opportunitles.

By thought/belief, you either bless or curse yourself. By thought/belief, you bring into your life success or failure, health or disease, happiness or unhappiness, poverty, or prosperity. A thought/belief of failure tends to produce failure. A thought/belief of disease tends to produce disease, and so on. There is no (God) that punishes you *unless you choose to believe this*. You punish yourself, or rather your thoughts/beliefs of evil punish you. It is all in your consciousness and character of thoughts/beliefs.

Whatever there is in your life of disharmony, lack, sickness or unhappiness, is the result of your out of alignment, out of frequency, out of tune, out of harmonious thoughts/beliefs with the Divine Intelligent Source of Power, 'Eternal,' 'ALL THAT IS,' "The One – Source Energy,"

You live in an orderly Universe, but you do not react harmoniously to your environment; you are not in correspondence with the hidden laws and order around you. The universe doesn't need to be altered; what is needed is for your consciousness to evolve. Within your thoughts lay the cause of the disorder in your reality. You each live in a little world of your creation; therefore, the disorder and trouble that afflicts you or the lack that restricts your life can never be overcome, save by a change of mind, a habit of thought/belief, and mental attitude. All change comes from within.

The fact remains that believing in terms of success and achievement, at the same time maintaining a consciousness of abundance and prosperity, tends to attract these things to you. The mind is creative to a degree undreamed of by most people, and your beliefs attract things to you after their kind. Opportunities for achievement and more abundant circumstances, on the one hand, or failure and lack, disappointment, and discouragement on the other.

Your outward reality is nothing more than a reflection of your individual inward 'BELIEFS.' According to your consciousness, you 'people' your world around you with hate, discord or love, and harmony.

Over time, your life tends to express the type of thoughts habitually dwelt upon. Your life is filled with evil or good to the extent that you fail or succeed in harmonizing with Divine Order, which is the only true 'ISNESS'.

By changing your 'Beliefs' and mental attitude, you will "reverse the lever" and come into harmony with the One Divine Universal Consciousness. And by doing so, success is liable to become your master and you, its slave. Therefore, it is crucial that you choose the highest form of success that you can. When this is accomplished, your life will blossom like the rose, shine like a full moon and flow like the mighty stream. "You shall be led forth with peace; the mountains and the hills shall break before you into singing, and all the trees of the field shall clap their hands. " Selah!

02/24/2014
By: Dr. Ali

3
"UNCONDITIONAL LOVE"

1. Unconditional Love does not punish!

2. Unconditional Love does not seek revenge!

3. Unconditional Love does not test, try, or tempt!

4. Unconditional Love does not destroy, kill, or take life!

5. Unconditional Love cannot be provoked, angered, or hurt!

6. Unconditional Love does not argue, fuss, fight, cast blame, or hate!

7. Unconditional Love does not want, require, need, or desire 'worship'!

8. Unconditional Love does not require wages or payment for anything!

9. Unconditional Love does not express sympathy, sadness, sorrow, pity, regret, or pain!

10. Unconditional Love does not command, demand, force, impede, or intrude!

11. Unconditional Love does not show Favoritism, is not bias nor views any Person, Place, or thing before or after another!

12. Unconditional Love – Love's you so unconditionally that – you are allowed to believe that Unconditional Love does NOT love you unconditionally!

13. Unconditional Love will even allow anyone to believe that which Unconditional Love is NOT!

14. Unconditional Love is 'UNCONDITIONAL'; and the essence of... 'ALL that IS'!

Nothing more, nothing less!

12/05/2012
By: Dr. Ali

4
THE FREQUENCY OF UNCONDITIONAL LOVE

Everything, all things vibrate! Nothing can exist without vibrating or possessing a frequency! Nothing does not vibrate. This is why nothing does not exist. That is what nothing is, a lack of something, a lack of vibration.

Unconditional Love is the highest vibrational frequency tone! Unconditional Love does not ever change its state of being by lowering its vibrational tone! All existence exists because of this source of energy; generated by this state of being. Did you get that? Source is not energy! Source is that which gives energy its power! Unconditional Love will give of itself for an eternity and never lose or become depleted in the least minuscule degree! PERIOD!! It never needs RE-vitalizing, RE-plenishing, RE-generating, or Rest! Why? Because Unconditional Love is a self-perpetuating source! Always expanding - Forever growing - Eternally evolving - Yet Never expanding - Never growing - Eternally the same - Why? Because it is already... 'ALL THAT IS'! Now wrap your mind around that!

Sympathy, Sorrow, Sadness, Pity, Regret, or Pain of any type are expressions of a state of being that is out of alignment, balance, focus, or out of being a perfectly matched frequency with Unconditional Love! To believe that such a state is normal, natural or human, and anyone who never expresses any one of those states is just cold-hearted Beings, are still thinking behind the veil of an illusional 3rd dimensional, holographic duality. This is Unconditional Love experiencing itself in all of the ways that it can, through you, me, and all other things. Only as one begins to Awaken out of this mysterious illusional 3rd dimensional, holographic duality, will one become more consciously aware that it is all only an elaborate dream!

To express Compassion or Empathy is a projection of Caring or Concern in order to grasp a better, clearer, or deeper Understanding without matching or lowering one's vibration to that of sorrow. This process is natural, this is normal, this is Unconditional Love! Did you get that? If not, it is Alright.

It only means that there is more for you to experience in 3D.

Of course, this is only my perspective; Nothing more and nothing less!

12/05/2012
By: Dr. Ali

5
"FEAR & UNCONDITIONAL LOVE"

1. Fear will punish!
   Unconditional Love, **Omnistand**!

2. Fear seeks revenge!
   Unconditional Love **Forgives**!

3. Fear will test, try, and tempt!
   Unconditional Love is **Omniscient**!

4. Fear will argue, fuss, fight, cast blame, and hate!
   Unconditional Love **agrees with your perspective**!

5. Fear needs, wants, requires, desires, and demands worship! Unconditional Love is **'UNCONDITIONAL'**!

6. Fear requires payment or wages for acts of violations! Unconditional Love is once again **'UNCONDITIONAL'**!

7. Fear can be disturbed, irritated, provoked, invoke jealousy, angered, thus be hurt! Unconditional Love is **Omnipotent**!

8. Fear will aggravate, segregate, compartmentalize, discriminate, desecrate, annihilate! Unconditional Love **Unifies, Organizes, Creates**!

9. Fear deceives with expressions of sympathy, sadness, sorrow, and pity!
Unconditional love expresses **Care, Compassion** and **Empathy**!

10. Fear impedes, intrudes, commands, demands, and forces! Unconditional Love allows **Freedom of Choice**, self-will, without reprisal!

11. Unconditional Love, love's you so unconditionally that you are '**ALLOWED** to believe that Unconditional Love does 'NOT'... love you unconditionally!

12. Unconditional Love is so unconditional in its loving that everyone is allowed to believe anything about Unconditional Love which Unconditional Love is NOT!

13. Unconditional Love is '**UNCONDITIONAL**'; the essence of '**ALL that IS**'!

Nothing more, nothing less!

12/31/2016
By: Dr. Ali

6
RECALIBRATE YOUR LIFE
"BY KNOWING WHAT YOU BELIEVE & BELIEVING WHAT YOU KNOW"

1. You are always supported unconditionally by creation in whatsoever way **you choose to believe!**

2. You are naturally and totally abundant in **all ways that you believe!**

3. Everything is fundamentally neutral. So choose carefully what you prefer to believe, you will automatically **create that immersion reality!**

4. Always act on your highest joy because creation will always support your actions!

5. Unwanted feelings and emotions always carry an underlying hidden belief! You must find out what that belief is and eliminate it!

6. Look through this illusion duality at what you think you see around you and use this illusional immersion duality to create your new intentional illusional duality!

7. All life is an expression or reflection of your deepest thoughts or beliefs.

Through personal intent or collective intent, your illusional immersion duality is created before you physically, as the life you live!

8. Every choice you make defines who you are and creates the illusional immersion duality you will experience!

9. Your creative abilities are not actuated by what you think! They are actuated by what you Believe!

NOTHING MORE & NOTHING LESS!

05/15/2014
By: Dr. Ali

7
Evil is a Subjective Experience!

All things, all reality, all experiences exist **within** the mind or consciousness of 'The One'; (God, Jehovah, Elohim, Yahweh, Allah, Brahma, etc.). It is **illusional** to think that your experiences are outside of 'The One' consciousness, which is **UNCONDITIONAL LOVE**. We have been deceived into believing that we are 'Separate' from 'The One'; that there is an 'Out there,' an 'Outside' of the 'One' consciousness, the **UNCONDITIONAL LOVE** of 'All THAT IS,' 'The One'; (God, Jehovah, Elohim, Yahweh, Allah, Brahma, etc. **This 'thought' of 'Separation,' when believed, is the illusion; it deceives you into thinking of yourself as a 'Victim'!** Love thy neighbor as thyself- *(Because they are 'thyself')* Matt.19:19; Take heed that you be not deceived. Luke 21:8; *Which deceiveth the whole world. Rev.12:9.* Deception originates by thought and seats itself within your consciousness. You must **remember** that all your experiences are by your created **choice**. We exist within an <u>attraction based</u> construct, all created for our learning or remembering 'Who U R', so learn or remember - Thy Self! Your thoughts are electrical energy in motion. These thoughts become your beliefs. They create feelings and emotions which becomes your state of being, your particular frequency! From this frequency your reality is created.

What you think most about becomes your belief and is materialized into form! As one thinketh in the heart, so are they. Prov.23:7 There is no 'Out there,' out there! There are no 'Victims'! There is truly nothing "Outside" of your 'Consciousness'! It is all like unto a dream. No-Thing can 'Separate' you from **UNCONDITIONAL LOVE** because that is 'All THAT IS'!

When you **choose** to accept that you are One with 'All THAT IS,' then something very interesting will happen. Something quite beautiful and magnificent will start to manifest in your reality (Life Experience).

Every moment of every hour of every day that you contemplate this thought, you will inevitably begin to realize & believe that your very 'Being' exists within the mind or consciousness of 'The One'; (God, Jehovah, Elohim, Yahweh, Allah, Brahma, etc. Because that is 'All THAT IS'! And the degree to which you come to know this thought to be true will be the degree to which you will no longer experience evil, which is, lack of choice. Evil does not exist within the consciousness of 'The One,' which is 'UNCONDITIONAL LOVE'!

You can only experience evil through an illusion. By believing in the conscious state of separation or duality, can you experience **the actions of another being evil or consider enacting evil upon another.**

Once you finally <u>remember</u> and accept your intrinsic Oneness to 'All THAT IS,' <u>*you will no longer experience evil being done to you*</u> unless you creatively choose/allow that experience within your reality construct.

This is only my perspective. Nothing more & nothing less!

4/07/2014
By Dr. Ali

8
HOW & WHY DUALITY EXIST

There are four main Universal Construct Laws/Thoughts. 1. You Exist! 2. Everything exists, Here & Now. 3. The ONE Is All and the all are ONE! 4. What you put out is what you get back! 5. Everything changes, except the first four Laws/Thoughts! Not to know any ONE of these Laws/Thoughts places you in a 'Duality Mind Set.'

"KNOW THYSELF." One most intricate ways to experience/know 'SELF'; is to forget that you are of **UNITY-CONSCIOUSNESS**, a **CREATOR** of your reality. For any Being, desiring to experience/know 'SELF,' on this mastery level of extreme challenge, an illusional 3D Duality type game was created, yet all the experiences had, are QUITE REAL. Many constructs hold this 3D duality game together. To experience this illusionary realm and for it to operate/function properly, all that is necessary is for any Being to **fall asleep**, disbelieve, or 'forget' any One of the Universal Laws/Thoughts and thus create within their **Consciousness** or **'Self'**...

NEW LAWS/THOUGHTS OR BELIEFS SUCH AS:

A. BELIEF IN **'SEPERATION'**

B. BELIEF IN AN **'ADVERSARY'**

C. BELIEF THAT YOU ARE A **'VICTIM'**

D. BELIEF THAT **'I AM RIGHT** & **YOU ARE WRONG'**

E. BELIEF IN AN – 'OUTSIDE OF SELF' – **'OUT THERE' – 'OVER THERE'**

So, there we have it; the fundamental essence of this illusional game in which we "live, move, and have our Being." You cannot believe that you need to be **saved from** outside of your - 'Self,' by an outside agency or 'person,' without first believing in a **'Separation,'** an **'Adversary,' 'Victimhood'** or having a... I am **'Right,' and** you are **'wrong'** attitude! The more you complain & fight against this reality *(What you resist-persist!)*, the deeper you dig yourself into it. It is a self-perpetuating system; an illusional duality world. *"What you put out is what you get back!"*

Of course, this is only my perspective! I do not claim to be right or wrong. Nothing more, Nothing less!

01/9/2014
Dr. Ali

9
You are all Divine Transcendent Beings (2012 Explained)

Once upon eternity now, **the Original Eternal Creator** 'IS'! As far as wide and as deep as thought could glide, Omniportance, Omniscience, and Omnipresence **AM**... During eternity now, **AM 'Thought'**! I extend my **consciousness** into multiple unified **sparks** of eternal **Co-Creator** expressions, each with their octave, all existing as **ONE. I AM** thought them in their dimensional universe for the prime purpose of exploration in Love, Joy, and compassion. And, so it is!

So, once upon eternity now, these multiple unified **sparks,** eternal **Co-Creator** expressions also thought to extend their **consciousness into** multiple unified **sparks** of eternal **Co-Creator** expressions; Each with their individual octave; all existing as **ONE**; They **too**, in their dimensional universe for the prime purpose of exploration in Love, Joy, and compassion. And, so it is!

And yet still again, this **thought** was repeated. Perhaps, yet again, and again, and again. **Over** one-hundred and forty-four thousand individual eternal **Co-Creator** expressions, all from the Original 'I AM,' all dancing to their octave, yet all vibrating harmoniously as ONE and all synchronized in frequency as ONE!

As Co-Creators, these Exalted Ones continued to **will** their thoughts into various creations. They created multi-verses, galaxies, and solar systems, and **they became** suns, stars, planets, and moons. They continued exploring and experimenting in ways never done before. Beautiful, glorious, and magnificent in variety and **all dancing to their** <u>octave</u>, **yet all were vibrating harmoniously as ONE and all synchronized in frequency as ONE!** Worlds are filled with firmaments and duality; "As above, so below." Atmospheres, magnetospheres, and stratospheres are also evolved: From the collective consciousness throughout the multi-verse, worlds <u>were seeded.</u> Gender is created; language and the **spoken word** instituted. One planet is named **Gaia, or you may know it as Earth**, and the expressions thereon are named **Hue-Mans. All dancing to their** <u>octave</u>, **yet all vibrating harmoniously as ONE and all synchronized in frequency as ONE!**

With rapturous ineffable excitement did the multi-verse extend and abound. Waters filled the planets; Grass, flowers, bushes, and trees after their kind; oceans, seas, lakes, and pond with **expressions** of swimmers, wigglers, and floaters after their kind; land creatures, walking, sliding, crawling, and creeping after their kind; winged fowls that fly or glide after their kind and all are rejoicing, **all dancing to their** <u>octave</u>, **yet all vibrating harmoniously as ONE and all synchronized in frequency as ONE!**

Creation continues, and **only** **Gaia** is bathed with **Free Will** and chosen as the metropolis of all that is. Free will being introduced made Earth the most unique and esoteric expression in all existence. Gaia received eternal **Co-Creator** expressions or now (Gods, Angels, Monads, Souls, or Light Beings) from all over the multi-verse. **Gods** met and shared experiences and ideas for even greater explorations in thought. It was decided that **Hue-man** would not **have** a Soul; Instead, Hue-man **will be a SOUL.** Now Hue-man is the most prestigious and most magnificent of all creation and **Gaia,** the most challenging and sort after of all mystery schools in existence. All is in a sacred harmony of ecstasy, and every new thought evolves and expands the collective. Earth stands now at the **leading edge of thought** in the multi-verse, all dancing to their octave, yet all vibrating harmoniously as ONE and all synchronized in frequency as ONE!

But! Some **Gods** began a thought process that caused a firmament to form as layers. Layers formed upon layers, which caused density or weight. A firmament of a thickness began to appear.

Since Gaia was a **free will region**, every **Light Being** is free to experiment at will. At some eternity now, the frequency of some of these Light Being's **lowered** ever so slightly, causing their dance to alter.

Their higher **'Co-Creator Self'** lovingly caution them about this lower thought they were expressing.

Solidification resulted, a mutation was brought about, and creation **devolved** into a world of **the third dimension** (3D). Again their higher **'Co-Creator Self'** lovingly attempted to caution them. At some moment in eternity now, **<u>'time'</u>** was created, which made it possible for the sensation of longevity. Again and again, their higher **'Co-Creator Self'** lovingly attempted to caution them. Hue-Man is also being manipulated into this **lower** vibrational frequency. These once glorious Light Beings have given up their High Vibration and accepted a lower, different tone and dance with a different frequency. Though still master geneticists, they placed meticulous and intricate attention into **their** now more controlled, enslaved **Hue-man Kind**. These Dark Cabals began to alter the most intricate of Hue-Man's **D**eoxyribo-**N**ucleic-**A**cid.

Hue-man's glorious crystalline body was changed into a dense carbon-based disgrace. Time and time and time again, their higher **'Co-Creator Self'** lovingly attempted to caution them**.**

Ever so, imperceptible did an unconscious change manifest into a mysterious <u>state</u> of mind, which we will refer to as **Deception or SLEEP**. Hue-man also was a part of this mysterious mental state. These **Demi-Gods** began spending more and more time, even merging and *mating* as they came to see the daughters of man as fair.

By now, these **Demi-Gods** state of deception was much deeper, and their reception of all thought was being processed through this mental state, which we call today the **'EGO.'** A **lower** energy grid was developed because, in their new world, there was no energy to sustain their life. They inconspicuously willed themselves lower and lower, thought upon thought, until **these gods** caressed themselves by **incarnating**, more in-depth into this lower vibratory world of **'EGO,'** at which time they were swept into the *illusional thought!* – *'This newly created world is real; we are separate, and so they no longer could remember who they truly were!*

Hue-man thought continued to degrade, while an entirely new consciousness developed. Separation, civilizations, societies, countries, rulers, rules, statutes, customs, and laws were enacted. As time continued to pass, experiments in mind alteration began.

At first various types of plants were used to sedate the mind, then more potent chemicals.

Lawful prescription drugs and non-prescription drugs came into use. These drugs were then placed in the food supply, water, and other liquid beverages. These drugs were placed on plants and in the ground on farms. All to keep the hue-man mind **weak & sedated** so that they would not, could not, thought not, to ever wake up.

Thoughts of competition, games of Win or Loose, television, etc. are all lower frequency distractions; **sedative type drugs** of a different sort.

Dedication to and childish beliefs in **religions** are also inextricable mind-altering drugs that bind one to negative thoughts, strange concepts, and twisted principles. These traits empower the very illusion you will someday seek to escape. Deep-rooted religious beliefs drowned Hue-mans in a drunken stupor of **impatient discuss**ion, **anger, fear**, and even **hatred** against all that do not believe as they. This low vibrational egotistical thought that believes, *"I am right, and you are wrong,"* has lasciviously bathed the mind so thoroughly that it may take the passing of a comic year before one ever free themselves from such debauchery.

All desperately fight for approval from a god who is believed to intervene in daily affairs. From battles won or loss, illnesses imposed or cured, good fortune given or taken away – you believe.

The demands this god places on you by asking for the death of your child as a sacrifice for sins and just before the unthinkable;

One is stopped, only to be told that this was all done for their benefit. What an evil, sadistic trick, yet you explain it away.

You are told who and when to kill but at the same time commanded, "Thou shall not."

Your highly respected kings are reverenced, even though they too indirectly commit the formal 'Thou shall not' and all because of uncontrollable lust for another man's wife. The service of obedience that you render is **not** done by a **love** of **free will**. But instead, your obedience is rendered because of an ever-present threat, producing a subconscious fear that constantly looms overhead concerning an everlasting punishment in a lake filled with **Fire!** This type of belief renders you a helpless victim to a demanding and cruel tyrant.

Believing that you are unworthy, filthy, disgusting sinners in need of blood from a human carcass will render forgiveness and thus salvation. A human sacrifice, but you believe it without question, hook, line, and sinker. These cabals <u>feed</u> upon such low energy vibrational thoughts. This is why they introduced this manner of insane thinking. Many of you are even **possessed** by these cabals, without ever being aware. Perfection need not be obtained, only remembered. There is a Law based on Attraction; it is a universal law. It has enabled every one of you to attract (create) by **will**. Though what you attract appears right or wrong, moral or immoral, negative or positive, you will always get the very essence of your beliefs.

The world that you live and see today is the manifestation of all of your life's thoughts. Thoughts become things. Very many cosmic days have since past. *(4.3 Billion of your Years = 1 Cosmic Day)*

You have always been and will always be **Loved** and Connected **to Original Eternal Energy Source**. As Light Beings, extensions of Prime Creator thoughts; you must put forth an effort to remember that you are having a **hue-man experience**; Yet we dare not overlook the fact that though you have been intentionally altered and now **seemingly** have drifted out of frequency; to be **incarnate** on Earth at this time is a most wonderful and magnanimous opportunity and the experiences you learn will benefit you and the multi-verse. And **I AM** said, "It is Good!"

This cycle or **shift** of 2012 is causing **higher energy** on Earth to increase to peak intensity. This higher energy will ensure that all who desire may accept, evolve, and awaken during this shift. As this conscious shift continues, a new awareness is spreading over the entire planet.

However, many of you will still experience rejection of this seemingly new perspective in consciousness because you stubbornly harbor low frequencies such as prejudice, jealousy, anger, resentment, fear, and other egotistical thoughts.

Yet this illusion, though seemingly a sleepy mistake, is continually providing a multitude of unlimited learning opportunities. You and the multi-verse have and will continue to benefit from this exploration throughout the ceaseless ages of eternity.

Lessons of **acceptance, forgiveness, compassion** are all attributes of **UNCONDITIONAL LOVE.**

Remember, you are at the leading edge of thought in all of the multi-verse. No Sovereign Being has ever traversed so deep into such negative illusional thought through sleep or danced so far out of frequency **and returned**.

Consequently, it is essential to keep reminding yourselves that you are manifesting an illusion; this experience never happened. **Nothing real can be threatened, and nothing unreal exists.** Remember, all things work together for good. A spark has always connected you to **'I AM.'** As you open your hearts to release low unloving vibrational thoughts of **ego** and accept the abundance of Prime Creator's Infinite Love, the dance of your vibrational frequency unequivocally **retunes** itself and intensifies in strength within you.

Forgiveness of yourself and those you **think** have hurt you is essential because an unforgiving attitude is another low vibrational (energy) thought supporting and maintaining your illusion. You must let go of all old 3D (Third-Dimensional) low energy thoughts. Only in this illusion is it possible to hate, resent, judge, and condemn, as these are unreal mental concepts that do not exist.

The more intensely people express these unloving attitudes and beliefs, the more they continue to vibrate at a lower, out of tune frequency.

By forgiving those that hurt you, loving those that hate you, and blessing those that despitefully use and prosecute you, a new consciousness evolves in your heart. Your vibration is increasing. Your original frequency is returning. By accepting and forgiving, you can now see the divine spark within everyone, including yourself. You have come to realize that there is nothing to forgive because you and others are loving expressions of the original **I AM**.

You have been buried under layers of illusional beliefs in worship, obedience, sacrifice, pain, and suffering.

But it is now time to awaken and remember that we are all one, joined and connected, yet having an individual hue-man experience. And now as Mother Gaia, Earth, comes to the end of another 26,000-year cycle, this illusion, for many, is approaching the moment of its dissolution.

Many of hue-mans are preparing to fully awaken from this mysterious nightmare we call sleep and enter into an **Eternal Spiritual Reality**.

As stated before, many cosmic days have gone by in the ever so loving attempts to awaken you from this illusional world of low frequency thought. As you increase your efforts to adopt and put into practice a loving attitude, the supports upon which this illusion depends will continue to erode.

Many of you are soon to awaken from this sleep into the stunning realization of your divine heritage and recognize yourselves and all others as Beings of Light, thought extensions of Prime Creator. This illusion will be gone for many, and with it, all that made life an apparently losing struggle against the **EGO**, servitude, disease, lust of the flesh, and death. Many of you have already awakened, and as the moment of ascension rapidly approaches, many others will awaken also. I urge you to believe this missive, and I promise that you will not be disappointed because disappointment is impossible in reality.

www.bibliotecapleyades.net/pleyades/pleiadiansbook/pleiadian sbook_contents.htm

Now is the time to Wake Up!

9/11/2010
By: Dr. ALi

10
THE RISKS OF LIFE!

"The person who risks nothing, will do nothing, be nothing, have nothing, and become nothing. In this domain, decisions must be made every single day that somehow and in some way, constitute a risk. They may avoid some hardships, sufferings, and sorrows, but they will never learn how to consistently Advance, Feel the necessities of Change, Understand the Essence of Love nor the Aspirations of how to Live."

9/11/2010
DR. ALI

11
THE PERVERSION OF IMAGERY!

Every thought of the mind is an image, act of the will, determination, or desire. Every thought is a frequency, a vibration expressed on the invisible pool of ether or energy, as a request. Tell me, what have you been requesting lately? Since we are all one with the Universe, All that IS, Source or God, then there is never a time during our existence that any individual thought is not co-creating. All thought is automatically metamorphosized into our reality, transformed, or crystallized into physical reality.

TELEVISION IS ONE OF THE MOST <u>DESTRUCTIVE DRUG</u> KNOWN IN THIS DIMENSIONAL PLANE! Images that are not intentional are drugs to our minds. The unwanted images that are flashed before our eyes keep us in a daze of confusion. These images keep our mind bathed with a thick slime of pleasurable fulfillment or ridiculous entertainment. These images become so inextricably messed & meshed within our thoughts that many are unable to escape them even during hours of intimacy with sleep.

Be warned! Spiritual Attainment is by thought! Whatever interferes with thought interferes with Spiritual Attainment! Selah!

Of course, this is only my perspective, Nothing more, nothing less!

10/24/13

Dr. Ali

12
RELIGION?

Dr. David B. Barrett spent about forty-four years and enlisted the help of over 350 specialists in a study to discover how many different religions might there be in the world. The study found that there are over 10,000 distinct religions globally – of which 150 boast over 1Million followers. Dr. Barrett went personally and visited most in 238 nations and territories around the world. He found that within Christianity alone, there are at least an incredible 38,830 different denominations, splinters, factions, offshoots, or sects.

So, with 38,830 denominations in Christianity, not counting the denominations, splinters, factions, offshoots, or sects from other religions, this would exceed well over 100,000 more individualized groups. These findings concluded that there are at least or more than 150,000 various individual religious denominations, splinters, factions, offshoots, or sects, in competition around our now known world! Most groups found their beginnings from one book translated over hundreds of times since its original written copy. BUT!

There is one universal thought or concept that ALL religious groups have in **common**.
I mean literally – they **ALL** will sit down at any table and **AGREE** to this one Absolute **FACT!**

Do you know what that one absolute **FACT** might happen to be?

They **ALL** believe **emphatically**, **positively** & most **certainly** that...

They are **RIGHT**, and you are **WRONG!**

BUT! WAIT! THIS DOES NOT MEAN **'YOU'** AND YOUR RELIGION! Oh! No! YOUR RELIGION IS THE RIGHT RELIGION!

Of course, I do not claim to be right; this is only my perspective, Nothing more, Nothing less!

http://www.religioustolerance.org/worldrel.htm

12/05/2013
By: Dr. Ali

13
R U THE CREATOR
OF YOUR REALITY
OR A VICTIM IN IT

This is only my perspective, but many Christians are quite bodacious in their defense against anyone trying to tell them that they are a 'Victim.' "NO!' They say, "Not me." "I am Victorious in Christ Jesus." Alright, let us see what the difference is between a Creator and a Victim.

Creator – One who creates.

Victim – Someone or something injured, harmed, offended; suffered a loss from some act, condition, or circumstance:

Syllabus – Anyone or anything that can have unwanted action taken against it/self in any way, shape, or form thus needing to be Protected, Rescued, or Saved is a 'Victim.'

So then, we think that one is not a victim unless one has been 'Victimized.' But! I ask; What does one call anyone or anything that has been 'Victimized'? Then what were they before they were 'Victimized'?

Often the statement is made; "They went looking for an innocent 'Victim.'" *Only victims need victory, to live a Victorious Victimized free life*!

Here is one last thought.

Adversary – An opponent, an enemy. Anyone or anything that is 'Against.'

Now, in 1st Peter 5:8 it states; *Be sober, be vigilant; because **YOUR** adversary (Anyone who believes!) the devil, as a roaring lion, walketh about, SEEKING (a target/victim) whom he may devour:*

In conclusion: ONLY those who **believe** and **can** be injured, harmed, offended, suffer a loss; In need of a Protector, Rescuer, or Savior from an ADVERSARY; Always has been and always will be a **'VICTIM**.'

On the other thought; A **Creator** can NOT be injured, harmed, offended, suffer loss neither **has nor believes in** an 'Adversary'!

Once again, this is ONLY my Perspective, Nothing more & Nothing Less.

09/01/2013
By: Dr. Ali

14
IT IS JUST A 'GAME'

Of all the glues that hold the third and fourth dimension together and the paths that keep you moving steadily in a low vibrational delusion towards darkness; None is found to be as deceptive, more luring than that of the art called 'Game.' Understanding and choosing to let go of this glue requires a special recognition through centripetal thought. Let us begin.

Games were first introduced as innocent fun! They were eagerly and enthusiastically grasped by all whom these games were introduced. Games have become an evolving-subtle and very inextricable personified entity. It was first accepted as past time entertainment but later as amusement for social gatherings. So tell me, dear friend, what real harm could 'Game' play?

Game first originated as singular enjoyment; it was a solitary challenge always to perform better the next time around. Then it became a test of personal intelligence. After a while, the thought of playing **'With'** someone was conceived. Game is tightening its line as it evolves and subtly sinks its self-perpetuating beliefs deeper into the crevices of the heart.

Game is now a mighty psychological opponent. It always wins! If you choose to play, you will always lose!

Your friend who you at first played **'With'** has become your opponent and is now played **'Against'**! You have now learned a new motivation named **Competition**! Game's hold is ever so tighter, its grip more secure. You are mentally, emotionally, and physically trapped, and believe it or not; it's very severe! Game has you spiraling into an emotional decay. You are continually lowering your vibration every time you play.

You have placed meaning with great value to 'Win or Lose.' It has become an intricate part of your culture and to everyone that choose. Aggression is encouraged; winning is exalted. The lower animal propensities are once again awakened, and the concept, 'I Beat You,' has taken on a precarious meaning. Deeper and deeper into delusional thought, does Game drag you. Losing has been formulated within the mind to be disdained, loathed, and disgraceful! It is disgusting, humiliating, and downright despicable to 'Lose.' No one wants to 'Lose'!

Winning has taken on an even more psychological entrapment! The winner is given a false sense of superiority, physical strength, and self-empowerment! Winning is likened to an intoxication.

The reasoning faculties have been compromised, and you will now go to extreme measures, irrational tactics to WIN! You are now engulfed in winning. And losing is not an option. You have become a slave to 'Game' in whom you crave. You have given so entirely to 'Game' your will, that now to win, you would even 'Kill'!

Do you remember how it feels? It runs deep, doesn't it? And the very thought of another basking in their victory can leave you feeling shameful. The body may even respond in clumsy movements. Your speech may stutter for expression, while your feelings sink lower into a mood of depression.

You played 'Game,' my man because it was cool; Now how do you feel, you Loss-Fool! Everyone knows it shows on your face; You know it too, by the feeling of disgrace! Something has been lost, but how do you explain; you do not have the words, but you do have the shame!

I demand a rematch; I demand a new game; by any means necessary, I refuse to live in shame! It's all about me. My reputation has been scared; I've been living a lie, my life's a façade! I am willing to kill to re-establish my name, and if I lose again, my response will be the same! How did I become that which I disdain? Could it possibly be over, something so simple as a **'GAME'**?

12/27/14
Dr. ALi

15
R WE ALONE?

Our present-day scientist has developed very powerful telescopes. Their range will allow us to gaze far into outer space. Science has developed a measuring system which can determine distances in outer space quite accurately. It has been determined that our planet is about 25 million light-years away from the center of our galaxy. And that our galaxy is about 100 million light-years across!

With these powerful telescopes, we can also count stars, solar systems, galaxies, and this has allowed us to realize that there is not just a universe but there are Multi-verse! We estimate over 100 Billion stars within our Milky Way Galaxy alone. And some galaxies are 100 times larger than the Milky Way. And we have observed that there are over 100 Billion galaxies within our one universe. Let us just estimate…

100 Billion X 100 Billion = 1e + 22 (10 Sextillion)

One would have to be very egotistical, quite arrogant, or even somewhat impetuous in thought – to assume that we earth hue-mans are the ONLY children at the playground!

Of course, this is only my perspective! Nothing more,
Nothing less!

01/03/2013
Dr. ALi

16
CREATOR & CREATION
R THEY ONE & THE SAME?

We humans, more often than not, by giving names, titles, genders & labels to things, tend also to place limits on these things and place them into boxes and categories. We will attempt not to do that here. Instead, when referring to every religion (God, Brahman, Jehovah, Yahweh, Allah, etc. We will use the term Creator, All that 'IS' or The ONE!

All will agree that **their** "Creator" is Omniscient, Omnipotent & Omnipresent, Omni-Limitless & Omni-Infinite! In the consciousness of "The ONE", there is no such thing as past or future, before or after, sooner or later, over here or out there; ONLY 'ISNESS'! Anything and everything is possible. Time does not exist. In actuality and practicality, "The ONE IS" ALL there is…

It stands with rationale and balanced reasoning *(so I think)* that everyone and everything consists of nothing more and nothing less than "ALL that IS"! Everyone and everything is indivisible aspects, expressions, manifestations, personifications, sparks, or conscious awareness of "ALL that IS"; which is HAVING a neutrino, quarks, particle, atom, molecule, cellular, Earth, water, fire, air, insect, animal (Wo-Hue)-Man EXPERIENCE!

This has been done by some creation of a holographic 1st, 2nd, or 3rd dimensional, illusionary duality!

So, who in Heaven or in Hell do you think you are?

No one can fully understand or fully know that which is so vast and unlimited. But! By learning one's 'Self,' one can begin to KNOW!

"Thy Self"

Of course, this is only my perspective: Nothing more, Nothing less!

02/04/2013
Dr. Ali

17
'MY' SPIRIT'

Religion has taught us many negative thought processes that we would be wise to unlearn. It is by hue-man habit that we also speak many of these habitual expressions. Let us look at the word **"MY."** It means 'Mine' or belonging to or possession of; When we say, "My Spirit," "My Body," 'My Mind,' "My House," etc., it denotes a **separation**; A duality! It is the same as me saying, "My Dr. Ali," or you saying, "My (*your name*)." when speaking about yourself. It expresses that there is **YOU**, and then there is this spirit, body, or house that **BELONGS** to **YOU!** Sometimes we do not mean what we say.

As Multi-Dimensional Beings, we are energy **SPIRIT** Beings! Spirit cannot possess Spirit or itself, Holy or Unholy! Even the Bible, which we all respect, has GOD speaking in such a manner; "The Spirit **of** The Lord," "The Spirit **of** God,"; **"My** Spirit shall not always strive with man," etc. We have been programmed to **identify ourselves** as a Body, possessing a Spirit! This is why we make statements like 'MY Spirit,' 'My Mind,' or my 'Sub-consciousness'; Which, by the way, is no such thing! So, if you can see this, understand; unity-consciousness does not think this way.

All things are Spirit, vibrating at different frequencies.

All matter is solidified energy, Spirit, or consciousness. Matter is Energy, Spirit vibrating at a slower frequency. **Your body is solidified Energy** – crystallized Spirit. You, as Spirit, are not in your body. **Your body is in your Spirit, inside your consciousness!** As you raise your vibration, you become more Spirit-like in thought, moving closer towards fluid-like Spirit, thereby making your created reality more malleable and easily changeable. We all use this form to materialize into this three-dimensional physicality. Our body is only a holographic **projection** in our consciousness, as is all that we see. Do we say, '**Our** Hue-Man'? NO!

We say being hue-man, as hue-man or as a hue-man. It is even misleading to say, 'I am **A** Spirit' as though you are separate in some way from other spirits. We should speak about ourselves **AS Spirit!** This reality has programmed and brainwashed us into using such terms so that automatically we will perpetuate this illusion of separation! An awakened unity-Conscious mind recognizes that there is **ONLY ONE SPIRIT!** But while in this duality, we are all (*apparently individual*) aspects, sparks, or expressions of that **ONE vibrating Spirit!** BUT! In actuality, we are **ALL ONE INFINITE SPIRIT, MIND, CONSCIOUSNESS, HAVING A (HUE, WO)-MAN EXPERIENCE!**
Of course, this is only my perspective. Nothing more, Nothing less!

05/26/2014
Dr. Ali

18
Hindrances to Awakening

Awakening takes focusing on the intent of changing one's unloving attitudes and thoughts of separation, back towards unity and Unconditional Love. By choice, you must hold a unity-conscious, indiscriminate attitude of unconditional love.

Until you release attitudes of judgment, blame, and the nurturing of desires to see those whom you feel have offended, hurt, betrayed, or *done you wrong,* in any way, shape, or form – punished!… You cannot begin to awaken! For those are the very attitudes that self-perpetuate this duality in which you are presently experiencing. The more you seek revenge, payback, or simple justice, the deeper you sink into this holographic duality called LIFE. The reason for this is that while you hold such thoughts or beliefs, it causes you to vibrate a frequency of **separation**. This frequency of **polarity** places you totally out of harmony with Unity-Consciousness. It will make anyone extremely uncomfortable to be in a place where all **are one** and unconditionally loved.

It would seem to you to be unfair that those miserable, selfish, and deceitful people, who had done you so wrong, could be accepted wholeheartedly and lovingly by "The ONE" (*GOD*).

It would be a total mismatch, a state of utter incompatibility and shock! To be in such a place (Heaven) would be excruciatingly painful for you and anyone holding such thought vibrations.

Of course, this is only my perspective! Nothing more, Nothing less!

04/23/2014
Dr. ALi

19
"EXISTENCE"

The first universal law is 'You Exist.' The fundamental quality of existence is existence itself. Any-Thing and Every-Thing that exist always has and always will because "THE ONE," whom most may address as God, Brahman, Jehovah, Yahweh, Allah, etc., is all that ever has or ever will be. "THE ONE" is all-inclusive! No-Thing exists 'outside' of "THE ONE"; For there is no existence outside of "THE ONE" except non-existence and even that is up for discussion but for another topic and time. "THE ONE" is OmniPotent, OmniScient, OmniPresent, and in actuality, "ALL THAT IS"! Do you agree, or do you even understand?

Then it stands to reason that All-Things and Every-Thing consist of & are a reflection of or a creation of that "ONE THING." Since there are no rules, laws, statutes, or codes that govern "THE ONE," "THAT ONE INFINITE, ALL KNOWING & ETERNAL THING" may express itself in all the ways that it chooses. PERIOD! "THE ONE" is so "OMNI-POWERFULL" that "THE ONE" even knows what it feels like, by personal experience, **'NOT'** to be "THE ONE"! Q – How is that? Ali – Well, thank-you for asking?

"THE ONE" experiences this as your hands – by everything that you may touch; as your feet – by walking everywhere you may walk; as your eyes – by looking everywhere you may look; as your heart – by feeling everything you may feel; as your ears – by hearing everything that you hear; as your nose – by smelling everything that you may smell! We are all aspects, indivisible sparks of light that "ALL THAT IS" has created for the purpose of looking back at itself, of experiencing itself, and of expressing itself. You are the very essence & epitome of "THE ONE," HAVING A (WO & HUE-MAN) EXPERIENCE!

And when we all finally wake up from this forgetfulness or dream; We will say, "WOW! That felt Soooooo! Real! BUT! That was not fully me. That was only a part of me. This is who "I Really **AM**"!

So then, who in Heaven or in Hell do you really think you are, since 'YOU EXIST'?

Of course, this is only my perspective! Nothing more, Nothing less!

01/28/2013
Dr. Ali

20
DOES NON-EXISTENCE EXIST!

Many people believe that you can create something from nothing. Many people believe that you can make something disappear. And of course, some believe in non-existence. What one chooses to believe on this subject will determine their direction of reality shift to a staggering degree. What one chooses not to believe can be pathetic; yet valid and warranted.

Belief is the basic/foundation for all things. All that you see and all that you are is because of a 'Belief.' Every emotion that you express and every feeling that you sense are all because you first believed something.

There could be no real experience, no solar system, no galaxy, no universe or multi-verse! There could be no time, no space, no dimensions in any place; There could be no 'UP' or 'DOWN'; no 'IN' or 'OUT'! You could not look forward or even turnabout. But most importantly, non-existence would not exist!

That is right! Non-Existence exists; if it did not, you could not speak about it. Though the fundamental qualities of non-existence is non-existent, it still occupies a position in a realm that cannot be reached. Nothing can go there nor come from there. Why?

Because it is 'NON – EXISTENT! The very quality of 'Non-Existence' is NOT to EXIST!

Non-existence is already full of all of the things that do not exist, and existence is full of all of the things that do! This is a universal law and the structure of existence and non-existence. Though they appear to be two things, they are only 'ONE.' Yes, they both exist but with separate and individual qualities.

A magician can make some – thing disappear from present sight, but it still appears somewhere in another sight. Energy cannot be created or destroyed! This, too, is a universal law. What is will always be. What is not will always not be!

Of course, this is only my perspective; No – thing more and no – thing less!

08/23/2017
By: Dr. Ali

21
NON – EXISTENCE

Abracadabra is a term used quite often in your world. It started with magicians of old. It means, By my words, do I Create! These magicians loved to fool their audiences by deceiving them into believing that they could create something from nothing. What do you believe?

Source Energy, The Creator, ALL That IS or I AM, etc. is 'ALL' there IS! It is 'ALL' inclusive! To even speak of non-existence outside of... 'ALL THAT IS'; is an oxymoron! The thought of no-thing in non-existence acknowledges identification. But, how can you identify no-thing? How can you refer to no-thing as 'Non-Existent' without at the same time giving this no-thing that does not exist an actual place, holding a thought in your mind? Logically and metaphysically speaking, there would have to be an existence for 'Non-Existence' not to exist within. Are you still with me?

There would have to be someplace that exists for 'Non-Existence' to be, where there is... 'No-Thing'! 'No-Thing' cannot be/exist because existence is already filled with all and 'ONLY' the things that 'Exist'! Now, this 'No-Thing' has become 'Something' because you speak of 'IT.'

One cannot speak or even think of 'No-Thing, which does 'Not Exist'! By definition alone, the primary and fundamental quality of 'No-Thing' or 'Non-Existence' means just that! As is the primary and fundamental quality of 'Some-Thing' or that which 'Exist'! 'Some-Thing' that 'Exist' cannot become 'No-Thing,' that is 'Non-Existent' as 'No-Thing' that is 'Non-Existent' cannot become 'Some-Thing' that 'Exist' because… 'NO-THING' DOES NOT EXIST' and 'SOME-THING' DOES! These two basic qualities are inherent to each and cannot exchange their basic fundamental qualities!

BUT! (NO-THING IS REALLY SOME-THING AS NON-EXISTENCE REALLY EXIST!)

In conclusion:

Source Energy, The Creator, ALL That IS or I AM, etc. is 'ALL' there IS! Everything is possible and impossible for it! It is never this OR that! It is 'ALWAYS' this 'AND' that!

Of course, this is only my perspective; I do not claim to be right; no-thing more and no-thing less!

10/09/2017
By: Dr. ALi

22
SO! YOU WANT TO
IMPROVE YOUR LIFE

Most people have such a difficult time attempting to improve their life; Always focusing on the outside rather than the inside. Allow me to explain. Understanding the world in which we live is one of the utmost importance. First and foremost – believe it or not – this world, reality or duality that you think we are presently living in, is all an illusion. That's right! An illusion! All that you see around you is only a digital, sort of, representation of your innermost deepest beliefs. These beliefs are thoughts, and all thoughts are energy. This energy is crystallized into dense physicality and reflected, holographically, in 3D, right back at you. Did you get that?

Life itself has no inherent meaning. We all give life the sense we individually choose. As co-creators, multi-dimensional beings, 'what we put out' vibrationally by our most profound beliefs or thoughts, will always be 'what we get back'! Your thoughts are electrical energy, and they become your beliefs, thus creating your conscious state of being and your particular frequency!

Your consciousness emits that particular energy frequency moment to moment and attracts/creates or manifests the very essence of that frequency into a physical 3D expression for your enjoyment within this illusional duality! Are you getting this?

You see, we all agreed to come into this illusional physical duality at this time to experience such a dimension of apparent separation from "ALL THAT IS" *(God)*. But! Each of us is experiencing our reality joined collectively by agreement. You are the Creator of your reality, and no one can do anything that can *'matter'* against you unless you match their frequency with consent. And that can be done through guilt, jealousy, anger, hate, fear, etc. Get the picture? This construct or world is only a collective agreement by similar energy – signature – frequency variables that allow us to intermingle. Everyone and everything are only reflections or versions of our thoughts, like in a play. You are the main character, and everyone and everything else is supporting actors or backdrops. The ONLY thing that is real is the experience! We are not in a real-world; this world is WITHIN US! Within our consciousness! There is no – 'Out There,' out there. All is inclusive, because "ALL THAT IS" *(God)* is all that is, and we are all sparks, aspects, or conscious expressions of "ALL THAT IS." Now, did you at least get that?

To be allowed such experience, you had to cross, let us just say, a veil of forgetfulness. We all had to agree to forget who and what we really are. That is when the joy or experience began!

So you see, your life is only a reflection for you to learn by and return to or re-member who you are and carry along with you the vast experiences you obtain. If you do not like your life and it is not what you prefer, then go within and make the changes. The outside will, in time, reflect the change within. But here is the essential thought. YOU MUST BELIEVE! And remember, you cannot fake a frequency! Impossible!

There are innumerable Beings throughout the multi-verse admiring your every move. You are exalted above all the various universal creations. None have ever dared to dive so far into the deepest realms of 3D dimensional darkness. None have ever unflinchingly braved such an unimaginable apparent separation from "THE ONE". None have ever slowed their vibration to such an extent and cast themselves out into the apparent, outermost leading edge of darkest thought! AND YET!

FOUND THEIR WAY BACK TO THE LIGHT! Your story will be told throughout the ceaseless ages of eternity! Your feat of bravery will be reverberated from planet to planet, from solar system to solar system, from galaxy to galaxy, from multi-verse to multi-verse, etc.

It is stories like these that put the 'Fin' into INFINITY! Because of willing, selfless, and unconditional loving Beings such as yourselves that sets the 'Mark' so majestically! It is nothing more and nothing less than,

RE'MARK'ABLE!

Of course, this is only our perspective, nothing more, nothing less!

06/06/2012
By: Dr. ALi

23
The Universal Law of Allowing

The Universal Law of Allowing means dropping all judgments and emotional attachments to what others **have**, **do**, or **say**. This is quite different from being tolerant. Being tolerant is not liking what someone else **is**, **have**, **do** or **says** and holding emotional-laden, negative thoughts about them, but letting them be, **have**, **do** or **say it** anyway. Practicing The Universal Law of Allowing requires granting others the same rights you demand yourself -- the right to **be**, **have**, **do**, and **say** whatever you choose. Here's one interpretation of that law:

I am that I am, and You are that which You are. I accept, honor, and respect you as you are. I honor, allow, support, and respect your right to be who you are, do as you please, have whatever you want, and say whatever you choose to say. I honor your right to live your life as you choose, to worship God, Brahman, Jehovah, Yahweh, Allah, etc., or not, as you choose. Now, I honor those same rights for me, and I humbly ask that you do likewise.

I honor the Golden Rule, "Do unto others as you would have others to do unto you" and I call for you to do likewise. As long as you avoid violating others' FREE WILL or destroying our collective environment,

I will honor your right to **be**, **do**, **have**, and **say** whatever you choose.

Here's another way of expressing this law:
Love God, Brahman, Jehovah, Yahweh, Allah, etc., love your neighbor and love yourself.

This concept may be vitally important because if the reincarnation belief system is correct, then God, Brahman, Jehovah, Yahweh, Allah, etc., your neighbor and you are all ONE and the same.

Christian tradition has done well at teaching about love for God, Brahman, Jehovah, Yahweh, Allah, etc., and your neighbor. Unfortunately, it has been a dismal failure at teaching people to love themselves. The teaching that labels everyone as *Lost*, *Ungodly*, *Wretched Sinners*, *Unrighteous*, as *Filthy rags*, in **need of forgiveness**, instills within the mind of the believer **Victimhood** and does not leave a positive image of oneself.

As you may already know, if you don't love yourself, your ability to love anything or anyone else is drastically reduced. Most Buddhists are quite skilled at practicing this law. You might also notice that Buddhism is the only major religion that has never started a war. You've probably also heard the Native American saying: Before you judge someone, you need to walk a mile in their moccasins."

Here is a way to practice the Law of Allowing:

When you have an emotional reaction to someone else's behavior, stop and tell yourself: "He (she) is neither good nor bad. I neither like them or dislike them. They just are. They are another human being doing the best they can. Given their conditioning, beliefs, circumstances, present needs, and desires, I'd probably be doing pretty much the same thing."

What Do You Choose to Support?

Your life force (the energy frequency that sustains your body) also goes toward the manifestation of your physical – illusional - 3D duality and is done by your innermost thoughts or beliefs. Do you want to live your life and keep your life force tied to all those things you think are wrong? If your answer is "no," then break the emotional ties.

.

Another way to practice the Law of Allowing:

Instead of making others wrong for who they are or what they do, become the observer and simply say, "That's something I'm simply unwilling to accept in my own life." Then allow the other person to be, have, do, and say as they will, without trying to fix anything, change them, or make them wrong for being who they are, for having what they have, for doing what they do, or for saying whatever it is that they may say.

Here's a brief quote from The Yoni Dance, Book One -
- Circles of Intimacy, Chapter 13, The Law of Allowing,
by R. Robin Cote.'

Herbert points toward the window and says, "Do you
see that lamp post over there across the yard?"

Yes!

"Do you have an emotional attachment to that lamp
post? — to what it does? — to the light is has? – to
what it does with that light? – to what it expresses by
that light?

No!

"When you can hold that same attitude for all of your
fellow human beings, you'll have **mastered the Law
of Allowing**. Our job is simply to allow all others the
free will choice to be who they **are**, **have** whatever
they want, **do** whatever they want, and **say** whatever
they choose. By giving others the same thing that we
asked for ourselves, we walk our talk. We also
become the role models and set the example for
others to follow."

"That lamp post stands there 24 hours every day, seven days every week, and at night, shines a light on the surrounding area. That is its purpose and responsibility. That is what it does. If you're mad, sad, angry, jealous, hate or hold any other negative emotion regarding that lamp post, is it going to change what that lamp post is, the light that it shines, what it does with that light, or how it chooses to express that light?"

"NO!"

"If you bitch, moan, and complain to the lamp post, is it going to change what that lamp post is, or the light that it shines, or what it does with that light, or how it chooses to express that light?"

Again I say, **"NO!"**

"If you bitch, moan, and complain to someone else about the lamp post, is it going to change what that lamp post is, the light that it shines, what it does with that light, or how it chooses to express that light?"

"NO!"

"The same is true for our fellow humans. We each are what we are, and we do whatever we do, we have what we have, and we say whatever it is that we choose to say.

We cannot change another's nature, and, short of violence or threats of violence, we cannot force them to do other than what they desire. And even if we force them to do other than what they desire, they remain who they are."

I ask, "What about using lies and deception?"

"You can con them, cheat them, lie to them, or otherwise trick them into being or doing as you would have them be or do, but if you do, you steal their soul, you steal their freedom, you steal their God; their granted right to self-determination."

Two things you should know about that:

First, "What you do onto the least of mine, you do onto me."

Second, "Whatsoever you put out is a frequency. You'd best believe that You will get the very essence of that frequency, manifested into physical – illusional - 3D duality, right back at you.

Of course, this is only my perspective, nothing more and nothing less.

06/06/2013
Dr. Ali

24
CREATION VS CREATOR

Often we hear the statement, 'God moves in mysterious ways.' I wonder if that statement is just an excuse. I ask this mainly because those who make it do not understand how God moves. The Bible reads, "There was war in Heaven; Michael and his angels fought against the dragon/Devil/Satan and his angels and prevailed not; neither was their place found anymore in Heaven. And were CAST OUT"! Rev. 12: 7-9

Now, wait just a minute! Some things are just common sense and contradicting according to its teachings. Doesn't the Bible teach us that the Creator is INFINITE! OmniPotent, OmniScient, and OmniPresent? Doesn't the Bible teach us that ALL things are created by ONE BEING (St. John 1: 3) whom many address as God, Jehovah, Yahweh, Allah, Buddha, Brahman, etc.? Which before anything was created, including time, past or future, would mean that this 'ONE BEING' was/is 'ALL THAT IS'! Then will you answer this question for me? **Why would an INFINITE, UNLIMITED, LOVING, OMNI (ALL) POWERFUL, BEING need to fight against its THOUGHTS!** Yes! That is correct, thoughts.
You, me, everyone and everything are nothing more and nothing less than the 'thoughts' of 'ALL THAT IS,' 'THE ONE,' God, Jehovah, Yahweh, Allah, Buddha,

Brahman, etc. Psalms 33:9 Now think about that for a moment before you start running off with an excuse that does not make any sense. It appears that Man has made the Creator in his image. Also, since the Creator is OmniPresent, then that type of existence makes the Creator ALL INCLUSIVE! All LIFE resides WITHIN 'THE ONE' Being! 'SEPARATE' does not exist. Meaning there is no such thing as 'OUTSIDE' OR 'OUT THERE.' The Creator has no boundaries! There is no, 'OUT THERE,' out there, to be cast out into. OmniPresent means, 'ALL PRESENT! EVERYWHERE! PERIOD! Another way of putting it would be that we exist WITHIN the MIND or CONSCIOUSNESS of the Creator as a 'THOUGHT,' he spake, and it was done! Ps. 33: 9

Look, listen, or read this with an open mind. If you eliminate the impossible, whatever remains, no matter how improbable, must be the truth! Like it or not, someone is lying, fooled, deceived, or just plain ignorant! Wake up, everyone! Take another look at what and why you believe the way you believe!

Of course, this is only my perspective, nothing more, nothing less!

09/01/2013
Dr. Ali

25
FORGIVENESS &
UNCONDITIONAL LOVE

Unconditional Love: Now what in Heaven or in Hell does that imply? Well, to start with; Unconditional means – without having any conditions PERIOD! Alright, forgiveness means – to release, give up, or let go of any type of resentment or claim to grant the one being forgiven a relief from any indebtedness or responsibility. Ok, I think that covers it.

The real question is this, can Unconditional Love, Love someone so Unconditionally, but at the same moment need to forgive that someone for something? For that someone to receive that forgiveness, that someone has to be penitent and ask for forgiveness according to specific guidelines. Does that seem like a condition to you? Does that seem like some type of atonement that will set you once again at one with Unconditional Love? Tell me if you feel like this. No matter what one may or may not do, even though some book written thousands of years ago and translated hundreds of times by hue-mans, may say is sinful, wrong or evil, etc.; There isn't anything that anyone can do against Unconditional Love that Unconditional Love, being what it is, would need to forgive them for!

Unconditional Love does not say, "I love you, Unconditionally, BUT! If you commit a sin, you will need to do something to receive my 'Forgiveness' because our relationship, as it once was experienced, has been altered. Possessing a need for forgiveness means that the relationship, as it once was experienced, has been changed or altered in some way. And to get that experience back as it once was, one needs to do something, and by doing something that would constitute a condition! BUT! Unconditional Love grants the fullness of its Love without conditions!

Well, this may only be my perspective, but that seems to be contradicting the term "Unconditional!" Only in an illusional third-dimensional reality can such a concept be possible. Meaning, in actuality, there isn't anything that we can do that would need to be forgiven. As free will Beings, it is our right to experience whatsoever reality we choose and not need to be forgiven for choosing it! Period!

Of course, this is only my perspective, nothing more and nothing less!

05/12/2013
Dr. Ali

26
WHAT IF?

The one thing that we have all done is to have taken for granted that our most basic childhood beliefs, our most essential parental, religious & moral foundation, which we dare not question; Could have been a Deception!

What if life is not a school, or a training ground, or a test, or a "bitch," but a fun PlayStation Game. What if life is like a ride in an objective, independent yet fear subjective, immersion 3D Illusional – Holographic – Limitation Duality – Disney World Amusement Park instead?

~ What if the purpose of life in this objective, independent yet fear subjective, immersion 3D Illusional Holographic Limitation Reality is not to conceive something by thinking but to perceive something by feeling?

~ What if we are like Players in a PlayStation game and are *supposed* to feel separate from our *Infinite Self's*, lonely and afraid"?

~ What if this connection to our *Infinite Self* has never been and can never be broken, but to enter this objective, independent yet fear subjective, immersion 3D Illusional – Holographic – Limitation Reality, the prerequisite is that each player had to believe that the connection was broken?

What if every experience we have ever had and will ever have is precisely how our *Infinite Self* wants it, and that there's nothing to be changed, fixed, improved, or corrected in our holograms?

~ What if all the things we have resisted are actually what our *Infinite Self* have wanted us to experience, and it is only our judgments and resistance causing our pain and suffering?

~ What if we can never and have never done anything "wrong," but only believe we have through various teachings, customs, and beliefs stating that we are wretched, flthy, unforgiving, sinners who need to be saved?

What if this planet Earth is actually a Being and doesn't need to be saved either – that it has its *Infinite Self,* who is creating the precise experiences it wants?

~ What if it is only our **ego** that says we have the power to create or change anything about our 3D Illusional Holographic Limitation reality but instead, all power actually resides with the *Infinite Self* on the other side of this Veil of Forgetfulness?

~ What if we don't need any self-help, magic formulas, *Secret*, spiritual laws, gurus, religious teachings, nor special techniques to try to make things different than they are?

~ What if, no matter what we do in the first half of this 3D Illusional Holographic Limitation Reality World – like meditate, pray, eat only organic food, fast, study, sing, shout, stand, sit, spit, sh-t, oooops, etc. It will not change anything until we have experienced all the imperfection, limitation, and restrictions our *Infinite Self* wants to experience, and only then is ready for us to play the second half?

~ What if all we need to do is relax, enjoy the experiences our *Infinite Self* creates for us (whatsoever they maybe), and stop judging those experiences to be "good" or "bad," "better" or "worse," "right" or "wrong," Righteous or Sinful?

~ What if humankind itself has never made any mistakes, but instead has explored the heights of limitation and restriction as a species precisely as the *Infinite Self* wanted?

~ What if, not understanding all this rhetoric, we made up many "stories" to attempt to explain what we experience – through religions, philosophies, and spiritual retreats – many of which contain some truth, but which are always altered, so they lead into more limitations?

~ What if it's now time in this objective, independent yet fear subjective, immersion 3D Illusional Holographic – Limitation – Disney World Amusement Park, for many more people to enter their metamorphoses. What if it is time to play the second half of this Holographic Limitation, to go over the top of the first hill on the proverbial rollercoaster and enjoy the ride back down to Infinite Knowing? It is time to 'WAKE UP'!

Again, this is only my perspective, nothing more, nothing less.

05/12/2013
By: Dr. ALi

27
STAYING FOCUSED AS A MULTI-DIMENSIONAL BEING in 3D

1. You **EXIST**, and you are an **Infinite, Eternal CREATOR** Being, an aspect, expression of **'All that IS'**!

2. Everything that exists, exist **'HERE'** & **'NOW'**!

3. **'THE ONE'** is all and **'THE ALL'** are **'THE ONE'**!

4. What you put out, according to your **Thoughts** and **BELIEFS**, manifest your **Holographic Illusional 3D** reality, which constitutes the life that you get back.

5. You must choose your highest excitement every **moment** and stay focused in the **NOW,** the only existence!

6. Continuum, Continuity, Time, or any concept thereof does not exist.

7. No thing, situation, experience, or event has meaning, except the meaning you choose to give it!

8. Therefore, ALL, Every & Any thing that manifests in your life works together for good! Rom. 8:28 'IF'! YOU BELIEVE IT!

Of course, this is only our perspective; Nothing more & Nothing less!

By: Dr. Ali
06/05/2013

28
Life is Just a Ride!

The world is like a ride *(Experience)* in an amusement park. When you choose to get on this ride, it appears to be very, very **REAL** because that is just how powerful our minds are. The ride goes up, down, round and round; It has thrills, chills and is very brightly colored and very, very loud! Please do not get me wrong about this ride. It is a very sophisticated, 3D Immersion – Illusional Holographic, Duality Ride. It is a whole lot of fun. That is, for a while. Some people have been on this ride for a very long time. Soon they begin to question, "Is this ride **REAL?** Or is it **JUST A RIDE**?

Some Beings begin to remember and get off the ride and, in time, come back to the ride and attempt to tell the existing riders that are still on the ride, "Hey, fear not! Be not afraid! Ever! **St. Mark 5:36** And the riders ask, 'Why should we not be afraid?' And the Beings answer… 'Because It's **JUST A RIDE!**'

And do you know what the riders do to those Beings? They **Rebuke**, **Judge**, **Condemn**, and **KILL those Beings! St. Luke 6:37** Why? Because they **believe** the Bible tells them so. St. John 16:2 Shut those Beings up!

They know not what they are talking about! They are Heretics! Lunatics! Crazy, Strange, Mixed up, Confused, and **Evil**! Who are they, and where did they come from anyway?

But! it does not matter what the riders say or do to those Beings who came back to enlighten the others. Why? Because

LIFE IS JUST A RIDE!

Nothing more and nothing less!

02/07/16
By: Bill Hicks
Edited by: Dr. Ali

29
Part 1, Life is Just a Ride

In order to participate within the 1st part of the ride, one must agree to the Beliefs, Judgments, Observations, and Perspectives that constitute that construct and, of course, the same with the 2nd part!

1. I must think I believe that I forgot who I really am (Infinite and Eternal Energy; Consciousness Focused into having a hue-wo-man experience, an aspect of 'ALL THAT IS') and believe that I am something else instead; Like a Body, a Victim or a, Sinner that needs to be saved!

2. I must think I believe that this life experience is real & what I perceive with my senses is really happening (Out There), in some objective, independent reality.

3. I must think I believe what I encounter (Out There) has power over me and the ability to affect my life.

4. I must think I believe in Fear, Competition, Protection, Judgment, Limitation, Right and Wrong, Better and Worst, Good and Evil, Life and Death.

5. I must think I believe there is something wrong with the reality that I see (Out There) that needs to be Changed, Fixed, Corrected, or Improved.

6. I must think I believe I have the power to change my reality and therefore, feel defective and deficient (more limited) when I fail.

7. I must think I believe that I can get myself out of this first part of this hue-wo-man experience by using my thoughts or Love my way out of it by using my heart.

8. I must believe I can make something happen, and when I fail, blame myself for not being smarter, better, or working harder at it.

9. I must believe that there are Goals to be reached, Agendas to be satisfied and Lessons to be Learned.

10. I must think I believe that I and I alone am responsible for meeting my own needs wants and desires; to obtain them I must put forth a physical effort.

11. I must think that Fear and Resistance, which are **Beliefs** are real. They are the **foundations** of the first part of this reality: Judgments and their resulting **Beliefs** are the **glue** that keeps the construct of this reality together.

12. I must believe in the **Foundation** of this Duality. It must never break down nor the **Glue** that holds it together or I would see through the Illusion and the first part of this ride for me would be over.

30
Part 2, Life is Just a Ride

In order to properly participate within the 2nd part of the ride, one must totally accept the first part of the ride, with no resistance and as being perfect just the way it is. And then agree to these new Beliefs, Observations, and Perspectives!

1. By feeling, I now know what I have been seeing; a 3D Immersion – Illusion, Duality - Reality that is not real at all. It is a Hologram created by my Higher (Infinite Self) to live my life experiences through me, it's (Lower-Self). I will be supported totally in Clearing and Freeing my thoughts towards a fuller, Awakening. My life is being lived by consciousness in consciousness and for consciousness. In fact, there is no "Out There" out there, no independent objective reality.

2. By feeling, I now know that I will never and can never perceive or experience anything in my life that my Higher Self has not created or approved for me and no one else can interface or affect me in my life experience that is not a match or within the vesica piscis of my own frequency. NO ONE CAN DO, SAY OR EXIST WITHIN MY 3D IMMERSION – ILLUSION, HOLOGRAPHIC LIFE THAT MY HIGHER SELF HAS NOT PREVIOUSLY APPROVED! PERIOD!!!

3. By feeling, I now know to stop focusing on Thinking and start focusing on Feeling! There is nothing to Analyze, Dissect, Understand, or Conceive! There is never any reason to ask 'Why'? Thinking and studying will never improve my Awareness!

4. By feeling, I now know not to assign any more power Out There which makes my hologram seem more real but instead, take my power back! Any life experience that is uncomfortable or undesirable in any way, shape or form becomes an opportunity to recognize this hologram for what it is and reclaim my power!

5. By feeling, I now know to let go of ALL Belief in Fear, Competition, Protection, Judgment, Limitation, Right or Wrong, Better or Worse, Good or Evil, Life or Death towards ANYONE or ANYTHING at ANY MOMENT!

6. By feeling, I now know everything is specifically created by my Higher Self and in sync with my existing frequency, there is never anything that need be Fixed, Changed, Corrected or Improved in my life experience. All that is needed is for me to focus on a more acceptable response towards everyday experiences which will set my frequency more in alignment with my Higher Self.

7. By feeling, I now know to be Perceptive and not Proactive.

I no longer have to try and MAKE something happen. **Following my greatest JOY from moment to moment to moment should be my main purpose in life!**

8. By feeling, I now know that there are no Goals, no Planning, no Targets, and no objectives. There is no Past and no Future Only this MOMENT! Here and NOW!

9. By feeling, I now know I can develop a TRUE UNCONDITIONAL LOVE & appreciation for ME, my Higher Self; everyone, everything and for all of my life experiences!

10. By feeling, I now know I possess the knowing that my Higher Self Loves Me Unconditionally and will take care of ALL my needs *(Including Money)* And there is never a need to worry about anything. I am now aware that my Higher Self will never create an experience for me without supplying me with everything I need for that experience!

11. By feeling, I now know I can awaken every day with curiosity and anticipation towards the 3D Immersion – Illusional – Holographic, Duality experiences that my Higher Self has created for me for that day. I simply set back, buckle up and enjoy the Ride! By: Stephen Davis
Edited by: Dr. Ali

31
So You Think You Understand
What is Truth

According to our system of beliefs and definitions, we construct the bases of our state of being. Unknown knowledge is judged by one's existing belief system and determined as true or false accordingly. But! The question remains. How can 'Unknown knowledge,' judge, 'Unknown Knowledge,' and determine its truth or falseness?

Uh-Ha! Everyone has the free will to decide what is right or wrong in their reality. Information is to the believer whatever the believer chooses it to be. From moment to moment, all information is decided whether true or false by the individual. Therefore, truth is within the mind of the beholder.

Each believer will live within the created reality of their beliefs and definitions about life. All beliefs and definitions emit outwardly like a pulsating charge of energy. Then, that energy frequency is converted, transformed into physical form, and reflected or mirrored back into their reality as an experience. What are your Beliefs and Definitions about life? Be careful because whatever they are, you are about to live them.

Of course, this is only my perspective. Nothing more and Nothing less!

07/12/2017
By: Dr. Ali

32
What Are You Focusing On?

What you are focusing on will grow: Faith or Fear? Every once in a while, check your Holo-Creation list. Make sure you are visualizing what you want. Not what you, 'Do Not Want.'

Faith is, believing that what you 'DO' desire will come to pass.

Fear is, believing that what you 'DO NOT' desire will come to pass.

When you are full of excitement, enthusiasm, and joy, it is because you imagine desirable future scenarios. When you are full of anxiousness, doubt, or fear, you are imagining future 'UN' desirable scenarios. It is not the role of the universe to know what you do or do not want. It only knows what you are imagining! What you are desiring! The universe does not omnistand what you are **'NOT'** desiring!

To eliminate fear from your life, remember, Fear is not real! It is the construct of thoughts that you imagine! Fear is a choice! Now, on the other hand, danger is genuine! And should be approached with caution, which is a more empowering and wiser construct. It is up to you to distinguish between the two.

Although there is no such thing as 'OUT THERE'; The only thing created by you that is 'Out There' is what you 'Believe' is out there.

There is never a need to fear, only the creation of a need to fear. You are 'ALL THAT IS'!

Of course, this is only my perspective, nothing more and nothing less.

10/28/2013
Dr. Ali

33
THE 'SPELLING' OF WORDS AND DEFINITIONS!

As we continue on our quest towards greater conscious awareness, we find ourselves under a 3rd-dimensional SPELL by our habits formed from the use of WORDS and DEFINITIONS. Such words and definitions have a hidden and mystical 'SPELLING' power that inextricably binds our thoughts towards VICTIMHOOD, LIMITATION, AND POWERLESSNESS. We must choose to put forth the effort and break this spell by eliminating such word defining thought forms from our vocabulary forever! Such terms and definitions produce a vibrational frequency in thought that is impossible to exist in the harmonics of a CREATOR. The tone expressed from such words and definitions is totally out of harmony with our Divine Self. *Did you get that?* Soon we will **eliminate** the use of 3rd-dimensional words and, in its place, incorporate the use of telepathy and, one day, **eliminate** the use of Extra Sensory Perception and, in its place, incorporate the use of 'Knowing'!

Here are a few of those hidden 'spells' needing to be eliminated... CONSISTANT, LOGICAL, HOPEFUL, FAITH, REASONABLE, SENSABLE, SEQUENTIAL, TRYING, ETC.
These words and definitions in all of their forms and tenses are poison to the Creator. Please omnistand,

there are NO laws, statutes, rules, codes, procedures, guidelines, or steps that a creator **MUST** follow. PERIOD! As CREATORS, we are 'LIMITLESS IN POWER'! Now omnistand this. Everyone and everything in existence have creative power. How one chooses to use their creative power determines one's STATE OF BEING; one's vibrational harmonic tone! That tone distinguishes one's purity and sharpness of pitch! Yes, anyone or anything may be able to create, but the overall question needing answered is, 'What is being created'? Take a moment and think about your life. Your life is a mirror, a reflection of your deepest thoughts, words, and definitions! It is by and through which you have created your individual reality in this agreed collective existence.

Let us keep in mind. We do not have to LEARN anything! All we need is to REMEMBER WHO WE ARE! All the learning we will ever need is within that knowing. KNOW THY SELF!

Of course, this is only my perspective, nothing more and nothing less!

10/22/2013
By: Dr. Ali

34
THE REFLECTIONS OF LIFE

Understanding life is made simple by first understanding that different universal laws govern the various aspects or divisions of space/time dimensions. Allowing everything to follow its purposeful role and knowing what those roles are, is the awakening experience. No one and no thing can 'Wake' you up. One must 'Choose' to see. One must 'Choose' to begin this arousing, awakening; this 'Re-Membering,' this 'Re-Collecting,' from the many lifetimes of reincarnating into this realm of forgetfulness or sleep. Although consciousness is "ALL THAT IS" and there have never been an 'Out there' – out there… We have all believed that there [was]. We all believed this before entering into this 3rd Dimensional, Illusional Duality because we made this agreement beforehand.

As expressions or aspects of "CONSCIOUS THOUGHT," we volunteered to 'Experience' how this seemingly 3rd Dimensional, Illusional 'Reality' actually feels. The only thing in all of this reality that is 'Real' is the 'Experience.' Everything that touches you personally, your health, family, pets, friends, neighbors, close associates, etc., is your vibrational offering, a 'Reflection,' or 'Mirror' of your 'Beliefs' and 'Definitions'; all manifested into physical form for your experience.

Some of us are starting to 'Re-Member,' who we 'Really' ARE! Beginning to 'Re-Collect' that we are 'Multi-Dimensional, Eternal Beings,' having a 3rd – dimensional, 'Hue-Man' experience! Did you get all of that?

What you see about other people, places or things, that conjure up within you Resentment, Anger, Hatred, Jealousy, Judgment, Malice, Irritability, Disdain, Dis-Ease, Uneasiness, any ill or Negative feeling are all perfect mirror reflections of ISSUES lurking within YOURSELF! All life is YOUR creation through 'Beliefs' and 'Definitions' which are reflected at you in physical form as your reality!

When we fully 'Remember' that we are Love, and begin to Love, Respect, and Forgive OURSELVES FIRST, then we will no longer possess Resentment, Anger, Jealousy, Hatred, Malice, Irritability, Disdain, Dis-Ease, Uneasiness, any ill or Negative feelings towards others. We will have truly 'Remembered'! We will have truly 'Awakened' to Self-Love, and at that moment, **'No-Thing Negative'** can touch us without our consent! At that moment, we will have chosen LOVE, which is, 'ALL THAT IS' anyway!

Of course, this is only my perspective; No thing more and nothing less.

11/06/2013
By: Dr. ALi

35
THE ESOTERIC NATURE OF META-PHYSICAL THOUGHT

The world that you have chosen to visit is the only one of its kind. It is the lowest in vibration, densest in energy, and the furthest in illusional separation, standing at the leading edge of creative thought! No other realm offers such possibilities; no other dimension offers such awakening growth; no other such 'ality' (duality, triality) offers such challenging experiences, mind-boggling feats, or death-defying tasks! You are there by choice. You are there because you were deemed 'Mighty' enough to handle the environment. You were found worthy by the hearts of an eternal counsel and trusted by such in their infinite wisdom.

As you continue on your awakening path, please keep in mind your new-found thoughts and conscious awareness are not for the faint of heart! As you have enjoyed your undisturbed journey, please do not infringe upon others' desire to experience the same. Why tell someone that they are having a surprise birthday party?

You have come to this point in your life through many incarnations. You have experienced many trials of seeming failures and many countless attempts to remember 'WHY'!

For now, just know this; When the moment arrives, you will leap with ecstatic joy, your heart will vibrate with unprecedented knowing, and you will acknowledge that it was all well worth the while!

Yet we reemphasize the importance of this one little thought. Where you have arrived consciously in thought, omnistanding is not for everyone. Please do not push, shove, or impose your thoughts on anyone. Besides, it is a violation of 'Free Will'! Let it be enough to know that all will follow the same course, on their path, in their own due time. For now, we all salute you… 'Masters of Limitation'!

Of course, this is only my perspective; no thing more and no thing less!

09/16/2017
Dr. ALi

36
MOST PEOPLE HAVE NEVER QUESTIONED!

Most people have never questioned what they were taught from their childhood to adulthood. Most people simply take for granted that everything that they have ever been taught was the whole truth, nothing but the truth, so help them, God! You should be grateful that you questioned Santa Claus! You should be grateful that you questioned the Easter Bunny! You should be grateful that you questioned Christopher Columbus discovering some people living on a continent for many, many years; before his arrival! You should be grateful that you questioned Health (Sick) Care! You should be grateful that you questioned Doctors, or you would have never learned that your body heals itself! You should be grateful that you questioned your school system, or you would have never come to know of Meta-Physics! You should be very grateful that you questioned your race, or some of you would have never known that Colored, Negro, White, Black, or African American are not the names of races! You should be very grateful!

You live in a duality that was designed for everyone. Whoever chose to go into that dimension to receive any particular unique experience was orchestrated to meet their peculiar and unique desires.

This beautiful world was one that existed at the very leading edge of thought in the multi-verse. No other Beings anywhere has dared to stretch their creative abilities into such depths of limitation & darkness! No other Beings in existence has ever and will never again; attempt to shut themselves off from the only true source of 'Light.'

You see, your world, as it became to be known, was designed to keep its inhabitants ignorant from ever knowing who they are. The inhabitants were never to discover their true-life stories. For if they did, they would wake-up from their sleeping stupor, and their purpose for going into such a realm would be over. Your world is exactly the way it was designed. There is nothing out of order going on there. No mistakes are being made. There are no problems that were not meant to be. There is no Right or Wrong. Only experiences!

You should be very grateful that you questioned your solar system, how your planets soar through the Milky Way Galaxy and circle your sun. You will be even more grateful to yourself if you questioned **RELIGION**. It will help you come to know… '**I AM**'!

Of course, this is only my perspective; no thing more and no thing less!

12/23/2016
By: Dr. ALi

37
U R A UNIQUE EXPRESSION OF
'ALL THAT IS'

Date: /   /20

By:

38
NATURAL SELF HYPNOSIS

The reality in which we live consists of Laws that govern and sustain its construct. In this, as in all other realms, creation operates in a precise order, with total obedience and respect to these eternal forces. Whosoever discovers such knowledge or directives will inevitably ascend or gain a more exceptional ability over one's own vastly powerful true Self. One such law is "Natural Self Hypnosis." This 3rd Dimensional Duality is an Illusion. It is a holographic display of digital energy interpretations, being reflected in a manifested physical form of your deepest and greatest **BELIEFS**! In this realm, whatsoever you choose to **believe**, the forces that be will consciously create a self-perpetuating system of support to sustain that **belief**! *Did you get that?* This is why you should never argue because everyone is right within their own chosen belief!

Some people **believe** in their Shamans, Priests, Witch Doctors, Voodoo, Sorceress, Wizards, Ceremonial body decorating and painting, Ritualistic Dances, and Chanting; with the eating of various plants and animals; baths in smoke, mixed solutions, mud or water, etc. While **Believing** such practices will ward off evil and sickness, thus bringing the happiness they desire and the much-needed healing they seek.

While other so-called more sophisticated thinkers **believe** in Preachers, Bishops, Elders, Modern Doctors, Nutritionists, Chiropractors, Herbalists, Ceremonial dressing in gowns for Ritualistic procedures called examinations; with the eating of deadly chemical prescription – psychotropic drugs; baths in poisonous radiation treatments, etc. While **Believing** such practices will Save them from contracting bad health and bring the homeostasis they desire and the much needed Heaven they seek!

All BELIEFS ARE SELF-HYPNOTIC! Whether it is true for anyone else or NOT! It governs and manifests, from moment to moment, **your** experiential existence in this 3rd Dimensional Illusional Duality! Life has no inherent meaning, and no one else can give your meaning of life to you! **You Determine** the meaning that life has manifested for you! Life becomes what you choose to buy into as the highest, most revealing thing you **believe** your life can be!

Of course, this is only my perspective: Nothing more and Nothing less!

12/30/2013
By: Dr. ALi

39
THE PERVERSION OF IMAGERY

Every thought of the mind is an image, act of the will, determination, or desire. Every thought is a frequency, a vibration expressed on the invisible pool of ether or energy, as a request. **We are Co-Creators!** Tell me, what have you been requesting lately? Since we are all one with the Universe, ALL THAT IS, Source or God, there is never a time during our life that any individual thought is not co-creating. All thought is automatically metamorphosized into our reality and physicalized for us to experience. Our life is of our very own creation.

TELEVISION IS ONE OF THE MOST DESTRUCTIVE DRUGS KNOWN IN THIS WORLD! Images that are not purposed are drugs to our minds. The unwanted images that flash before our eyes keep us in a daze of confusion. These images keep our mind bathed with a thick slime of pleasurable fulfillment or ridiculous entertainment. These images become so inextricably messed and meshed within our thoughts that many cannot escape them even during hours of intimacy with sleep. **Be warned!** Spiritual Attainment is by thought! Whatever interferes with thought interferes with Spiritual Attainment! Selah!

Revised!

Television and movie theaters are one of the most powerful spiritual distortions man has invented. The reason being is that it mimics a teach/learning/entertaining & innocent environment; which is a deceptive glue that helps to bind this construct as a normal existence.

Such visual activity lures, very gently, the finer sensitivity of the spiritual mind into an emotional glamour, a mental illusion, and an etheric Maya! Your already distorted vision has now taken you into a lower level of vibrational delusion! You have been had! And to top it all off, you feel emotionally glad! Mentally satisfied and ethereally subdued!

You have embodied and personified your reflection (reality), and now you are the reflection of the reality which you have given sentience! You are now the 'Created'; by your casual and careless visual exploits… *(What you put out is what you get back.)* You are the image in the mirror now and by Universal Law – the Attraction!

Of course, this is only my perspective; No thing more and no thing less!

03/19/15
Dr. Ali

40
NEVER DISCREDIT, REGRET NOR INVALIDATE!

You create your reality! If you believe that' statement, you should never Discredit, Regret, or invalidate any personal experience! Why? Because every individual experience is a reflection, a mirror; they are physicalized digital frequency impulses; emanating, 360 degrees from your present state of Beliefs. Your experiences are an exact balance, equal, or match to your Vibrational Resonance! Therefore, you created that moment of experience! Whether by deliberate creation or by default. What you put out is what you got back. Period!

You must come to fully accept every experience as a learning moment; and every learning moment as a step towards greater expansion, enlightenment, and awareness. One cannot Discredit, Regret, nor Invalidate any moment because it is from those moments that one sequesters the concepts necessary for the metamorphosis of thought, which grows into more evolved Beliefs. One cannot tear down the bridges that helped you cross the voids of illusion without tearing down your very own foundation from which your growth is exhumed.

Everything is Positive! If you say so! And since you believe that thought to be true, then every present moment has a gift in it for you. A glorious 'PRESENT' for you to enjoy, learn, and grow! The Universe does not make mistakes, and you are One with the Universe. Whether the moment was undesired, unintended, or disliked since the choice was made, it was necessary for your development! Period! You must unlearn such 3rd-Dimensional beliefs that set one experience better or worse than another. All experiences are beneficial! As is Life! As is Existence! As is the 'ONE' Experience, viewed from different perspectives.

You are waking up from an illusion! Grab hold of these concepts and wrap your mind around there vibration until you resonate in perfect harmony therewith. Repeat the idea often until the thought is no longer repeated from memory but a self-knowing, reverberating from your state of Being. This thought/truth as all other thoughts/truths must become you! Because you can never know a thought/truth until you become that thought/truth! Why? Because there is only ONE TRUTH... ONE BELIEF... ONE MOMENT... ONE EXPERIENCE... ONE – ONE! VIEWED FROM DIFFERENT PERSPECTIVES!

Of course, this is only one perspective; Nothing more and nothing less!

By: Dr. ALi
10/21/2015

41
EVERY MOMENT

Every moment of life is neutral; Created from your Vibrational Frequency, which is your Beliefs. That moment is 'Presented' to you in the 'Present' because it is a 'Gift'! That 'Present' moment has no meaning but is activated with purpose through your existing 'Belief System.' You automatically take on that meaning and simultaneously receive the affect or experience from it, which you come to know as your Life!

Everyone has free will, free choice! That is the beauty of this particular Holographic - Illusion, Immersion duality dimensional experience. 'ALL THAT IS,' CREATOR, GOD, JEHOVAH, ALLAH, YAHWEH, UNIVERSE, etc. only creates that which is Beautiful! It is the Free Will of all infinite Created Being's to view this creation as they choose after filtered through their Belief System.

There is no right or wrong way to view creation. All are vibrations and frequency interpretations, which is more or less in perfect alignment/harmony with 'ALL THAT IS,' CREATOR, GOD, JEHOVAH, ALLAH, YAHWEH, UNIVERSE, etc.

No vibration truly exists OUT of alignment/harmony with 'ALL THAT IS,' CREATOR, GOD, JEHOVAH, ALLAH, YAHWEH, UNIVERSE, etc.

It is all an illusion! Because all exist WITHIN the mind or consciousness of 'ALL THAT IS,' CREATOR, GOD, JEHOVAH, ALLAH, YAHWEH, UNIVERSE, etc.

For all is, No thing more and No thing less than the expressed 'Thought' of…

'ALL THAT IS,' CREATOR, GOD, JEHOVAH, ALLAH, YAHWEH, UNIVERSE' etc.

Of course, this is only my perspective; No thing more and no thing less!

12/06/15
By: Dr. Ali

42
SYNCHRONICITY

Life experiences occur naturally. Experience is Vibrating Energy flowing naturally in life. Energy is Un-Conditional Love, manifesting itself through experiences in your reality which flows naturally. Everything Vibrates at a particular Frequency, which establishes its self as a state of being! Everything 'IS' a Vibrational Frequency, and it is THROUGH your understanding/beliefs, which is a Vibrational Frequency of Unconditional Love that manipulates this Vibrating Energy and Creates or Manifests into material form, a Perfect reflection, match or balance, as your physical life experience. There are no accidents in life!

Though your life is Adventurous or Mundane, Exciting or Boring, Expectant or Disappointing, Encouraging or Discouraging, Enjoyable or Deplorable, etc., no one, not anyone can experience other than that which is of their creation! No one can experience what is not a PERFECT REFLECTION, MATCH, or BALANCE to their present Vibrational Frequency or State of Being!

Your entire life experiences have been no thing more and no thing less than an expression of Un-Conditional Love. It has been filtered through your very own Belief System, establishing your Vibrational Frequency, (Tone, Individuality, Personality, Attitude). This process manipulates Un-Conditional Love, creating the path and life which you have experienced! Did you get all of that? "What you put out… is what you got back"! It is never a Punishment or Reward; only an experience!

It is all Physics, though most will not accept nor agree. But to the wise, we acknowledge that if you do not prefer your present experiences in life, then go within. Change your Belief System, and your life experiences will change. Become more consciously aware of how to deliberately create the life you so desire. So stop resisting the natural flow of Life. Learn to apply a positive perspective to that which has no inherent meaning. For every moment is a Present! Given to you in that 'Present Moment' for the sole purpose of exploration, adventure & excitement, in learning who you are… "Know Thy Self"!

Your family, friends, associates, people you encounter, and those you observe from a distance; are reflections of your 'Belief System,' created by 'YOU,' in this infinite & meticulous, ever-evolving - inextricable plan, Called life!

Of course, this is only my perspective; No thing more and no thing less!

12/19/2015
By: Dr. Ali

43
STOP LOOKING BACK

Meta-Physically speaking, it may appear that there is no thing negative with reflecting on times past. But that concept is a very cunning deception unknown to the masses. 3rd-Dimension consists of many types of glue that bind that construct together. It keeps one from growing or ascending spiritually to grander levels of existence. Looking Back is one of them. You have been programmed to Look Back, remember the past, remember where you came from, quote historical figures, and dead authors as a custom of sounding or appearing smart or intelligent.

It is all a part of the most intricate and sophisticated matrix. This submersion illusion is a 'du-a-li-ty' and hypnotic in thought. This illusion teaches and enslaves one to believe that one is not intelligent enough to conceive an 'Original Thought'! And yet, that is partially true! (You do not 'CONCEIVE' any thoughts at all. Thoughts are placed within your brain, and you choose which you prefer to identify as your own). But that is another study. Your present realm teaches that truth must come from, 'Out There,' from someone else within your matrix. This realm is designed to keep you from discovering who you are.

If you base your belief on the past, then you will not focus on the Present Moment and yourself as the Creator of your own, Here and Now, Reality! Empowerment comes from within! Enlightenment comes from within the 'Present Moment'! **You are, and you exist within your own 'Consciousness.'** **LIFE DOES NOT HAPPEN TO YOU. LIFE HAPPENS THROUGH YOU!** All that you think is around you is not real at all and is only a REFLECTION of your innermost BELIEFS; All Created by YOU and for YOU to experience in physical form! The only real thing about your life 'Here and Now' is the experience! Did you get that?

What you put out (Vibrationally), is what you get back, (In physical form)!

Meta-Physically Speaking, the Past does not exist, nor does the Future, not even Time. The only real thing that exists in this 'PRESENT MOMENT' is the EXPERIENCE! IT IS ALWAYS ETERNALLY, HENSE FORTH AND FOREVERMORE, 'NOW'!

Of course, this is only my perspective; No thing more and no thing less!

01/10/2016
By: Dr. Ali

44
AT THE BASIS OF: Is the Ego

At the basis of an **Opinion** is Belief! One cannot have an Opinion without first creating a concluded or settled *Belief from the previously acquired information.*

At the basis of a **Belief** is Judgment! One cannot have a Belief without first creating a mental *Judgment* from the previously acquired information. At the basis of **Judgment** is Fear! One cannot have a *Judgment* without first creating cumulative Feelings, Knowledge, Sentiments, Prejudices, etc., from one's own life experiences, which determines whether to *Fear* or not to *Fear*. At the basis of **Fear** is the Ego *(SELF)!* One cannot have *Fear* without first having created a reason to *Fear!* And it is by your own doing that you have changed and created the *Ego* into that which it never was meant to be but now fighting to continue its imbued personification as you have created it.

One has always had an Ego. Ego is not its original title or name. To exist in this particular realm or dimension, you were created as a Personification, Personality, Individual Self, Physical Mind, or **Channeled Being**. As Consciousness, you agreed to forget who you are, so that you could experience physicality through a Physical Mind.
The Ego was assigned to you as a highly devoted partner, guide, protector, and loyal friend. The Ego's

primary responsibility was to help keep the illusion hidden so that the agreed experience could be accomplished. As Consciousness, Eternal and Multi-Dimensional Beings, You Fear NO THING! The Ego helped you through the use of Cautions, so as not to needlessly fall off a cliff, burn, drown, or be eaten by a carnivorous – less evolved Being! The Ego is always reminding you of your finiteness. Thus the life experience could continue without unnecessary interruption.

The Ego knows only what you tell it, and you tell or fed the Ego through your chosen Beliefs. The Ego then utilizes your System of Beliefs to assist you in your everyday life experiences. But, that which you have chosen to believe has developed the Ego into a malicious Micromanaging, totalitarian dictator that (It) you have become today. You now think that you are in control and have to *Conceive* of your way through life. But! You do not!

These are a few of the various aspects of the Self. You are Eternal and Multi-Dimensional. And now you are starting to remember! It is time to bring all of these expressions back into a unified whole from which you began.

You are Eternal Consciousness! It is time to start behaving accordingly!

Of course, this is only our Perspective; No thing more and no thing less!

01/15/2016

By: Dr. ALi

45
THERE IS ONLY ONE SOURCE OF FLOWING ENERGY

The ONE is all, and all that is - is ONE! This is the Second Universal Law. It is from this 'ONE SOURCE' that everything consists. There is only ONE, expressing itself in an infinite number of ways. Yet still only ONE expression. ONE thought, ONE knowing, ONE feeling, ONE emotion, ONE moment, ONE energy which is LOVE: You are an expression of the ONE LOVE SOURCE; expressed using the essence of the FLOWING ENERGY of this ONE SOURCE of LOVE. The ONE Source or Energy of LOVE is ALL THAT IS! There is no other thing.

You Exist! This is the First Universal Law. Existence itself is Eternal! So then, everything that exists has always and will always exist! That which you think is outside of you is controlled and Created by you, known as 'Life.' Life is not real, nor eternal. It is an illusion created by you for your experience. Life is a very sophisticated, immersion – holographic illusion and does not exist! The only real thing about your life is the Experience. Life is a reflection of your innermost Beliefs; it is a perfect balance or match, solidified, and physicalized into the theme of your life's duality as a result of your chosen Belief System.

Love Energy flows or is filtered through your Belief System, and as a result, you perceive your life and have experiences according to that perspective. Love and Fear are the same energy: Also, Peace and War, Care and Hate, Right and Wrong, Good and Bad. The same Love energy that flows through the hunter flows through the hunted. The same Love energy that flows through the Courageous flows through the Fearful. And it is the same Love energy that flows throughout the Creator as it is that flows through to Desecrator.

Remember, there is only ONE SOURCE from which flows LOVE ENERGY and by which all things consist. What each expression does with the flowing of that LOVE is determined by their chosen Belief System. That Belief System is accumulated through everyday life experiences. Yes, my friend, you are all given the very same gift of Flowing Love and are free to use it as you see fit. There is no Expectation, Judgment, or Condemnation by the ONE. Neither will you be Faulted, Blamed, or Censored. You will only be UNCONDITIONALLY LOVED!

Of course, this is only my perspective; No thing more and no thing less!

02/04/2016
By: Dr. Ali

46
IT REALLY DOESN'T MATTER

All that Exist originated from only 'One Source.' That Source is "All That Is." That Source is omnipotent – omniscient and Omnipresent! All creations are facets, sparks, or expressions of "The One," experiencing itself in all the ways it, infinitely, can!

All expressions are Good; Because Good is "All That Is." Only that which exists is Real! That which is out of vibrational frequency with "All That Is" does not exist and is not 'Real.' Therefore, only the 'Experience' from that which is not real is actually 'Real'! Did you get that?

No experience is 'Better' or 'Worse' than any other experience. Such an experience must be Believed, and such a Belief creates a wobble or an 'Out of Alignment' experience. 'Preferences' towards this illusional – Holographic, Duality, immerses you deeper into this self-perpetuating experience matrix. The very thought of wanting or desiring any experience over another, automatically, submerges you deeper. Your Belief System has you Self-Deceived, and you have no clue.

You see, this ride that you have willingly chosen to experience has many variations.

When you look at it, you must be objective; because it is all a matter of perspective! It goes up, down, over, under, out, in, around, and around! Though all experiences are different, all experiences are the same! All that you are experiencing is no more than a game! Except for this game, you cannot win or lose; it is all about the way you choose. That thought in itself does not give much relief; this one is better; check your system of 'Beliefs'!

It is now time to end this thought realization; It was intended to help you with deliberate creation. Don't get me wrong; you're expected to have joy! But all your manifestations are still just a toy. So, treat them that way, including those of the collective, remembering that there is only one valid perspective! So use this thought as a runner on a ladder; when it is all said and done,

It Really Doesn't Matter!

12/06/2014
By: Dr. ALi

47
EVERYTHING IS SACRED & VALID

There is an infinite number of paths to take on your journey back to the light. There are an endless number of thoughts to think and conscious states to discover as well. No one path thought, or conscious state is better or worse than another, although some directions, ideas, and conscious states do guide you on a more direct path back to the light of Unity Consciousness. The key is to remember 'Why' you are on a path to start with, and that reason is for 'ALL THAT IS,' 'SOURCE,' 'PRIME-CREATOR' or 'GOD,' to experience itself in all the ways that it can. And you, my friend, as an aspect or expression, in a most incredible personified form. You are multi-dimensional, and one of an infinite number of aspects or expressions used to harvest such experiences.

Everything that exists and created is Sacred and Equally Valid; that includes the light and the dark. It is through the freedom to choose or develop beliefs that bring about a self-hypnotized state of consciousness. This leads you to believe that you are out of Sacred Unity, sync, balance, harmony, or tone with 'ALL THAT IS.' Yet still, all choices are equal, the positive as well as the negative. Without Judgment or invalidation, choose the one you prefer.

You see, everything that exists is done so out of freedom of choice. It is entirely worthy of its existence and with the full intent for, 'ALL THAT IS,' to experience itself in all the ways that it can. No thing should be invalidated, or you would hold within your thinking a vibrational thought out of unity, sync, balance, harmony, or tone with 'ALL THAT IS.'

We all exist within the consciousness of 'ALL THAT IS,' and everything created as well. There is nowhere else to exist! We are all thoughts within the mind of 'SOURCE ENERGY'; for all is but the infinite energy waves of 'SOURCE.' There is no such thing as 'OUT THERE' or 'OVER THERE,' 'UP THERE' OR 'DOWN THERE.' 'ALL THAT IS' is all there is! As you journey closer to the light, your thoughts began to hold vibrational tones more in tune with Unity Consciousness. You begin to come more into sacred unity, sync, balance, harmony, and tone. Your delusional thoughts of separation begin to dissolve, and the hypnotic false beliefs lose their grip. You once more recognize yourselves for who you really are and have always been and will always be.

'ALL THAT IS'

03/07/2016
By: Dr. Ali

48
NO THING CREATED
EXIST BUT
EVERY THING CREATED IS ETERNAL

The nature of infiniteness is far grander than is your present cognitive ability to discern its true meaning. You cannot apply third-dimensional laws, rules, or codes when attempting to understand the infinite. Therefore, we will lay down a few eternal rules in this missive as we **attempt** to explain why... 'No Thing Created Exist, but Every Thing Created is Eternal.'

We Exist as ONE Consciousness! There is only one infinite Consciousness, in what is only the here and the now. This ONE Consciousness was not created. This One Consciousness simply 'IS.' It has always been and will always be! This ONE Consciousness is All that Is and all that 'IS,' 'IS' this One Consciousness. This ONE Consciousness can observe itself from different perspectives, thus allowing self-expression in an infinite number of ways, in an infinite harmonizing wave of conscious oneness. Inference, dancing in unique patterns of toned frequencies, in and out of forms brought on by focused thought, from various perspectives looking back at itself!

Infiniteness is UNCONDITIONAL! Infiniteness is LIMITLESS! Infiniteness is BOUNDLESS! Infiniteness cannot be explained by Conditioned, Limited, and bound minds! Only Infinite Consciousness can explain Infiniteness!

That which is created does not EXIST; it is a CREATION and thus only an illusion, but it is still some thing. And that which is some thing can never become no thing because it already is some thing! Everything created came from that which 'IS' and cannot appear like something else because something cannot be created from no thing! No thing can ever become some thing, or it would prove that no thing was always some thing. That which Exist, can never, Not Exist because Non-Existence does not exist! Existence is already full of all that exist, and nonexistence is full of all that does not! Did you get that?

Change is constant! But first, there must be a 'THING' from which a thing can change from. However, there are four Multi-Versal Laws that never change.

1. You Exist!
2. Every thing is here and now!
3. THE ONE is all & all are THE ONE!
4. What you put out is what you get back!
5. Everything changes, except these first four postulates!

This is only my perspective; No thing more and no thing less!

03/09/2016
By: Dr. Ali

49
ENERGY FLOW 'LIFE SOURCE'

The number one key to any being's existence is their 'Energy Flow.' Energy flow determines your state of awareness, which Gaia responds to by activating latent cells on a subatomic, molecular level; within your DNA. This activation increases your vibration, thus enabling more extraordinary personal abilities. There is only one source of pure energy but an infinite number of diluted and distorted variations after being filtered through the individual Being's belief system. And there are many, if not an endless number of realms, plains and dimensions from which they exist.

All existence and creation consist of this pure, electro-magnetic energy source, by which to maintain its present state of being! Therefore, your energy and its freedom of impediment, in the slightest degree, should hold your utmost attention! Whatsoever you eat or speak, drink or think, should all be done with the thought in mind of how it will affect your energy flow.

There is only One Consciousness; One Thought; One Thing! That One Thing is Omni-Present, Omni-Cient, and Omni-Potent! You presently exist at the leading edge of creative thought. You stand at the furthest and darkest point of believed separation from that pure source of energy.

Yet you still carry an untainted, unstained and pure spark of the original source of energy within. Discovering the knowledge of this spark and how to allow it to, once more, fill your entire Being is your journey in life.

This process is referred to as 'Waking Up.' How much one wakes up is an individual choice. This incarnation is not a race, nor is there a right or wrong path to follow by which one may choose in this process. You have all of eternity to evolve and ascend into more of your true resonant self. It is not so much what you learn as it is what you experience that means the most. It is your experience that is the only REAL thing during this journey anyway. The rest is only an illusional duality, submersion hologram of the most sophisticated and exquisite creating!

Your energy has been secretly, deceptively, and deviously sucked from you and your planet by Beings on a higher plain of dimensionality. After death, you have been kept here by reincarnation as a food source for these Beings.

But now it is time for you to know that cosmic help has terminated that looshing! You may now, at will, become more sensitively aware and choose to let go of this illusional duality, submersion holographic experience. By letting go, we mean, recognize your life for what it is, and stop resisting.

Every established belief connects you with other vibrations of similar thought. Be it high or low; you begin to ascend or descend. Your vibrational resonance creates a reflection in this hologram for your experience by your free choice of beliefs. On a subatomic, photonic level, you connect to that which you engage; on purpose or not, by action or by thought. How you relate to your illusional duality, submersion holographic surroundings, will determine the effect you receive from it. By relating we mean, what you choose to 'BELIEVE' about your surroundings.

Thoughts of jealousy, envy, ridiculing, arguing, anger, hatred, or ill feelings, opens a photonic channel for your life source to be drained! You must choose to keep your beliefs and thoughts elevated if you desire to receive your energy from a purer and lofty energy source.

Remember, everything is neutral in this illusion. You give everything the meaning it will possess in your duality, and the definition that you choose to provide will be the effect you ultimately receive from the experience. All is but a reflection of your innermost 'BELIEFS.' This is your ride, superimposed upon the collective ride, and you are all riding and enjoying this game of life together!

Of course, this is only our perspective! No thing more and no thing less!

11/17/2014
By: Dr. Ali

50
BETTER OR WORST
BELIEF SYSTEMS

I would like you to view 'BELIEF' as the densest solid substance known, created in any realm, reality, or dimension. View it as a shaft or rod of steel. And as another quality, it has awareness! All things, everything, owes its creation to 'BELIEF.' One description represents its strength while the other, its intelligence. All things, everything created, is founded upon, based, and self-perpetuated by 'BELIEF'! You are reading this and understanding this missive according to what you believe. And if you choose not to finish reading this, it will also be caused by what you 'BELIEVE.' There is only ONE energy source. And that ONE energy source is all 'LOVE'; of course, that too is a 'BELIEF.' Everything exists or is created by, with, and consists totally of this ONE energy source; yes, it is a 'BELIEF.'

Therefore, however, we may have slept the night before, whatever side of the bed we awakened on, whether it is raining or the sun is shining; cold or hot; clothed or naked; in your home or homeless; not hungry with food or hungry without food; job or jobless; rich or poor. It all has to be equally valid and 'GOOD' because it all comes from 'LOVE,' which, as we have stated, is a 'BELIEF'! Rom. 8:28

Our beliefs strengthen our alignment with "ALL THAT IS," or it will create a type of weakened out of alignment wobble. Since we believe that there is only 'ONE' source of energy from which all things and everything is derived, one can only conclude that there is NO difference in one experience from another! On the deepest and most intuitive level of cognitive awareness, there is no such thing as good-bad, right-wrong, better, or worst! They are all only experiences of your creation. Phil. 4:11 1Tim. 6:6

It is by our 'BELIEFS' that we divide, categorize, compartmentalize, and compare! We place value upon wants, desires, and dislikes! We become short-sighted and limited because of our beliefs. And it is all because we have forgotten who we are!

So, I would guess the most important question to ask is, "Who do you 'BELIEVE' you are? Because all that you have read, if you have gotten this far, will only mean to you, no more and no less than that which you 'BELIEVE.' And that which you believe determines who you are! You must come to accept totally, without any invalidation, every manifestation that appears before you. Why? Because by doing so, you express acceptance of yourself.

By: Dr. ALi
12/01/2014

51
PREFERENTIAL CONTRADICTION

Part A

How long has it been since you first heard, accepted, believed, and began stating, "I AM the Creator of my reality"? That is such an enlightened concept to become aware, accept, and of course, 'Believe.' You always create what matches your frequency! But! I have a most interesting question. Do you ever prefer any person, place, thing, circumstance, or situation over another? If you do, why would you create a person, place, thing, circumstance, or situation you do not prefer?

'ALL THAT IS,' does not make mistakes. And since you are 'Source Energy,' 'Infinite Being,' 'ALL THAT IS,' then it stands with absolute reason that you also do not make mistakes and thus create an exact balance or match as your duality, precisely according to your frequency. That person, place, thing, circumstance, or situation is precisely what you vibrationally conjured! Any known undesirable feelings against your now created life, only reveal a 'Wobble' and a lack of alignment with your Higher-Self

01-24-2015
By: Dr. ALi

Part B

You are totally and emphatically responsible for the creation of your reality. The frequency that you put out is the physical reality that you get back and live. It is an exact match with no mistakes! You always create what you believe is the most incredible possible life for you!

What is needed to be understood is that your thoughts and state of Being are in constant 'Contradiction'? Now, why is that? Your state of Being always reflects your present, past, and past incarnations. Your existence in your 3rd – 4th dimension required that you forget who you are. The illusional effects of that dimension added to and layered you with other "Belief Systems" that were Self-Perpetuating, which kept you in a 'Wobbling' state, out of alignment with your 'Higher-Self.' You must first remember who you are; how that - 'You' – believes, and "Believe That"! Then and only then will you always "Prefer" every created moment!

01-25-2015
By: Dr. ALi

Part C

Now, let us put it all together. Your life, reality, or present moment was fully allowed by your Higher-Self; all there is - is love. "ALL THAT IS" strongest desire for you is to be in joy, peace, and perfectly aligned with love! **Therefore, whatever present moment you are allowed to experience is emphatically and positively for your eternal good,** presented to you by your higher-self, according to your current vibrational frequency. Rom 8:28

You either believe in the previous statement, or you do not! Your 'Emotional Guidance System' will reveal your actual state of Being. The ever so slightest wobble will be detected, decoded, and reflected right back in your face! Your 'Emotional Guidance System' cannot misinterpret in the least degree, a distorted understanding of your present moment frequency. For you to think otherwise is a 3rd-dimensional distortion of thought.

So then, I have a most interesting question. Do you ever 'Prefer' any person, place, thing, circumstance, or situation over another or have any regrets? Someone's out of alignment!

Of course, this is only my perspective. No thing more and no thing less!

01-26-2015
By: Dr. ALi

52
THE VARIABILITY OF FREQUENCY

Believing that you are the creator of your reality is a concept now widely accepted. Though not fully nor intelligently understood by most. It is, however, a fundamental concept of becoming a deliberate creator. Everything that you experience has been previously filtered through your belief system and projected back at you 'as' your moment to moment experience. Nothing can happen to you unless it is an absolute match to your frequency. This is Universal Law; this is physics!

Your mind is very sensitive, impressionable, and powerful; it should be guarded with extreme care. The thoughts you express reinforce your previously formed beliefs and they determine your continually retuning of your frequency tone. This vibrational frequency-tone is a musical equation that comprises an infinite number of variable elements or notes. This is your signature statement that determines your state of Being or Melody. As you consider other variations in tones of concepts and express these to the point of belief; as a fixed melody or song, you have just altered, however so slightly, your previous associated tune – song; changed your next frequency – melody – song, thus your next moment of experience.

You are constantly shifting according to your change of frequency – melody – song; through matching reality picture frames, you experience each moment. It is by the music that you play vibrationally, from moment to moment, that determines everything you experience. The more crystal-clear and positive your pitch, the higher your vibration. The higher your vibration, the more harmonious your song! You play the instrument of beliefs every moment by caressing the Universe with new tones of thoughts and concepts. By blending and mixing, you create your very own personal signature song, and it is this song that is heard by the Universe. Remember, you create from your song or tone, not the notes or vibration; the notes or vibration only make up the frequency or tone.

The Universe does not make mistakes. The song you put out is the life you get back. To deny this thought only reveals one's lack of conscious awareness. The music you freely choose to play is what determines your ascension process. There is no Right or Wrong; Righteousness or Sinfulness; Good or Bad; it is all just a wave of experiences with infinite possibilities, all created by your signature melody.

Of course, this is only my perspective; No thing more and no thing less!

03/24/16
By: Dr. ALi

53
GAME

Of all the glues that hold the 3rd and 4th dimension together and the paths that keep you moving steadily in a low vibrational delusion towards darkness; None is as deceptively luring as that of the art called 'GAME'! Understanding and choosing to let go of this glue requires a special recognition through centripetal thought.

Let us begin. Games were first introduced as innocent fun. They were eagerly and enthusiastically grasped mentally by all to whom these games were introduced. Games were an ever-evolving, subtle, and very inextricable entity, first accepted as past time entertainment or as amusement for social gatherings. So tell me, my dear friend, what real harm could game play?

Games first involved single enjoyment as a sole challenge to always perform better the next time around. Then it became a test of personal intelligence. After a while, the thought of playing 'with' someone was conceived. Game has now evolved and subtly sunk its self-perpetuating beliefs deeper into the crevices of each player's heart. Game is now a mighty psychological, personified opponent; who always wins. If you choose to play, you will forever lose!

Your friend whom you were first playing with, has become your opponent and now is played 'Against'! Another new thought created by 'GAME,' why not 'Compete,' we can call it 'Competition'! Game's hold is tighter, its grip more secure; you are mentally, emotionally, and physically trapped and believe it or not; it's very severe! Game has you spiraling into an emotional decay. You are continually lowering your vibration every time you play.

You have learned to place meaning and value to the term 'Win' or 'Lose.' It has become an intricate part of your culture and to everyone that choose. Aggression is encouraged, winning is exalted; The lower animal propensities are awakened, and the concept, 'I BEAT YOU, I WON!', has taken on a whole new meaning. Deeper and deeper into delusional thought, does Game drag you. Losing has been formulated within the mind to be disdained, loathed, and disgraceful! It is disgusting, humiliating, and downright despicable! No one wants to lose!

Winning has taken on an even more psychological entrapment! The winner is given a false sense of superiority, physical strength, and deceptive self-empowerment! Winning is likened to an intoxication! The reasoning faculties have been compromised, and you will now go to extreme measures, irrational tactics to win! You are now engulfed in winning!

And losing is not an option. You have become a slave, and it's 'Game' you crave; you have given to 'Game,' so entirely your will; that now to win, you will even 'KILL'! Do you remember how it feels to win or lose? It runs deep, doesn't it? And the very thought of someone basking in their victory can leave you feeling shameful. The body may even respond in clumsy movements. Your speech may even stutter for expression, while your feelings sink lower into a mood of depression. And because of the way loosing has made you feel, you too will think that it is best to 'KILL!'.

You played 'GAME,' my man because it was cool; Now how do you feel, you Loss – Fool! Everyone knows it shows on your face; you know it too, by the feeling of disgrace! Something has been lost, but how do you explain? You do not have the words, but you do have the shame!

I demand a rematch. I demand a new game; by any means necessary, to get rid of this shame! It's all about me, damn it! My reputation has been scared; I've been living a lie, my life's a facade! I am willing to 'KILL' to re-establish my name, and if I lose this time, my response is the same! Lord!, how could I have become this which I once disdained? Could it possibly be over something so simple as 'GAME'?

12/27/2014
By: Dr. Ali

54
GAME! (Poem)

Game started as innocent fun; not to be serious, it was just for pun! But all along, there was a dark agenda; it was to grind your emotions as if in a blinder!

An unknown vice for solitary enjoyment; received applications for other's employment. With laughter and joy, you played with your friends; but soon, you're against them, and you played to defend!

New meaning in thought, and you have to choose; should I play to win or play to lose! Game has now taken on a personality; and losing's no option, in this reality.

I sense a new awareness, a new revelation; this game has become an intoxication! I put forth the effort to try not to play, but damn-it! I can't even cause a delay!

Whether I or a team, which I am a fan, to lose is a thought that I cannot stand. This 'Game' has got me, and I've lost control; I'm emotionally stirred up over a Super Bowl? At home, friends argued de-li-ber-ate-ly; Ding Dong! Who's there? The pizza delivery!

What in heaven or in hell could have happened to me; I never use to act, so emo-tion-al-ly. Could it possibly be this game that I play?

For a fact, I use to not act this way! Allow me, my friend, to make a suggestion; it's a mental creation, a manifestation! You played 'Game,' my man because it was cool, and losing has caused you to act like a fool! It's all a belief. It's a state of being; really and truly, you haven't lost a thing!

Don't dare tell me that, and expect me to believe, like nothing has happened, and I've been deceived! Something has been lost, though I cannot explain; I can feel it in my heart, it has left a stain! I demand a rematch. I demand a new game, by any means necessary, to get rid of the shame! It's all about winning, but I lost, and I'm scarred; my life has become, a hopeless façade!

I'm at the point now where I'd even Kill, just to win, so I can taste that pill! It's a crazy experience, an insane high, but I swear instead of losing, I'd rather die!

Yes, I will Kill to re-establish my name, so what's it to you? You've lost no Fame! How in this world did I become so insane? But please don't tell me, it was over a 'GAME'!

1/17/15
Dr. ALi

55
ISN'T YOUR GOD, GOD?

Date: /   /20

By:

56
THE ESSENCE OF PEACE

Empires, nations, countries, and individuals have lied, fought, and even killed for thousands of years in the name of peace. Yet peace still does not reign in the hearts of men and women. Now, why is that? Maybe Peace is not adequately understood for what it is, nor how to obtain it. Here is my perspective:

Peace is a higher frequency of thought, and one must stop thinking so third-dimensionally if one expects to obtain it. Also, one cannot lie, fight, or kill to obtain peace. Having peace is also not about protecting, defending, guarding, or controlling your thoughts. Lastly, peace cannot be acquired by using any lower vibrational thoughts or actions. It is all about what you choose to believe! There is nothing to fight against or for! Such an effort will only keep your vibration low and hold you in a state of peacelessness.

One must understand that there are many degrees of peace, which leads to more Intimate Degrees of Peace. And all along the way one may consider themselves at peace. Peace is a state of Being. So, it is to the degree or standard you hold for peace that will determine how far or close your state of Being will reflect more Intimate Degrees or Levels of Peace!

Peace is a particular frequency, vibrating at a specific rate of resonance. Peace is not something that you can gain or possess, but a mental state you become. Any degree of Peace can only be felt when one's frequency finally reaches that vibration in tone.

Ps. 119:165 states Great peace has they that love the law, and nothing shall offend them. Are you still being offended by what some person, place, or thing says or does? Are you still becoming upset, disturbed, bitter, or angry because of what happens outside of you? You cannot reflect Peace while holding on to such lower vibrational resonances. I wonder what law must one love, so not ever to be offended?

I believe that man's law cannot bring about peace since peace is not of man. I think that peace is 'ALL THAT IS'! It is by Universal Laws, which must be understood and practiced that sets one on the path to any degree of Peace. One such Universal Law is, 'The Universal Law of Allowing.' The Universal Law of Allowing means dropping all **judgments** and all emotional attachments to what all persons, places, or things **are**, **have**, **do**, or **say**. This is the path to Peace that passeth all understanding! Phil. 4:7

Of course, this is only my perspective; No thing more and no thing less!

05/01/2016
By: Dr. ALi

57

A CREATOR NEVER HAS VICTORY

Everything that you think do and say reveals what you believe about yourself. Make no mistake about this thought. You will always think, act, and speak as you Believe! These expressions reinforce your creative ability and do not cause materialization. Such words do not matter or become solid as a creation into your reality. **All creation is manifested by what you believe!** Belief is a rod of steel and is impossible to fake. What you believe is what you 'Put out.' It is what you will always create and 'Get back'! And the universe does not make mistakes! Period! So then it would be wise to pay close attention to how you think, act, and speak because these reinforce your beliefs.

As you move further into 5-D, you must continually delete, let go of various 3-D beliefs, recognize and keep up with the expansion of your conscious awareness. A victim, 'Wins & Looses, has Victory & Defeats, Successes & Failures, Conquers & is Conquered, make Mistakes, is Jealous, Argumentative, Envious, becomes Angry, gets Revenge, feels out of control, wants to be Right, so not to be Wrong, etc.

Where that a Creator CREATES, with Unconditional Love and is Omnipotent, Omnipresent, Omniscient, is neither Right nor Wrong, in total control and always at Infinite Peace!

You exist in a polarity realm where that a Creator and Victim are the same in nature but sit at opposite ends of the same steel rod of belief. So they differ only in degree.

It is your free choice to what degree you wish to exist on this rod of belief. How you feel, or your 'Emotional Guidance System,' will always let you know exactly where you stand in reference to Creator or Victim.

Of course, this is only my perspective; no thing more and no thing less!

05/09/2016
By: Dr. ALi

58
YOUR MOTIVATIONAL MECHANISM

We all have a personal Motivational Mechanism. That mechanism is simply this; you will always lean towards, buy into, accept, agree with or choose what you 'BELIEVE' will make you happy, joyful, satisfy you, benefit, or is best for you! There are no exceptions to this Motivational Mechanism.

Now, if your present life is not preferred, if it is full of drama, and a big disappointment, then that only means all of the DECISIONS which lead up to this moment in your life were brought on by DECISIONS that did not serve you, BUT you choose them because you BELIEVED that they would. Though these past decisions have proven to be far less than desirable, you still chose them based on that belief. Everything in life is created out of what you choose to believe. And beliefs are often built upon other beliefs, which are built upon other beliefs etc. Even now, you are deciding whether or not to choose to believe this missive!

If you choose to believe this missive, then this is how you can start creating or manifesting a more desirable life. First, you must figure out what it is that you believed, which has caused you to make such unsatisfying choices in life!

Take one choice or decision at a time and ask yourself, "What is it that I must have believed, for me to have made such unsatisfying decisions"? And, "What is it that I now need to believe that will motivate me to make my next more pleasurable decision"? If you can realize that a belief is outdated and no longer serves you, then delete that belief or replace that old, obsolete belief with a new updated version that better serves your joy, happiness, and wellbeing.

Everything is energy. Thoughts and beliefs are too. You, the world, and the universe are all a part of one significant metaphysical expression of infinite beauty! Understanding the physics, (laws), behind this beauty helps one enjoy a more delicious journey through this beautiful experience you call life.

Whatsoever the universe has presented to you, remember, it is all just an experience! Learn not to take this temporary life so seriously! Besides, you are a multi-Dimensional Infinite Being! This is only ONE of an infinite number of life experiences that you have had and will have.

Of course, this is only my perspective; No thing more and no thing less!

05/12/2016
By: Dr. ALi

59
Ultimate Self-Empowerment!

You have been lied to about your power from your birth and who has or does not have dominion over you. You have also been taught to 'FEAR,' which is the basis for losing your power. What you chose to buy into or Believe meant everything, and that is how you gave it all away! The Universal Law of Attraction; What you put out is what you get back; Positive Thinking etc. All hold their congruency - warranted through Belief, which is as a rod of Graphene, harder than a diamond and stronger than steel! All Solar Systems, Galaxies, Multi-Verses, Realms, Dualities, Dimensionalities, etc. hold their construct through Conscious Belief; and observation, which on such an infinite scale is actually, 'Knowing'! But that is another missive.

Everyone is a unique resonance, melodic tone, chord, pitch, or unique signature vibrational frequency! Whatever Vibrational Frequency you choose as your state of Being, Ultimately, determines the reality or parallel world you will experience! Physical reality does not exist; it is an illusional creation; as is LIFE. Yes! There is a state of Being you refer to as 'IS-NESS'; which is not life. Life is a 'CREATION'! Another thought for another missive. Let us continue. You are Consciousness and physical reality, as an Illusional, Submersion – Holographic Duality, exist 'WITHIN YOU.' Though 'sleep' does not exist either, let us just say you are sleeping and having a wonderful dream; only for many, it is a nightmare! Life is one big Matrix with everyone experiencing their own individually superimposed reality, like the negative to a photo, placed on top of each other.

Now, this is where it gets fascinating. Each negative frame is an individual, different, and separate possible reality TimeLine; in an independent parallel world! And every TimeLine or world consists of a different version of YOU! You are a different Being as you focus your consciousness through each Belief, creating each TimeLine or Static Reality world! Literally! Beliefs are self-sustaining. They must be re-established at infinite speed as you shift through every frame or world, always carefully matching Beliefs' slightest alteration. Your focus will be through the eyes of that version of you in the world that perfectly matches your beliefs or vibrational frequency at any given nanosecond. Do you ever wonder, 'What would have happened 'IF'?' Well, another 'YOU' did experience that 'IF'! There is an infinite number of 'IF' variations or realities, worlds, TimeLine possibilities, and versions of 'YOU.'

If you can cognize a thought within your imagination, then that version of you exist, in that world and Time Line of events! Your life is based upon or created from the most powerful thing that you BELIEVE it is capable of reflecting!

You can only create according to the prior collective agreement and overall purpose for the experience in this dimension and to the extent of what you believe is possible. You cannot experience what is not your vibrational frequency equivalent. Please understand your world, though it may appear exactly like or very similar to everyone else world, 'It is not'! It is your world, superimposed upon everyone else world, for the mutual collective interacting experience, and everyone is the Creator in their world! NO ONE CAN AFFECT OR CAUSE AN EFFECT TO YOU NOR YOUR WORLD WITHOUT YOUR PRIOR AGREEMENT, PRESENT CHOOSING OR BELIEF!

You shift from parallel reality worlds to parallel reality worlds, billions of times a second! All shifts are governed exactly and precisely by your beliefs. By focusing infinite pure energy, which is your beliefs or (Consciousness), through billions of static frame by frame reality worlds a second, your world is materialized, and motion is created. Wisely applying these quantum and meta-physical laws will help explain the structure of reality, and if practiced and perfected, one can better control the creation of anything they desire!

This is real Alchemy at its finest! It is the wisdom taught by the ancient Egyptians and in the mystery schools through the Order of Melchizedek. First introduced by The Great, Great, Great! The Master of Masters of Masters! Hermes Trismegistus!

This is knowledge kept secret from the whole world since the beginning of 'Yourstory,' 'Ourstory,' 'Mystory,' but **'NOT'** 'History'! What is above is below. The above energy is the same energy that is below! 1. You exist! 2. Everything is here and now. 3. THE ONE is THE ALL, and THE ALL are THE ONE! 4. What you put out is what you get back! 5. Everything changes (except those first four laws). If your life is not going as you desire, ask yourself one essential question; What is it that I believe? Dig deep because here dwells the wisdom of Ultimate Self-Empowerment!

You must let go of old 3rd-dimensional beliefs that no longer serve but disempower, limit, and restrain your expanded awareness. Your experience is the only thing real within this hologram. Your role in this wonderfully delicious & most sophisticated dramatic play is Creator; everyone else is only a version or reflection of 'Yourself,' as you are to everyone else. **(THE ONE is THE ALL and THE ALL are THE ONE!)**

You came into this realm by choice, with a prior agreement to experience interaction with your version of others in this simulated physicality of limitation, which is at the leading edge of thought in the multi-verse! To get the full extent of the experience, you had to forget who you are. Would you want to be told that you are being given a **surprise** birthday party? Now it is time for **MANY** to 'WAKE UP'!

Are you **'WAKING UP'**? **"THE LIPS OF WISDOM ARE CLOSED EXCEPT TO THE EARS OF UNDERSTANDING"**! R U OMNISTANDING?

Of course, this is only my perspective; no thing more and no thing less!

05/21/2016
By: Dr. ALi

60
ALL EXPERIENCES ARE VALID

You often use the phrase, 'I am only human,' 'I am trying,' 'Life is hard'! These phrases are all 3rd-dimensional excuses. Please understand that any use of thought that excuses a behavior is an open denial of one's power. You have learned many disempowering habits during your quest in 3-D. Believing that you are weak, without power, and giving excuses for that state of being are two such habits. You must come to the belief that you are all very, very powerful Multi-Dimensional Beings! Were you not, you would not have been allowed to incarnate into the most challenging dimensional realm, at the most challenging moment in linear time, of such dense physicality in **multiverstory**! Keeping your vibration as high as possible by **letting go** of old non-serving thoughts, beliefs, and definitions will bring conscious awareness to your real state and power. You always **believe** what is in your best interest! ALWAYS! By holding on to old, outdated beliefs that, in actuality, bring to you pain, discomfort, or ill feelings, only mean that you have an idea that if let go, it would not be in your best interest. The result would bring more incredible pain, discomfort, or ill feelings!

Incorporating positive concepts and beliefs that better serve you or are, according to your best interest, will bring to you greater joy, benefit, satisfaction, and shift you to a world more suited to your desires.

By understanding and accepting that all your life experiences are valid, empowers you most magnificently. You see, life itself is neutral, without meaning. It is up to you to give your life meaning. Whatever definition you give to your life's many circumstances, situations, and challenges will be the effect you will receive from them! All your experiences are valid and should be accepted with a positive attitude. To invalidate any experience is like removing the stepping stones of progress, to greater conscious awareness.

Although you may not favor a particular experience, that does not negate its infinite purpose. You cannot have an experience that is not purposeful! PERIOD! All experiences shape and mold you on your life's journey. Some of your most unpleasant, distasteful, and even horrible experiences have been most enlightening, fulfilling, and empowering! And if you deny such experiences by your negative thoughts, you lose the real benefit and growth in conscious awareness which is of infinite value and reward.

You must **let go** of every thought, belief, and definition that is no longer serving you! How do you know what thoughts, beliefs, and definitions are no longer serving you? If they bring you the slightest pain, discomfort, or ill-feeling! You must come to believe that every experience has an infinite purpose and find a positive meaning for every delicious experience in your life! Do it until you believe it! *SELAH!*

This is only my perspective; no thing more and no thing less!

05/28/2016
By: Dr. ALi

61
THAT PERSON USE TO BE ME
BUT!
I HAVE NEVER BEEN THAT PERSON!

As we step into the world of meta & quantum physics, there are rules and laws that govern that realm. Consistency must be followed, or one will find themselves in a delirium state while figuring it all out. If you are prepared, we will now go down the proverbial rabbit hole and enjoy a most provoking and enlightening thought.

As multi-dimensional Beings, you exist, at once, in an unlimited number of realms, dimensionalities, realities, dualities, trialities, etc.! In one moment in one space and time, as ONE THING! This ONE THING is being viewed from different perspectives. Linearity does not exist except in your space-time continuum. You are 'One Thing' and 'Everything' all at the same time and all at the same moment. Always remembering that, 'there is no moment and there is no time'.

Every nanosecond, you focus energy through a new static formed reality created from your Beliefs. It is a perfect match or reflection of your entire belief system. As you drift in and out of what you buy into as a changed/new belief, so does your focused energy through your life frame or still photo reflections.

Also, no matter how small a new static frame change, it literally & totally presents a different 'YOU'; in a literal & totally different growth experience. Whoever you think 'YOU' were before, 'YOU' never were… **nor ever was**! Why? Because the past is created from the Present Moment! There is no Past, and there is no Future. ONLY THE HERE AND NOW! That other person was them, them, them and this person you are now, now, now is You, You, You!

When you bring a child into this world, the child looks like YOU, the parent! YOU, the parent, do not look like the child! The Bible teaches that "Man & Woman were created in God's image"! BUT! God is not the image of Man or Woman! How often have you seen a shadow, but that which is casting the shadow is different from which the shadow is portraying? Some people can cast shadows with their hands and fingers and make the shadow appear like a bird, dog, or even a butterfly. Quantum is the vibrational bridge to 5th-dimensional physics. The more 3rd-dimensional you think vibrationally, the less you can, seemingly, conceive 5th-dimensional quantum mechanics. What the @#$%* did he just say?

Of course, this is only my perspective; no thing more and no thing less!

5/31/2016
By: Dr. ALi

62
LIFE HAS NO INNATE MEANING, EXCEPT
WHAT YOU DEFINE IT TO BE!

All life vibrates as one infinite present moment. Energy also vibrates in an endless number of moments. These two statements are both correct and will be explained but in a different missive. Your life is one of those vibrating moments. It is free of meaning. There is no defined intent nor purpose innately meant. Life is neither positive nor negative, good nor bad, right nor wrong. This is very true. Life has no meaning. And no one can tell you what your life was meant to be, nor what life means to you! It is a balanced, harmonious, and perfectly synced tone of incredible ecstasy. As you gaze at your life, you will find that it also consists of present individual moments. And so, through your eyes of chosen beliefs, you automatically bestow upon your life, and each moment, its meaning and intent.

Your life or experience has always been neutral. It is a gift or present to you from 'ALL that IS.' This is why it is referred to as 'Present Moment'! A moment's present. You create your life. So if you are angry or at peace, sad or joyful, bored or motivated, discontent or content, you have no one to blame but yourself.

As you observe your present, you attach a fixed frequency to it by your beliefs. You are free to observe, then settle on whatever meaning you choose for each present moment. But, be very careful and cautious about how you choose to define your life experiences. Why? Because however, you describe your experiences will determine its effect on you. Are we teaching that life effects the one living the experience? Yes, we are! So, why not give every moment a positive meaning. This way, you are sure to get a positive effect from moment to moment. Make sense?

Of course, this is only our perspective; no thing more, and no thing less!

06/09/2020

By: Dr. ALi

63
I CREATE MY REALITY

I create my reality; no matter how much I may like or dislike my life. The sole Being responsible for my holographic, illusional & yet physical reality is me. Of course, if I do not like my life, I can change it quickly, but I must understand how. My belief is a self-empowering rod of steel! Belief is self-aware and is the secret behind me waking up into a greater conscious awareness of my true self & infinite state of being.

Belief is no less than 'ALL THAT IS.' Belief is the initiator and source that gathers and holds all constructive thoughts in form. Belief is conscious and ever-present; aware, ever anxious, always eager to extend itself into action. Belief is 'ALL THAT IS'! Belief is the very essence & actuator within all thought. To think a thought without belief is thoughtless. Belief is the core, the binding substance of 'ALL THAT IS.' Go now and 'BELIEVE'!

If we willingly respond negative to life in the slightest degree, this attitude is the most unambiguous indication how much we still believe in this immersion, holographic, illusion we call reality. Why would you respond negatively or get disturbed by that which is only an illusion or hologram?

The only thing that is pertinent upon the present moment is that which you choose to believe. Actually 'ALL THAT IS,' 'KNOWING,' is a state of Being, (Epilief), beyond belief.

Guilt or Fear represents the opposite of Love in 3rd – dimensional belief. Love has no opposite! Nothing can reflect the is-ness or the perfection of 'ALL THAT IS.' This so-called opposite is such only because it represents the furthest in thought away from Love. I create my reality. My life is a reflection of my innermost beliefs. To accept my life totally, completely & wholeheartedly; increases my vibration & alignment with my higher self. Any complaint, disagreement, or regrets are clear indications of a misalignment, disharmony, or a lowering of my vibratory resonance. My life is a hologram, an illusion of infinite manifestation and complexity! The more I believe this thought, the greater my control over this illusion. Soon my 'Deliberate Creative Powers' will begin to manifest, and my innermost desires will present themselves into physical form sooner, faster, quicker! But first, I must learn to hold my thoughts and emotions in a balanced and harmonious tone!

Of course, this is only my perspective; no thing more and no thing less!

6/17/2014
By: Dr. ALi

64
YOUR PERSONAL REALITY

Part A

Concepts previously have been expressed in third-dimensional terminology, only for more superficial learning. But now that you have advanced in your conscious awareness, we may be more fifth-dimensional in our teach/learning techniques.

Your life/reality is an individual realm. There is only 'ONE' & that is YOU! Every moment of every day, your life/reality will reveal the most extraordinary experiences you 'BELIEVE' is possible. And all that is possible lay within you. Your life/reality is but an illusion or hologram. They are single framed static pictures, with your consciousness focused through each frame, trillions of frames a second. Thus allowing continuity, linearity, and the appearance of smooth motion. Each frame is created or chosen from countless trillions of perfectly matched life/reality frames based on what you have chosen to believe. But still, through all of this, the ONLY thing that is 'REAL' is your experience. Even 'YOU' are not 'REAL'; yet, you 'ARE'! You are a channeled 'BEING'!

Nothing is ever Attracted, Created, or Changed! You do not attract, create, or change anything in any life/frame/reality.

Every experience is valid. Neither better nor worse than any other. You are everything, and everything is you! **Everything already 'IS'!** Everything always already exists as you desire it but within a different frequency life/frame/reality. You only 'Shift' your consciousness through the particular life/frame/reality you choose to experience by frequency; as they perfectly represent any new beliefs. Every life/frame/reality always stays as is. **The only thing that ever changes is your 'BELIEF'!**

Your life/frame/reality is separate and individual from everyone else. Within this hologram, your life/frame/reality is totally yours to control. Keep in mind that your life/frame/reality is superimposed upon the collective. Everyone lives their personal/separate/individual - Life/Frame/Reality – their personal unique tone! You are free to experience within your Life/Frame/Reality – tone or dance, whatsoever 'TUNE' you are able to 'Sing/Believe.' Just as long as it is relevant to your previously contracted, locally agreed, dimensional realm theme.

Nothing ever has to be done outside of your thoughts! There is nothing to physically 'do,' attract, create, or change out there. **Everything already 'IS'!** You are **always** experiencing the life/frame/reality, which is perfectly reflecting the most incredible illusion you believe is possible for you at any given moment.

Remember! All you have to really 'do' is believe the experience you desire, and you will experience that belief! **Period!** Now go continue telling yourself **"Yourstory"**!

Of course, this is only my perspective; no thing more and no thing less!

08/23/2017
Dr. ALi

Part B

You are now gradually sliding out of 4th density; through the Vesica Piscis and more fully into 5th-density or dimension. You must be as transparent as possible with what will soon become quite apparent. Your reality is experienced as 'ONE' static picture frame at a time. Trillions of them every moment, smoothly, consecutively, and at an infinite speed. This personal reality was given to 'YOU'! It is yours to do as you please. You are in 'TOTAL CONTROL'! You are the 'Leader, Ruler, Creator 'GOD' of your reality! **Remember?** Your reality is reflected before you in physical form, as you focus your deepest core beliefs through each frame. The stage is your present world. Your theme has been predetermined. It is your play; you are the main character. Everything and everyone are all illusions, props, other versions of 'YOU,' or background fill-ins.

No thing, no one, not even 'YOU' are real! The only thing that is real is the 'EXPERIENCE'!

Now, those that are the closes to you, family, friends, acquaintances, usually reincarnate together and remain close from incarnation to incarnation. There are agreements with other soul group game players as well. But for now, know that every individual conscious reality is 'Superimposed' upon all as a collective. The more you get involved, a photonic connection strengthens with other physical realities in the illusionary game, and your power to control your reality or life experience weakens. These realities all appear to be 'ONE' big world reality with everything systematically affecting each other. Nothing could be further from accurate. No one else can affect you from their reality unless you believe or agree to be affected. **Remember?**

Shortly your vibrational resonance will shift you into a fluxing state. This shift makes you invisible to those outside and in a lower vibrational octave. Yes, you will be able to see and, to a degree, communicate with them. But they will not be able to initiate interaction with you! It is at this moment that more generous galactic, universal, and comic laws will govern your existence. Always honor these laws as you continue on your journey towards the light, or you will, by consequences, create negative karmic repercussions.

Remember! Be the **'OBSERVER'**! Stop getting so involved! You are only passing through this matrix, subjective – immersion illusional, holographic realm. Your intermingling was only for the experience. You just got a little sidetracked, a little overly involved. It is now time to **Remember** the 'Creator' that you are! No one and no thing in a lower reality octave can affect you nor cause an affect to you within 'Your Reality', unless you choose to be affected~! **Remember this?**

Of course, this is only my perspective; No thing more and no thing less!

01/28/2018
By: Dr. Ali

65
FEAR, HATE & LOVE
ARE ALL THE SAME ENERGY

The ONE is ALL, and the all are ONE! This is the second universal law. The ONE is limitless and without any rules, guidelines, codes, regulations, procedures, processes, and is not subject to anything! The ONE can do whatever it chooses! There is no space; there is no time, there is no, in there or out there, there is no over there; there is nowhere but here and now! Nothing is ever being created because everything already 'IS' and everything that 'IS' is 'ALL THAT IS.' From this one thing do all other things appear to be created. It is by the observance of the ONE thing from different perspectives that the ONE THING seems different or separated. Since there is only ONE THING, ONE THOUGHT, ONE CONSCIOUSNESS, ONE 'ALL THAT IS'; there can be only one Omni-Source, Omni-Power, Omni-Energy.

The 'ONE THING' is Omni-Present, and you exist at the same infinite place because there is only one infinite place, one infinite here and one infinite now! Things are not 'THIS' or 'THAT'; they are 'THIS' AND 'THAT'! So, nothing ELSE needs to be created! All are the unique personality structured thoughts of the 'ONE CONSCIOUSNESS' and exist within and **'IS'** the 'ONE CONSCIOUSNESS'!

All unique personality structured Beings are given a free appearance to possess their own beliefs, which provides a sense of individuality. Each live, breath, and move by what has become their belief system.

To Exist, you receive Pure Energy of Love from 'ALL THAT IS,' and you filter that LOVE through your belief system. What evolves from that filtering determines your thoughts, motives, action, or in other words, your unique personality structure. Once this energy is filtered, you may appear different; even identify yourself as separate, making all judgments through your established belief system. It is by your belief system that you give meaning to what you now see. Fore nothing has inherent meaning, it just 'IS.'

Remember, there is nothing else by which to receive sustenance. All are of the ONE THING! You are not 'THIS' or 'THAT'. You are 'THIS' AND 'THAT'. Experiencing 'YOURSELF' as many other things appearing different. Viewing 'YOURSELF' as something other than 'THE ONE THING,' not knowing yourself as 'THE ONE THING' while experiencing the remembering that you are 'THE ONE THING' because there is NO OTHER THING BUT THE ONE THING!

Of course, this is only my perspective; No thing more and no thing less!

06/12/2016
By: Dr. Ali

66
ENERGY ALIGNMENT

Alignment is another word for choice. You are placed in alignment with what you focus on. What you align with you create and attract more of that into your life. So, what are you focusing on the most in your life? This is why your life has been what it is. If you are satisfied, focus more on the same. If you are not happy, then change your focus, and you will change your life.

Of course, this is only our perspective; no thing more and no thing less!

12/29/2019
By: Dr. ALi

67
See a Sermon

People would rather, see a sermon, than hear one any day: They'd rather one walk with them, than merely point the way. The eye is a better student, more comprehending than the ear. Wise counsel can be confusing but an example is always clear.

The best of all the preachers, are those who live their creed; Seeing good put into action, that's what we mostly need. I could soon learn how to do it, if you show me how it's done. Pretend that I am just a child, experience, I have none.

If a person hold a position, of honor and respect, But their words and actions conflict, them we should reject. Are you paying attention, to this in which I teach? All I am saying is, you should practice what you preach.

This statement has been made, many times before today. You need not do as I do, just simply do as I say. Am I suppose to assimilate, this thought you think is profound. To me, this is a sophistry, you can tell by the way it sound.

Eloquent lectures, recited so well, maybe quite wise and true. But still, I'd rather get my sermons, by watching what you do. I could misunderstand, some of that great advice you give. But there is no misunderstanding, how your Act, and how you **Live.**

Revised 7-2-02
By: Dr. ALi

68
DIMENSIONAL VESICA PISCIS

You are now standing in a unique position within a great and wonderful convergence. It is a very sacred and necessary path that is entirely unavoidable. You are somewhat at a cross point. It is a type of interconnecting or superimposed realm between two dimensions. Significant change and transformation are taking place within all. Your present position within this shift we will refer to as a Dimensional Vesica Piscis!

You exist within two dimensions at once, but you can only experience one at a time. You can view both but only to the extent of your awareness. You can use more of your fifth-dimensional abilities to manipulate your third-dimensional experience and focus more on settling yourself further into the fifth-dimension if you choose! You are a multi-dimensional Being. Very shortly now, you are about to discover more of this through your conscious awareness. All that you had ever attempted before now and failed, attempt it again for the first time. Your new awakened abilities are online, and you will prevail!

Be brave, my friend. You are evolving into more of your true exalted 'Self.' Your 'HigherSelf' is now able to merge more fully within its lower form of existence, which is 'YOU';

all because the lower form is aligning more fully with its higher. It is to the degree by which the lower expression finds alignment does this evolving take place. You and your Higher Self are 'ONE'! But! You must remember and 'Believe,' and as you do, the process happens naturally.

We congratulate you on your successful journey further into the light! Your travels have taken you to the leading edge of creative thought, where many are still experiencing but are yet to start their journey back. When we say 'We,' what is meant is, 'All of Creation'! For it is through amazement that 'All of Creation' marvel at such mesmerizing accomplishments! We lay in wait for your testimony as to how you so stealth-fully maneuvered such an incredible feat! For even on our level of such a superior evolved state, we cannot fathom how and what you have done. 'All of Creation' is on the edge of their proverbial Seat! 'All of Creation' waits to communicate with you more; after you completely pass-through this… 'Dimensional Vesica Piscis'!
We salute you!

12/25/2016
By: Dr. ALi

69
ENERGY WAS CREATED

Consciousness is 'ALL THAT IS.' There is, literally, NO THING ELSE! It is ONE THING! Consciousness being 'ALL THAT IS' is not subjugated to; bound by any rules, laws, guides, codes, or stipulations of any kind and can express itself in any way that it chooses! PERIOD!

Consciousness, knowing itself, chose, in eternity, to look back on itself, and in doing so, created what we refer to as a 'Vesica Piscis.' This Vesica Piscis is an intersecting caused by consciousness reflecting on itself, which created a perspective with a Density, another 'Awareness' or Consciousness. That perspective – density of consciousness is what we refer to as energy. Now, within that energy exist what we know as vibration, and that vibration represents the intention of consciousness looking back on itself.

Third-dimensional wording is limiting in nature. Words created by the casting of spel-lings are categorizing, departmentalizing, and limiting expressions. Any term used to explain, describe, or define 'ALL THAT IS,' is in itself, self-defeating. 'SOURCE', IS! Period!

'THE ONE' cannot be explained, described, or defined with 3rd-dimensional words. If within your 3rd-dimensional thinking, you think that you can conceive any thought of what 'ALL THAT IS,' is, then rest assured, 'SOURCE' is not that but more. Even the words used here to refer to 'ALL THAT IS,' fails us in our attempt.

Do not feel discouraged, because this thought alone, if believed, creates an empowering just by knowing that such a 'BEING' exists!

Of course, this is only our perspective; no thing more and no thing less!

06/19/2016
By: Dr. Ali

70
THERE ARE NO ACCIDENTS

Nothing happens by accident, chance, or happenstance. There is no such thing as coincidence, luck, or serendipity. The multi-verse cannot express a MISTAKE! 'ALL THAT IS,' 'SOURCE,' 'I AM,' 'THE ONE' or 'CREATOR,' is Omni-Present, Omni-Potent, and Omni-scient! Such an 'INFINITE BEING' is incapable of an expression that could or would ever be a mistake. Also, there is no such thing as 'ANOTHER' or 'DIFFERENT'! There is only 'THE HERE,' 'THE NOW,' 'THE ONE'! This is one of many paths to 'PEACE THAT PASSETH ALL UNDERSTANDING'!

Once this thought has become accepted by you, it will prove to resolve ALL situational and circumstantial experiences you consider a mistake. You can never – ever disagree with this thought nor create excuses that would some way give warrant for any unwanted experience. The attempt would automatically misalign you with your higher self, lower your vibration, and alter your frequency.

Any experience that disturbs you, in the least degree, is clear evidence for you to reconsider the belief that caused such an experience.

It is a signal from your 'Emotional Guidance System, ' allowing you to recognize the present thought and reconsider its servitude.

Life does not need correcting, improved upon, or helped! Life is perfect just the way it is. The more you come to believe this thought, a resolve of calmness will overshadow you with a peace never before experienced! This thought is a Master Key to remembering who you are. It shoulders all other ideas within. As you move further into the 5th – dimension, such 3rd – dimensional thoughts just fade away. You must replace such thoughts with;

"ALL THINGS HAPPEN EXACTLY THE WAY THEY HAPPEN BECAUSE ALL THINGS HAPPEN"! IF THIS THOUGHT WERE NOT TRUE, THEN 'THE ONE' COULD NOT BE DEFINED AS, 'ALL THAT IS'!

Of course, this is only my perspective; no thing more and no thing less!

06/25/2016
By: Dr. ALi

71
THE CORE OF EVERY THING

Everything began. Everything that is some thing began! Every thing that did not begin is no thing, just as it was before it began! No thing is still some thing though it never began or existed! That thing is beyond your words of expression. So let us just say if it began, then it exists!

At the core, center, crux, root, heart, or nucleus of the most diabolical, ruthless, vile, heinous, wicked, fiendish, ugly, hellish, cruel, negative, evil, disturbing, filthiest, disgusting, nasty, obscene, worthless, trash is;

'SOURCE ENERGY', 'ALMIGHTY', 'THE ONE', 'CREATOR, 'LIGHT', 'ALL THAT IS', 'BRAMAH', 'GOD', 'ALLAH', 'JEHOVAH', 'YAHWEH', 'BUDDHA'...

No thing is separate from or stands outside of or is other than 'THE ONE SOURCE ENERGY.' WHY?

BECAUSE BEFORE ANY THING 'BEGAN', 'THE ONE SOURCE ENERGY' – 'IS'! Not was, 'IS.' Even time began! The Past, Present, and Future also began! Up, Down, Over, Under, In, Out, Left, Right, Here, There, Center, All began!

At that infinite moment of **'Is-ness,'** there 'IS' NO THING ELSE! Even the expression of 'Moment', as a thought, began! No thought or inference can shed even a glimmer of understanding of that which **'IS'** before all things 'BEGAN.' Your deepest, most profound, philosophical, or intelligent thoughts fail to express 'ALL THAT IS' which 'IS' before anything 'BEGAN'!

And now even the phrases and words used to reference that which is Primordial, Infinite, Eternal, Omniscient, Omnipotent, Omnipresent in nature, fail in the attempt.

BUT! Knowing all of this, you should also omnistand how you respond, react, treat, handle or feel toward 'ANY HUMAN, ANIMAL, BEING OR THING' is a reflection of your level of understanding towards **'LIFE'**!

Of course, this is only my perspective; no thing more and no thing less!

7/12/2016
By: Dr. ALi

72
SELF-RESPECT

You have been taught to believe that there are right and wrong choices. You have bought into the belief that only the choices you perceive to have brought about your desired outcome are the only choices capable of bringing about your ultimate goal. You have come to believe that such so-called wrong decisions are not capable of leading you to your desired experiences. You think that different choices have different outcomes that are separate and completely disconnected. By this method of programmed beliefs, you belittle, devalue, denounce, find fault with yourself and become discouraged whenever you perceive making bad choices. By this method, you are programmed into believing that your preferred goals are lost or gained by judging yourself based on right or wrong choices. You have chosen a method of thinking that is disempowering!

What you perceive as 'Out There' is only an illusion; a hologram. Nothing 'Out There' can 'Empower'! All empowerment comes from 'WITHIN'! I would have you to know that there are no right or wrong choices, and no one preferred experience is better or worse than any other. All choices are valid, and all experiences are equal in value. All choices are intimately & inextricably bonded with all other choices and with who you are at that moment.

All choices are equally capable of guiding you to obtaining your desired experience; they vary only in the paths taken! Choices are the very essence of your signature vibration, and they determine your frequency. For you to belittle, devalue, or denounce any choice, is to criticize, devalue, and denounce yourself! To disrespect your choices is to disrespect yourself!

Belief is as graphene; harder than a diamond and stronger than steel! The definition you give to anything determines its effect on you. You are an aspect of 'SOURCE ENERGY,' a creation of 'ALL THAT IS'; thus, you cannot make a mistake or a wrong decision! You are worthy, imbued with self-respect, and unconditionally loved! As you gain greater knowledge of 'SELF' you will come to know this to be true! You must embrace all of your choices, actions, and behavior as ONE POSITIVE ACT! You must come to believe that all are 'ONE' because 'THE ONE' is all! There is only one creation; one moment, one 'HERE,' one 'NOW'. Yet they are all, the one same thing, seen from various perspectives!

Of course, this is only my perspective; no thing more and no thing less!

07/17/2016
By: Dr. ALi

73
ALL THINGS ARE
ALL OTHER THINGS!

There is only **'ONE THING'**! There is only **'ONE CONSCIOUSNESS'**! There is only... **'THE ONE' 'I AM'**! There is no 'OUT THERE,' 'OVER THERE,' 'UP, DOWN, or BACK THERE'! There is only the 'HERE and the NOW! And 'HERE' is not 'ANYWHERE.' And 'NOW' is not a moment in time because time does not exist in eternity! But, this **'ONE THING'** cannot know **'ITSELF'**; nor experience **'ITSELF.'** Why? Because there has to be **'AN-OTHER,'** from which to draw 'Reflection.' Therefore **'THE ONE'** created **'ALL THAT IS,'** from which **'THE ONE'** gazes back at 'IT'S SELF' from a point of observation, from the **'FIRST REFERENCE POINT'** of perspective! Yet **'ALL THAT IS'** is still **'THE ONE THING'**~! Gazing at **'IT'S SELF.'** Observing and forming an opinion, settling on a perspective, establishing, forming, creating a **'NEW BELIEF' about it 'SELF'**! The most obvious question to ask is, "Then how could **'THE ONE'** be omniscient? We leave that for another missive.

And then **'ALL THAT IS'** creates from its first perspective an **'EXPRESSION'**! Gazing at **'IT SELF'** from yet another (2nd) perspective as **'THE ONE THING.'** Observing and forming an opinion, settling on a perspective, establishing a **'SECOND BELIEF'**!

And then that **'SECOND EXPRESSION'** creates from that second perspective another **'SPARK'**! Gazing at **'IT SELF,' from that perspective as 'ALL THAT IS'** and **'THE ONE THING.'** Observing and forming another (3rd) opinion, settling on a third perspective, establishing, forming, creating a **'THIRD BELIEF'**! Thus on and on and on; experiencing **'IT'S SELF'** in all the ways that **'IT'** can!

This process is repeated; Perspectives, Expressions, Sparks, Shards, and Personifications an innumerable amount of times; times an innumerable amount to an innumerable power time infinity! Yet, in all of this and in all of that, one has to remember, that is, if you have forgotten, there is only **'ONE THING'**! There is only **'ONE CONSCIOUSNESS'**! There is only **'THE ONE,'** **'I AM'**! There is no 'OUT THERE,' 'OVER THERE,' 'UP, DOWN, or BACK THERE'! There is only the 'HERE and the NOW! And 'HERE' is not 'ANYWHERE'. And 'NOW' is not a moment in time because time does not exist in eternity!

If you do not mind, I am a little puzzled and would like to ask a question? Since there is only **'ONE THING'**! There is only **'ONE CONSCIOUSNESS'**! There is only **'THE ONE,' 'I AM'**! There is no 'OUT THERE,' 'OVER THERE,' 'UP, DOWN, or BACK THERE'! There is only the 'HERE and the NOW! And 'HERE' is not 'ANYWHERE,' and 'NOW' is not a moment in time because time does not exist in eternity!

Then where did all of the various Perspectives, Expressions, Sparks, Shards, Personifications, and I come from?

Simple: You and the various Perspectives, Expressions, Sparks, Shards, Personifications are all **'THE ONE THING'; Moving at 'INFINITE SPEED,' appearing as all other things! Because there is, was and forever will only be... 'THE ONE THING'; Experiencing 'ITSELF' in all the ways that 'IT' can!**

Of course, this is only our perspective; No thing more and no thing less!

04/07/2019
By: Dr. ALi

74
'THE ONE' IS NOT SELF – AWARE!

There is only 'THE ONE ETERNAL CONSCIOUS THING' in 'THE PRESENT HERE & NOW MOMENT'; Holding 'ONE INFINITE THOUGHT PERSPECTIVE.' It is Omniscient and Omnipotent! There is no omnipresent. There is no other here & now moment. There is no 'OUTSIDE' and no 'INSIDE'; There is no 'Then or When'. There is no over there, over here or where. No past no future; No up nor down; There is only 'THE ONE ETERNAL CONSCIOUS THING' in 'THE PRESENT HERE & NOW MOMENT'; Holding 'ONE INFINITE THOUGHT PERSPECTIVE.'

There is not even 'No thing'; Because 'NO THING' constitutes 'SOME THING' and so there would be 'ONE THING' and 'NO THING,' which is 'SOME THING'; the equivalent of three things. Stay with me now! So then, there is only 'THE ONE ETERNAL CONSCIOUS THING' in 'THE PRESENT HERE & NOW MOMENT'; Holding 'ONE INFINITE THOUGHT PERSPECTIVE.'

Also, there has been no creation. Everything that appears to have been created already 'IS'; existing as 'THE ONE ETERNAL CONSCIOUS THING' in 'THE PRESENT HERE & NOW MOMENT'; Holding 'ONE INFINITE THOUGHT PERSPECTIVE.'

For 'THE ONE' to become 'Self-Aware,' it must observe itself from a different perspective, from a different frame of reference, from a different position, angle, view, or thought. But since there is only, "ONE INFINITE THOUGHT PERSPECTIVE', for such to 'BE'… There would have to be 'An-Other' 'INFINITE THOUGHT PERSPECTIVE' expressed; A conscious personification, spark, entity, 'THING' or 'BEING,' Fractal or Facet… which would exist in another 'POSITION,' viewing from a different perspective; in a 'DIFFERENT HERE & NOW MOMENT.' Like a child becoming aware of itself, 'THE ONE' is now… Omnipresent!

BUT! BOTH ARE THE SAME 'ONE CONSCIOUS THING' in 'THE PRESENT HERE & NOW MOMENT'! BUT NOW OBSERVING ITS SELF AS…

'I AM'

Of course, this is only my perspective; no thing more and no thing less!

08/18/2016
By: Dr. ALi

75
YOUR LIFE IS SELF IMPOSED!

No one can blame another for their life experience. Each must take responsibility for their creation. No man, woman, or child can experience anything other than that which was previously agreed upon. Every thought is a vibration. Many like vibrational thoughts evolve into a belief, a frequency, or tone. That tone creates a physical hologram for the believer to enjoy as their life experience. As goes the proverbial expression… 'What you put out is what you get back'!

Understanding this simple universal law of creation can help you create a life more enjoyable. Casting this thought off as nonsensical will continue a life uncontrolled and ever more challenging. Become the master of your destiny and learn the cosmic laws that govern your existence. Practice every day how to apply and deliberately create a more joyous life. Let go of old, outdated, and corrupt beliefs that no longer serve you and replace them with newer and more invincible, self-serving beliefs.

Of course, this is only our perspective; no thing more and no thing less!

10/01/2016
By: Dr. ALi

76
EVERY WAKING MOMENT

There is only ONE Consciousness, and it consists of everything that is. There is no other state of Being, awareness, reality, dimension, nor plane where this ONE Consciousness dwells. This ONE Consciousness does not get tired, does not sleep; thus, it is at all times Awake! Now, this is because the state which you refer to as 'sleep' does not exist. The very nature of Consciousness is to be what it is; Conscious! It cannot possess the character of both.

YOU are an expression, spark, manifestation, personification, or fractal of this Consciousness. And you also do not sleep. You are infinite & eternal thought energy. During the **moment** when you think that you are sleeping, your dreams are the focusing of your energy through another particular expression of yourself. All expressions are YOU! You are a multi-dimensional Being, remembering who you are and experiencing your way back to knowing, through an illusional, holographic, submersion duality called life!

As you look out into reality, all that you see is YOU; Reflections of your innermost beliefs; physicalized for you to experience. You are special; you are unique, you are 'ALL THAT IS'; experiencing yourself in all the ways that you can. There is nothing else other than this ONE Consciousness.

Every Being or thing that you see are only other expressed versions of YOU, from a different perspective. So, you are all other Beings and things.

As you continue to awaken out of this mysterious state called sleep, you will find and begin to utilize powers heretofore unknown. You are 'Creator'! You are that which always was and will always be. Relax and get to know yourself. Relax and accept your real identity. Relax as you continue to remember, Every Waking Moment!

This is only my perspective; no thing more and no thing less!

09/29/2016
By: Dr. ALi

77
SEXUALLY TRANSMITTED DEMONS

Part A

One should be very particular who they choose as their 'Physical Therapy' partner. At the point of orgasm, your aural field, which is your vibrational frequency and soul signature, is entirely open and merges with your sexual partner who you now have become inextricably intertwined with as ONE!

Intimacy at this level intertwines your aural energy with the aural energy of the other person. These powerful Physical Therapy Sessions, regardless of how insignificant you may think they are, leave spiritual, vibrational debris, particularly with people who do not practice any type of cleansing, physical, emotional, or otherwise. The more you interact intimately with someone, the deeper the connection and the more of their aural vibrational tone intertwined with your own.

People who sleep with multiple partners carry around with them a mixture of energy vibrations from every person they have joined with in physical therapy. If any of these partners possess a low vibration or dark energy, with whom you involve yourself, such therapy can cause you to start repelling positive energy and instead attract more negative energy into your life.

Of course, there is the other side of the coin. If you are powerful enough, you can counteract another's negative energy by grounding out or short-circuiting their low vibration. You have the power to raise their vibration. But! It will all depend on the willingness and openness of your partner. Force can never be used to help raise another's vibratory resonance.

Of course, this is only our perspective; no thing more and no thing less!

10/02/2016
Dr. ALi

Part B

One needs to be very particular with whom they have Physical Therapy. From the very beginning, you open your aural field to whatever may be within the aural field of the one with which you are intimate. At the point of orgasm, your aural field, which is your vibrational frequency and soul signature, is entirely open and merged with your sexual partner. You both briefly become inextricably intertwined as ONE!

Intimacy at this level intertwines your aural energy with the aural energy of the other person. These powerful connections, regardless of how insignificant you may think they are, leave spiritual vibrational debris from your partner, particularly with people who do not practice any type of cleansing, physical, emotional, or otherwise. The more you interact intimately with someone, the deeper the connection and the more of their aural vibrational tones intertwined with your own.

People who sleep with multiple partners carry around with them a mixture of energy vibrations from every person they have joined in physical therapy with; **until they cleanse themselves of such trash or low negative vibration!** If any of these partners, with which you have involved yourself, possess low, dark & negative energy, you can absorb some of that energy and now cause you to repel positive energy and attract more negative energy into your life. Such energy is also the primary cause of illness and disease. There exist Beings that actually feed on such low energy, as do people that love 'DRAMA'! *Ephesians 6:12* Meta-Physically speaking, Negative Beings, Negative Angels, or Demons are quite real! Only the ignorant deny their existence. Spiritual matters are spiritually discerned. Unless you are inclined towards the light, you will not understand the depth of this `missive. *1 Corinthians 2:14*

Beware! You are as children when compared to these highly evolved and mastermind entities. Some have existed, inter-dimensionally & hyper-dimensionally for countless lifetimes, in a karmatic state well over one cosmic year. Counting years as you do, that would consist of 3.4 BILLION of your linear years! So you see, such Beings have existed long enough to master consciousness on a level of thought that you could never understand in your present state of conscious awareness. They toy with you as you might with a worm, insect, or single-cell organism on a lab dish, in a laboratory.

If you are drawn to drama, being upset, angry; If it feels good to hear people fussing & arguing; If you like watching movies involving negative drama, deceit, revenge, jealousy, killings, etc. Then you are being used for 'LOOSHING'! You are being fed upon by negative Beings or 'SEXUALLY TRANSMITTED DEMONS'!

Remember, dear ones; everything is 'ENERGY'! Nothing more and nothing less!

07/2/2018
Dr. ALI

78
R U MORE CONCERNED WITH HAVING THAN BEING?

You have a saying; 'You want your cake, and you want to eat it too;' which is about how much one wants everything their way. Many of you would like to evolve further into fifth-dimension, but you do not want to give up third-dimension things. This is an impossibility! You see, the vibrational energy of 5D cannot support 3D resonance. The energy is far too great.

If you find yourself more concerned with having the things of 3rd-dimension rather than letting go and exploring future possibilities well, rest assured, you are not ready for 5D. Now that does not mean that you have done something wrong or that you have failed. Everyone will evolve at their own pace and advance according to their own divine time. There is no right or wrong time for anyone. No one can make a mistake, and no one can choose incorrectly.

As multi-dimensional Beings, you have the rest of eternity to experience this life you call, 'Living'! There is nothing to worry about, nor anything to fret over. That is unless you choose to experience them both.

So, I would suggest that you stay in the moment and enjoy the ride! The reason being, you will never pass this way again, unless, of course, you choose to Make the most of it and live life to the fullest! It is a most beautiful adventure, even if you do not know it, you still know it to be true!

Of course, this is only my perspective; no thing more and no thing less!

12/14/2016
By: Dr. ALi

79
YOUR THOUGHTS ARE NOT
YOUR THOUGHTS!

The moment has arrived for you to learn more about who you are. Yes, you are Spirit, in a Human Body, having a human experience. But did you know that only your **Higher Self Conceives**, your **Human Brain Receives**, and your human **Mind Perceives**? You were never created to 'DIRECTLY,' 'Conceive,' '**Create'** your thoughts or reality! You simply live by the thoughts you choose to identify with that are received by your brain from your Higher Self, and of course, by other Beings as well! Your only purpose is to give feedback from the experiences created from the beliefs formed from all your perceived thoughts, which you have chosen to identify as your own. As stated, your thoughts are already conceived and placed within your brain, thus the reason for a 'guide,' which is your Higher Self. Which is the GREATER YOU!

You are at the very leading edge of creative thought in the multi-verse. Before now, no other creation had dared to dive so deep or stray so far from 'The Light' or Source Energy! All of creation is, proverbially speaking, 'on the edge of their seats in anticipation,' as to how you will choose.

Your original creation was altered by Beings with a different, more negative, NOT EVIL, motive in mind. They were allowed to play out their 'free will' course of action rather than be immediately stopped. You refer to these Beings as Demons! Soon, they began to place thoughts in your brain, which is how you gained 'Free Will.' With the freedom to choose your Higher Self's thoughts or those of Demons. The only thing is, you did not know which were which. You are now waking up, sorta-speak, from this, 'Altered State.' You are now more consciously aware and can choose more wisely the type of person/Being you prefer to be.

The construct in which you find your existence is a Holographic, Immersion Illusion – Reflective – Attraction Based Duality. Though you are, seemingly Real, you also are not! Though you exist, you also do not! Though you think you are conceiving your thoughts, you also are not! You are not experiencing this 'OR' that, you are experiencing this 'AND' that! As we previously stated, you were never designed or created to conceive for yourself. You were only to live the experience of the thoughts given to you by 'YOU,' from a more evolved dimensional plain.

You are now free to choose any specific thought, negative or positive, as 'your' own. In that choosing, you decide what you will Believe and which of the more advanced and evolved Beings will guide you.

Some Beings will lead you further from 'The Light' (Demons), while others will lead you back towards 'The Light' (Guides/Higher Self). It is your sole purpose to find your way back to Source Energy, 'The Light,' from which you originated, and in actuality, you are.

Of course, this is only my perspective; no thing more and no thing less!

12/11/2016
By: Dr. ALi

80
With Who, What, When, Where
Do you Identify Yourself

If one restrains a baby elephant to a stake driven deep into the ground, by one leg, to prevent escape; that baby elephant will struggle to free itself, time and time again. That baby elephant will attempt to free itself over and over and over and over until the moment when a final choice will be made to believe I CAN NOT BE FREE! **'Who'** gave that baby elephant such a belief?

Elephants have a fantastic memory and express many human-like emotional, sensitive, and consciously aware qualities. As the years pass by and the baby elephant continues to grow into adulthood, it will become the strongest and largest of all the land mammals. As an adult elephant, it can weigh well over twelve thousand pounds or six tons and can carry eighteen thousand pounds or nine tons! With that amount of strength, it could easily pull itself free from the restraint of any stake driven no matter how deep into the ground. BUT! Circus elephants will not! Do you know why? The reason is because of **'What'** the elephant has chosen to 'Believe'! They learned a limitation and held on to that 'Belief' from **'When'** they were a baby elephant.

The reality that you live every day is a precise, exact, distinct match to your vibrational frequency. Your life is solidified energy of your deepest, purest, and most cherished 'Beliefs'! Your life represents the fullest of what you believe is the most probable and possible reality for 'YOU'; based on its relevancy and purpose according to your previously chosen theme or path for this dimensional adventure!

Who, what, when, and where you identify yourself is who, what, when, and **'Where'** you will shift yourself in the levels of reality! You shift trillions of times every second through framed like realities! You are continually matching the unique precise, exact & distinct reality that best represents your every second to second or moment to moment 'Belief'! You cannot escape the photonic connection made by the simple decision to place identification with any person, place, or thing! Be not deceived! 'Belief' is **'ALL THAT IS'**! Through 'BELIEF,' you become more or less consciously aware, and you either ascend or descend in spiritual growth!

Of course, this is only my perspective; no thing more and no thing less!

By: Dr. ALi
12/18/2016

81
THIS IS NOT YOUR EXPERIENCE

Date: /   /

By:

82
OMNISTANDING!

All of your life, you have acquired information. From your parents, siblings, family members, friends, teachers, preachers, leaders, and customs. All of these sources helped to form your overall 'Belief System.' It is by this 'Belief System' that you have developed your character traits and personality. This is who you have become. This is who you now are!

Each belief formed a corresponding frequency, which formed more vibrations or thoughts, which formed even more beliefs. As your life continued, beliefs formed upon beliefs; frequencies upon frequencies, and they all created 'ONE' distinct, particular, unique 'TONE'! That tone represents your life's belief system, at every moment along the way, up until this very day. You are a 'Note,' a beat, within the Orchestra of Creation! This musical note pulsates throughout 'All THAT IS'! And "ALL THAT IS' would not be if 'YOUR' note ceased to resonate! Therefore, you must be as much of 'ALL THAT IS' as 'ALL THAT IS' – 'IS'! Because 'ALL THAT IS' cannot be – 'Parted.' You are an intimate expression of the heartbeat of 'ALL THAT IS,' as is each and every other 'TONE.'

Having considered 'ALL' possibilities! Having caressed 'ALL' probabilities! Having balanced and explored 'ALL' inferences! You have decided to 'Stand' on said 'Belief.' And as the 'Creator' you are, you accept all responsibility for the life you created for yourself! It is my hope that you Omnistand!

Of course, this is only my perspective; no thing more and no thing less!

By: Dr. ALi

01/21/2017

83
HIGHER SELF! HUMAN BRAIN! HUMAN MIND!

For many thousands of incarnations, you have been enshrouded in the concept of separation, physicality, limitation, victimization, win/loss, victory/defeat, right/wrong, etc. Some of you now remember. These are they whom we convey this missive.

You have never conceived nor generated one idea within any of your thousands of incarnations, even to this moment. Maybe you have heard this before. "The Higher Self – 'CONCEIVES'! The Physical/Human Brain – 'RECEIVES'! The Physical/Human MIND – 'PERCEIVES'! And **'YOU'** are the Physical/Human MIND or CONSCIOUSNESS! It has never 'CONCEIVED' an idea; NEVER! The Physical/Human MIND was never designed to figure things out, conceive ideas, or create plans. It is not within the capacity of the Physical/Mind to know 'HOW' things will happen! Its sole responsibility is 'ONLY' to understand how things **ha**ve 'HAPPENED'! It is the total, exclusive, and complete responsibility of the 'HIGHER MIND' to Figure, Conceive, and create 'HOW' things 'WILL' happen! This is why **'YOU**,' Physical/Mind, do not have to be concerned, stressed, or worried about 'HOW' things will work out or get done! This is physics; this is Universal Law!

As for the 'EGO,' it is not your leader, Lord, GOD, or Higher Self. It was your **'Conscious Companion,'** which made it possible for you to experience limitation within the 3rd – dimension. Its sole purpose was to caution, alert, or remind you that you are now experiencing Human Life. 'Please do not stick your body's hand into a fire; throw your body off a cliff; stab your body with a knife, or shoot your body in the head with a gun.' Your Physical/Mind nor the 'EGO' has never been and will never be in charge! Although, as time passed, you did create your experience to appear as though this was the case. Simple caution by the EGO has now become 'FEAR' and, in some cases, 'Terror'! You have created the 'EGO' into a 'Negative Tyrant'! The 'EGO' was to be your **'Willing Servant/Companion'** and was never imbued with the character of leadership. You are now remembering. You are now 'Waking Up'; it is time for you to reassign the 'EGO' to its original responsibility and choose wisely thoughts that are vibrationally in tune with your 'Higher Self.' Did you get all that?

YOU ARE NOT REAL! Feels real, doesn't it? You are within a 'Submersion, Holographic, Duality Matrix. YES! You 'ARE' a 'HOLOGRAM'; a very sophisticated, marvelously designed hologram! But you do have 'FREE WILL,' that has helped bring to you great and wonderful 'experiences,' which, by the way, is the only thing that is real!

Your 'EXPERIENCES' and your 'EGO' has helped you reach this point of remembrance in your 'Spiritual Growth'; as you journey back into 'GREATER LIGHT.' Please omnistand, you are going through a process of 'Realignment.' This process helps you to find your way back to 'GREATER LIGHT'! It was always your goal; it was always your intent.

This 'Realignment,' path or journey, leads back to your 'Higher Self.' WHICH IS **ANOTHER 'YOU'**! **'YOU'** are Omniternal Spirit/Consciousness and have been your leader, Lord, GOD, or in charge, from your first incarnation. That is until your 'Lower – physical/mind – Self' got mislead, out of sync, out of tune, or confused. This state of being happened when other more 'Highly Evolved Negative Beings,' not with your best interest in mind; began to fight for dominance over your 'Lower – physical/mind – Self.' They did this by enslaving, changing your **D**eoxyribo**N**ucleic **A**cid and then placing 'THEIR THOUGHTS' within your brain. Now you have got to figure out who is whom! You have NEVER been the one calling the proverbial shots. NEVER! *Your main and only role, in this Play-Station Game, has been to 'CHOOSE' what thoughts you wished to identify as 'YOUR OWN' and convey to your Higher Self, how that experience 'FEELS.'*

You are an extension, a personification of a far more infinite, omnipotent Being, which again, is **'YOU'**! You are living a Play-Station game, and you are the main character within it! Crazy weird – right?

All thoughts that have ever been thought still exist. Thoughts are only energy and do not become personal/personified until 'YOU' claim/believe them as your 'OWN'! Then and only then does your unique frequency change to match the vibrational resonance of your new-found beliefs. And your consciousness shifts through the new framed reality/experiences that match perfectly, precisely your new unique tone! This is how your reality 'Reflects,' in physical form, what you believe. This is the third Universal law. **What you put out,** as a belief (frequency), will determine **what you will get back,** as your reality experience!

The thoughts you have chosen to identify as your own will determine what 'Higher Being' you pattern your disposition, character, and tune your vibrational frequency after! This adds new meaning to; The Devil made me do it! Demon Possession! And I do not know from where those thoughts came!

You are within the Vesica Pisces of The 4th & 5th – Dimension! It is far time for you to choose more wisely which thoughts you identify as 'YOUR OWN'!

Of course, this is only our perspective; No thing more and no thing less!

11/04/2017
By: Dr. ALi

84
WHOSE THOUGHTS
ARE YOU THINKING?

Omnistanding the construct of your reality within your dimension can prove to be of great help. Especially when it comes to 'Preferential Creation,' but it is an even more significant benefit if you happen to have a basic omnistanding of how 'Thought Beings' play a role in that same realm. You see, there are many Species, Entities, or Beings. There are many levels from which they exist within the realm of your dimension. You may not see them, but they do see and toy with 'YOU'! These 'Thought Beings' are masters at vibrational frequencies. They can meld into any tone below their own and even a few slightly above. They are not bad, evil, or necessarily demonic. Most of the time, they are only toying with you, though their actions may be viewed otherwise. Never the less, they are very, very powerful, persuasive, manipulative, mesmerizing, enchanting, and deceptive! Pay attention because this is where you will need to polish your skills and develop them so that you can distinguish between tones of a lower or higher vibration. It will be a challenge, no doubt! But with practice, you too can become a 'MASTER TONER'!

Now, a little more about these 'Thought Beings.' 'Thought Beings' helps you to be 'Free Will.'

Allow us to explain. No thoughts that you think you are thinking are actually **'Conceived'** by 'YOU.' Let us use the terms 'Lower & Higher Self' to make this discussion a little easier. As 'Multi-Dimensional Beings,' you exist on more than just one level of dimensionality. Originally you had only your 'Higher Self,' Guides, and benevolent Beings with which to communicate. This 'Higher Self' is also 'YOU.' YOU want only the best for YOUR – Lower - SELF! Your 'Higher Self' conceive thoughts and placed them into a 'personification, aspect, spark or Lower Self' **'Physical Brain.'** That 'Lower Self,' 'Human Mind' – 'YOU,' 'Perceives' these thoughts as its 'Lower Self's' own personal thoughts. This may sound strange, but as a human or lower expression of your 'Higher Self,' your primary and only responsibility is to **'Choose and Feel'**! This expression of 'YOU' can only make 'Choices' and experience how something 'Feel.'

As time passed, your realm was invaded by other Beings having a somewhat different agenda. They caused much havoc on mother Gaia, and your planetary vibrational frequency dropped. This left all humans vulnerable and now receptive to 'Thoughts from other more maleficent Beings.' As other Beings visited your realm, they also placed thoughts within your physical brain, sometimes referred to as 'Demon Possession.' And all this time, you thought you were just going crazy!

But now it has come time to 'Wake Up' and start choosing thoughts more accurately that are from your 'Higher Self,' Guides, or more benevolent Beings.

You determine your character and personality by the thoughts you identify with by choice. Thoughts are not personal until you accept them as such. Only then does your state of being reflect the vibration that matches perfectly with every chosen thought. As you settle into a belief, your frequency at that moment becomes established. That is your personal, unique, and distinct signature tone! There are no other such tones in ALL existence! There is only 'ONE'! 'YOU'! And you decided that by every personal thought you choose which inevitably becomes a 'Belief'!

So, lighten up on yourself. If you do not like the thoughts you are thinking, then dispel them as nonsensical or undesirable. This is true empowerment, always having the freedom to choose the darkness or choose the light. Remember, you are in total control of your life at every given moment. You always have been, although at times it may not seem so evident. You are very, very powerful Beings that know what you are doing. No other realm gives such a class in negative, low dark energy. This incarnation upon your planet is considered a 'Master Class.' It is a part of the illusional construct you chose to experience. This is what helps to make you 'MASTERS OF LIMITATION!

Of course, this is only my perspective; no thing more, and no thing less!

01/28/2017
By: Dr. ALi

85
WHAT IS AILING YOU?

This missive is very personal, necessary, and omnipotent. It is our hope that you will pay close attention to every detail. A great and glorious shift is upon you. You cannot turn back, but you can create an illusional holding pattern that will inhibit you from truly moving further into the 5th- dimension. Yes, you are within the vesica piscis of the 4th & 5th dimension. However, you are still holding on to chatter, debris, or lower vibrational contaminants. These must be brought up so that you can make a choice to hold on to them or 'LET THEM GO'! Now, let us use a teach/learn process we call 'Centripetal Thought.

'First, you automatically collect 'Energy' or 'Data.' By 'Choosing' or 'Identifying With' specific data, you group segments together and form personal 'Information.' This personal information automatically becomes your 'Knowledge.' All of these mental energies that you have identified as personal has determined your ability to 'Understand,' or the term we prefer, 'Omnistand.' Now, if you eloquently, skillfully and methodically apply this acquired omnistanding, you will have obtained 'WISDOM,' and there are infinite levels of 'WISDOM.'

If any person, place, or thing upsets, irritates, anger, frustrates, or disturbs you in the least manner, it is because of an issue that you have not resolved within 'YOURSELF'! You must find out what that issue is and eradicate it. So then, why does this special someone so easily anger you? Do you expect them to indulge in an intelligent conversation with you? Do you expect their reasoning to be of a more superb rationale? Do you long to offer your academic help and share the secret of what you have learned, but it frustrates you because they choose not to accept your offer and believe? **Bingo!**

The 'Universal Law of Allowing' is one of the greatest of universal laws. As an initiate in the Cosmic Order of the Melchizedek Priesthood, a basic omnistanding and degree of attainment or progress must be achieved before you can move forward. Though you cannot ever get anything wrong, you can delay your journey home. You must keep in mind that the greatest teacher/learner is 'YOU'! You must stop thinking that it is your place always to teach/learn someone else! This is not your primary responsibility! Masters do not go to others, pushing their wisdom! They wait for others to come to them. Then and only then will that wisdom be more fully accepted and appreciated! Let go and give in to what you know to be the way home! You have found your way home, now let others find theirs!

A new day is coming! All will be seen for what it is! Be patient, and all will see you for who you are and what you have accomplished. Your name is on the lips of many family and friends. They have all observed your life; it has not gone unnoticed! Do not let your pride undo such a wonderful and miraculous journey! We are all waiting for the moment when we can visually reveal ourselves to you! We all ask that you no longer let your Ego delay your journey home!

REMEMBER WHAT YOU HAVE LEARNED AND APPLY IT! TIME IS SHORT! YET TIME IS NOT!

Of course, this is only our perspective; no thing more and no thing less!

02/23/2017
By: Dr. ALi

86
DIS-EASE!

You have been programmed in life to take many things for granted. Take, for instance, the base, bottom line, root cause, or principal reason for a dis-ease. First, you must recognize dis-ease for what it is, and all dis-eases are nothing more and nothing less than a symptom of a deeper issue from within. One should not treat symptoms, or they will reappear as a different symptom.

Dis-ease is not a curse, nor is it negative or bad. All dis-eases are good! Why? Because they reveal to you that you are out of alignment with who you are. It is a way to help put yourself in check. It is a way to inform yourself that you are not centered or genuinely aligned. The attempt to heal others without proper omnistanding is a very juvenile approach. Dis-ease is a very wise and omnipotent process of helping to awaken one to higher conscious awareness. For centuries now, dis-ease has not been appreciated nor omnistood for its sole purpose.

If dis-ease is not a part of your life's theme or chosen journey and you are not restricting the constant flow of energy into your torus by negative low vibrational thoughts or beliefs, then you could never become dis-eased! It is a learned experience and can be avoided.

By keeping your vibration high and consistent, disease cannot exist in your body. It would be impossible, even in your duality.

Healing with chemicals or drugs is not healing at all. It is considered meddling or toying with life and on a rudimentary level at best. But of course, your culture thinks this procedure is advanced medicine. Such a practice is only a 3rd-dimensional temporary fix. Sure the symptom may seem to disappear. It is only one of the glues that support your existing construct. It serves to delude your mind more into the illusional grip of the hologram in which you exist. True healing is therapeutic, yogistic, and deals more directly with the 'Mind'!

REMEMBER! *True 'Healing Is By Thought'*!

So then, if you wish to improve your health, do not start by treating symptoms; look at your 'Belief System.' Take a profound observation of your thought process. It is there that you will find how 'ALL' Dis-Ease begins and ends.

Of course, this is only my perspective: no thing more and no thing less!

02/26/2017
By: Dr. ALi

87
ASCENSION SYMPTOMS
DREAMS OF EMBARRASSMENT

By now, my child, you are well within the 5th-dimension. You are beginning to notice that nothing is quite the same and never will be again. Your eyes are clearing as you yawn into greater conscious awareness. Even as you sleep, you find it more challenging to discern which state of experience is real. Pay close attention, my dear, THEY BOTH ARE!

Have you recently found yourself in this mysterious state, which you refer to as 'Sleep Wetting *(Urinating)* in bed?' Do you dream of being in your room for baths and using the apparatus for bodily waste disposal, but your physical body is still fast asleep in bed? Have your attempts to control such an embarrassing act failed, time and time again? It is alright; the information in this missive is that which you can 'COMPLETELY **DEPEND**'! Pun definitely intended!

Please omnistand; your entire physical complex is changing. Your very **D**eoxyribo**N**ucleic **A**cid has changed, and every cell in your human body complex as well. You are crossing out of the 'Vesica Pisces' of the 4th & 5th dimension! Everything is blending. You are beginning to take on more of a multi-dimensional awareness, but for the moment, everything seems to be your chosen experience.

Be patient; in time, you will, as most have already learned, how to stay more focused vibrationally, within your desired dimension and reality of choice.

You are ascending at more incredible speed now, and one of the signs is 'BED WETTING/URINATION'! You are caught in moments of time between two-dimensional drifts; two timelines. Every moment will become more challenging while attempting to discern which eyes you are gazing through and in which reality you have your chosen experience? You are ascending, and your physical complex is doing all that it can to keep up with your conscious awakening. Relax. Yes! It will pass, as well as the limitations of old 3rd-dimensional embarrassments!

You have arrived, and we are all very proud and delighted! You have all walked under the swords of victory! Now it is up to you;

'TO BELIEVE IT'!

Of course, this is only my perspective! No thing more and no thing less!

03/16/2017
By: Dr. ALi

88
WHEN LIFE NO LONGER REFLECTS ANY ISSUE WITHIN YOURSELF

If any person, place, or thing; upsets, irritates, frustrates, disturbs, aggravates, or angers you in the lease degree; it is only so because of an out of alignment issue or issues that lay, unresolved, from within yourself! A low vibrational state of 'Being' is one that is out of alignment, out of tune, or resisting your HIGHER SELF, All THAT IS, SOURCE ENERGY, GOD, JEHOVAH, ALLAH, BRAHMA, ETC. If this is your state of being, your frequency can only reflect unpleasant everyday life experiences. When you have a car accident, or it gets repossessed when your house lights get turned off, or you get fired from your job, you may have a breakup in a relationship, you may get sick, fall, crack a bone, stump your toe or even bite your tongue. These are all due to an 'Out of alignment,' being out of tune, negative karma, being resistant to your 'Higher Self.' This state of being creates issues within your physical self and thus in your life experience.

You journeyed to such a dimension to experience 'Limitation'; to experience what it must 'feel' like to be 'separate' or out of alignment with your HIGHER SELF, All THAT IS, SOURCE ENERGY, GOD, JEHOVAH, ALLAH, BRAHMA, ETC.

This is the essential fundamental purpose for your presence in that domain. Nothing is 'Real' except the 'Experience'! Remember that! All reality is a highly sophisticated illusion; a 3rd-dimensional, holographic, submersion duality! Such life/duality is created from your deepest and most secretive 'Beliefs' through you! Not to you, before or outside of you! You exist 'Within' your consciousness! Consciousness is not something within you; you are 'CONSCIOUSNESS,' and your experience is from within! Now wrap your mind around that thought! Therefore, life is a perfect match for your frequency, reflecting your deepest 'BELIEFS'! In time you will resolve all unconscious and consciously known inner issues while living in your present duality. It is what happens next that is most invigorating!

At that moment, when every issue from within is dissolved, you will shift to a higher vibrational resonant frequency – dimensionality and to an increased level of conscious awareness! At that moment, everything will change dramatically!

Unless it is a part of your contracted journey to experience, you will no longer experience undesirable circumstances such as having an automobile accident or having your automobile repossessed; having your house lights turned off, or getting fired from your job, having a relationship breakup, getting sick, falling, cracking or breaking a bone, stumping a toe, or even biting your tongue.

Every waking moment will be one of miraculous everlasting joy! Full of unimaginable bliss and utopia; to the degree, of course, of your present conscious awareness! There will always be greater awareness to be had. You see, one does not have to experience 3rd-dimensional evil, negativity, harm, or emotionally stressful circumstances to learn, grow, or become more self-aware. That is simply how it is done on this planet, in this 'Master Class'! There is no other existence, dimension, realm, or plain anywhere, that one can experience such learned knowingness at the very leading edge of 'Created Thought'! Only on this planet has creation been allowed to stroll so far out from the light into the deepest, darkest voids of empty nothingness, where Beings, such as yourself, find their way back towards the 'LIGHT'! The multi-verse is on the edge of their proverbial seats in multi-versal awesomeness!

ALL CREATION, IN EVERY HIGHER DIMENSION, IN EVERY REALM, ON EVERY PLANE, THROUGHOUT EVERY FORM OF EXISTENCE, ETC! ARE WATCHING IN EVERLASTING INFINITE EXPECTATION TO SEE JUST HOW YOU ARE ACHIEVING SUCH NEVER EXPERIENCED PHENOMENAL JOURNEY!

Most of you have graduated and shifted to the fifth-dimension already, but most of you still are not aware of this most beautiful feat.

We say feat because, for the first time 'EVER,' the physical body has been taken along with you in this significant shift, and it has been done without first transcending through what is known in third-dimension as death! Rejoice, my fellow Beings, You have graduated and are ready for your next most glorious new episode in your Soul's Journey back towards the 'LIGHT'! **Namaste!**

Of course, this is only my perspective! No thing more and no thing less!

04/10/2017
By: Dr. ALi

89
YES, I SAID 'NO'!

Many people find it challenging to tell another 'NO' when asked to do something. Now, why is that? Most of you will find it fascinating that you were raised with principles and moral values based solely on your culture's most prominent religion, even if you or your parents were never members of that religious sect, group, or organization. Still, your life reflects, by your unconscious chosen beliefs, many of its religious teachings. Your very government has based its standards, whether it follows them or not, on these same teachings. Your television and radio broadcast them, and your schools promote them. Every day of your life, you are constantly bombarded to believe THE TEN COMMANDMENTS! We are about to discuss one of many brainwashing, mind programming, and learned behaviors of 3rd-dimension. One system created to teach this tricky concept is called religion. It is one of the many types of glue (concepts) that binds the 3rd-dimensional construct in existence.

Are you your brother's keeper? Genesis 4:1-9 Help your brother in need? 1John 3:17 Do not neglect to do good. Hebrews 13:16 Give, and it will be given to you. Luke 6:38 Many will be hungry, give them food; Some thirsty, give them drink; welcome everyone, even strangers.

Will you visit the sick: Will you go to the prisons? Matthew 25: 35-40 Would your answer be 'YES' to these questions and statements?

Religion has taught you how to love, be friendly, kind to your neighbors and strangers. It has even gone as far as to demand or require this action as your humanitarian duty, responsibility, and or obligation! But religion has also taught you something very unnoticeably subtle, cunning, and graciously **'mephistophelian.'** It has led you to feel 'Guilt' if you do not perform such obligated or responsibilities commanded by its definition of 'Love'! Most are ignorant of the 'Fear' factor that has now been created. Guilt is a third-dimensional term used to cover up the deeper and more distorted undertone of 'FEAR.' True love can never be required, obligated, made to feel responsible to express. The nature of true unconditional love cannot be commanded!

Such a vibrational mental state is by design. You must have as clear as possible, and the most accurate omnistanding of 'Unconditional Love' because if not, you will become mentally, emotionally unbalanced and vibrationally out of sync/tune with your Creator. Such thinking causes you to create an inherently contaminated mixture of energy flow. This low vibrational tone is 'Looshed' or feed upon by Beings on higher levels of ascension.

But they are in a lower state of chosen conscious development. They created the concept on your planet eons ago called **'We-live-on' or 'Re-li-gion'**!

Yes, they feed upon such emotional energy or frequency, created by your chosen beliefs. Did you know that 'Guilt' is actually 'FEAR' in disguise? Do you know what 'FEAR' does to your vibrational frequency? Yes, religion has a shadow teaching. Without careful attentiveness and centripetal focus, one would miss the 'mephistophelian' undercurrent and systemic education of contradicting vibrational thoughts.

You see, to feel 'FEAR' means that you have succumbed to believing that you do not have a 'Choice'! You think that you must do a thing whether you want to or not, whether it is in your best interest or not, whether your heart is in it or not, whether you genuinely 'Love' or not! You are just doing it because you feel 'Obligated'! In essence, you have been taught to be a **'Hypocrite'** while at the same time, you think that it is perfectly normal.

Unconditional Love is not something you receive or possess! Unconditional Love is not something that you can learn by study and then express! It is something that you **'BECOME'**! Unconditional Love never moves one to feel to the slightest degree, 'Guilt' or 'FEAR.' As you become more consciously aware, remember…

'YOU' are the first, the only, and most important thing in existence! **Period!** Because there is only 'ONE' consciousness, "ONE' spirit, 'ONE' thing in all of existence! And that is 'YOU', **'I AM'**. Like a hologram, every piece contains the whole! Everyone's reality is superimposed upon the collective. Everything is an expression, shard, personification, or extension of that 'One Thing'! Everything came from this 'ONE' Omniscient, Omnipresent and Omnipotent thing! Everything is THAT ONE THING! Which you refer to as, CREATOR, GOD, JOSHUA, ALLAH, JEHOVAH, ALL THAT IS, SOURCE ENERGY ETC!

It is just that you have forgotten and are now beginning to remember that everything is also 'YOU'! Everything is connected! Your duality exists for your experience only. Nothing is real in it except for the experience. So, what you do and how you treat anything and everything is how you are treating 'YOURSELF'!

Now that you have a greater perspective and omnistanding about the knowledge of 'Self,' you can approach the above scriptures with far more wisdom; without feeling obligated, required, responsible, or commanded. All of which are low vibrational third-dimensional terms.

The bible teaches spiritual stories about other people lives. Spirituality teaches stories about your spiritual life~!

It is now time for you to start thinking more 5th-dimensionally since some of you are there. It is time to begin applying such greater expanded conscious awareness to your spiritual soul's journey.

To LOVE UNCONDITIONALLY, one can say **'NO'** and feel no GUILT or FEAR!

Of course, this is only my perspective: no thing more and no thing less!

04/14/2017
By: Dr. ALi

90
WHATEVER YOU BELIEVE
IS TRUE

Most people spend their whole life arguing that they are Right and you are Wrong. It is a natural mindset for those believing they are still living in third-dimensional reality. And of course, we would not dare have you think that we are Right; oh no, what we offer here is only our perspective. It is up to you to decide whether such a position is worthy of your support or if you prefer another.

'Belief' is the foundation, the building block, the actual creative tone that materializes the life you experience from moment to moment to moment. Everything you see, touch, taste, feel, or hear is a perfect match to your 'Belief,' tone, or 'Frequency.' Let there be no misomnistanding, 'BELIEF' is the key and essence of 'ALL THAT IS'! 'ALL THAT IS' has no origin. But for the sake of conversation, we will hold that thought for another missive.

For now, simply follow the thought that all physical life as you know it has its materialization because of and by that which you choose to 'BELIEVE'! Universal Law teaches us that 'THE ONE IS ALL AND THE ALL ARE ONE.' If you choose to accept this as a premise, then this flowing thought would be as follows.

All is 'ONE' eternally conscious – expressed thought, behaving as if separate and experiencing itself in all the ways that – that 'ONE' eternally conscious – expressed thought can appear as separate! Did you get that? Every supposed single person, place, and thing is experiencing their own personal, 'Individual' reality, but superimposed upon the collective within their chosen realm, plane, or dimension. Every person, place, and thing is living their own eternal 'TRUTH'! Whatever is believed is supported by the universe and proven by the same with self-supporting evidence that what is believed is TRUE! Why? Because it is 'THEIR' individual 'TRUE' reality! This leaves no room for Right and Wrong because the Universe does not discriminate with such third-dimensional principles. It only wants to experience itself in 'ALL' the ways that it can. **All the ways that it can!**

Therefore, each reality and that which exists within can 'Believe' whatsoever, he, she, it chooses. Period! And be supported by the Universe for having believed it. So then, to argue with someone is, in actuality, an argument with the Universe! Within this thought is much wisdom, and within that wisdom is much PEACE!

Of course, this is only my perspective; no thing more and no thing less!

06/08/2017
By: Dr. ALi

91
HEALING OR PREFERENTIAL SHIFTING

Every moment and from moment to moment to moment, greater conscious awareness is being impressed upon our mind. As we pass further into Alcyone's photon belt, our central sun, we are all being drenched with more significant amounts of this photon energy. Our deoxyribonucleic acid is also changing from moment to moment to moment. Many of us are becoming smarter, more intelligent, wiser! Thoughts that we have believed all of our lives are now no longer believed in the same manner but with more clarity and greater insight!

Healing, for example; There is no such thing as healing! That is a third-dimensional term used only to express a concept heretofore not fully omnistood. You see, every possible version for every circumstance, situation, or event that could ever happen to you are in separate unique, still frame realities that already exist. That includes the version where you see yourself as healed. No reality is ever changed! That would constitute – the original reality no longer existing, which would mean that 'ALL THAT IS' is no longer all that it could be. The only thing that ever changes are the eyes through which you are looking at any given moment!

You are everything, and everything is 'YOU'! But! You focus your conscious attention through 'ONE,' seemingly, version of 'YOU' at any single moment in time. And yet, there is a version of you that can view millions of versions of itself/you all at once. Whatever version is your present preference does not mean that the other versions do not exist! They all exist in their individual vibrational frequency realm; in their individual still frame reality.

Nothing is ever 'Healed' or changed in any individual reality! All reality frames must remain as they are. You only shift by frequency to the preferred reality that represents your new desire or belief, which already exists! You do not have to 'Attract' anything from afar, nor do you have to 'Create' anything new, from what you think is nonexistence, which, by the way, is impossible. All one needs to do is match their frequency with their preferred reality. Then you will shift to and experience that reality. Now, looking through the eyes of a different 'YOU,' having that new experience.

If you can believe this thought, you are well on your way to mastering the art of… 'Preferential Shifting'! Everything that you could ever want, desire, need, or prefer is within 'YOU'! Or already exist but in a different vibrational frame reality! Remember, match the frequency to your preferred experience, and you shall witness that experience!

Of course, this is only my perspective; No thing more and no thing less!

07/01/2017
By: Dr. ALi

92
SHOULD OF, COULD OF, WOULD OF!

Many of you go through your life journey with regrets, wishes, hopes, and feelings of loss. Often contemplating what you **Should of, could of, would of 'IF'**! You must remember the second universal law. "Everything exists here and now,"! You are not a separate entity. The first universal law states, "The ONE is all and the all are **'THE ONE'**! You are multi-dimensional, and thus by nature, you contain it all because you are **'THE ONE'**; Presently experiencing itself as 'YOU,' an Earthly (Gaia) Being! As am I, and 'THE ONE,' experiencing itself as 'ME'! A higher/greater version of 'YOU' in the future on a different timeline.   Even though you are only witnessing one experience at a time, countless other versions of you are experiencing all of the other versions of experiences you think has been missed. If you can think of another scenario, then that too exists as an experience. You cannot think of any experience that does not exist. As a matter of fact, you cannot imagine nor create anything that does not already exist! Because everything already exists **'Here and Now'**!

As you expand your consciousness into greater awareness, you will learn how to keep your thoughts organized more adequately as you contemplate various levels of concepts. You cannot apply 3rd-dimensional rules or laws to 5th-dimensional thoughts. You must keep them properly separated. 5th-dimensional ideas do not have to make 3rd-dimensional sense! You are crossing over now. You are absorbing more of your greater self. This transition may become awkward at times. But just remember to remain open-minded and willing to let go of any belief that you sense no longer serves you or no longer feels right for you.

Soon you will no longer possess the need to listen to, read, or get information from 'Out there;' just to feel that a thought is right! You will come to that conclusion from within yourself! You have experienced that need but now are moving past that stage and on towards greater experiential awareness.

Relax, you need not worry, wish, or regret anything. If you can accept this concept, you will soon recognize the senselessness of ever thinking; **I should of, could of, would of 'IF'!**

Of course, this is only our perspective; No thing more and No thing less!

By: Dr. ALi
11/30/2018

93
REGRETS OF LIFE

Regrets of the past, fear for the future can make one's present moment so miserable! Some have shifted and are now within the Vesica Pisces of the fourth & fifth dimension. Many are still unaware. Are you one of them? If not, then it is far time that you rid yourself of old, outdated, third-dimensional thoughts such as I regret, I forgot, I missed out, I will have to make that up, I must catch up, I made a mistake, I wish I had made a different choice, I should of – could of – would of – if.

BUT! You are presently experiencing an illusional, duality-hologram of separation. You are only able to witness 'ONE' experience, in 'ONE' moment, in your space-time reality. There is nothing in your present moment holographic/illusional world, as it 'REAL-ly is. Even 'YOU' are not 'as' you real-ly are! The only thing that is 'REAL' is the experience itself.

You see, you cannot possibly regret, forget, miss out, make something up, catch up, make a mistake, have made a different choice, should of – could of – would of – if, anything! Nothing requires 'Fixing', 'Correcting', or 'Changing'. You cannot 'Forget' nor 'Remember.' Memory is created from the present anyway.

You always express what at the present moment 'is' and what you, at the present moment, 'know'!

WHY? Because every experience that you witness is witnessed as a result of your present moment, innermost belief! It is the most perfect, precise, and accurate match - reflected as your life/reality; physicalized into material substance for you to experience. It is all based on the tone of your vibrational frequency! All versions of every probable and possible choice exist as an individual still reality frame. Your consciousness is shifting through these frames as light does through the plastic negatives on a real, at your motion picture theater, which by the way, is an illusion! The pictures on the large screen are not actually 'Moving'! Also, for you to believe that you can make a mistake would ultimately mean The Universe can make a mistake! Now that is 'IMPOSSIBLE!

You see if you can think of something you regret, forgot, missed out on, have to make up, have to catch up, made a mistake on, have not done, wish you had made a different choice about it, should of – could of – would of – if; then those versions of reality experiences 'exists' and you experienced all of those choices as well.

BUT! you simply did not 'Witness' the experience in the present moment. Why?

Because your consciousness could only be focused through the reality that best synced most perfectly, precisely, and accurately with your present moment's innermost belief!

Every experience is valid. Every experience is justified. No experience is 'Better' or 'Worse' than another. As you move further into the fifth dimension, it is crucial for you to begin acknowledging every experience you witness as 'Valid' and 'Acceptable'! For all are just that and not a ONE can be negated, invalidated, or regretted! You must come to know that 'EVERYTHING' is exactly as it ought to be! Nothing ever needs to be Healed, Changed, Corrected, or Fixed! That is if you wish to continue increasing your vibrational resonance and ascend further into The 5th-Dimension.

Your life experiences are formed around your innermost beliefs! You are always focused through the reality that perfectly represents the vibrational frequency of every present moment. Every version that could have happened in any situation or circumstance did happen and was experienced by 'YOU'! Know that in your realm, you can only witness 'ONE' chosen 'Belief' experience at a time.

Every experience that you probably or possibly could have experienced does and still exist! **Everything exists 'Here & Now'! 'EVERYTHING'!**

Nothing ever is regrettable, forgetful, missed out on, have to be made up, need catching up, is a mistake, is a wrong choice, should of – could of – would of – if! This is why 'ALL THAT IS' is all there is! The experiences of Itself is witnessed through 'YOU' and everyone and every other person, place, and thing in existence! 'YOU' are 'SOURCE ENERGY; experiencing Itself in 'ALL' of the ways IT possibly can!

You are a spark, an expression, a personification of 'SOURCE ENERGY'! Experiencing Itself in an illusional separate singularity; of a different quantum – mechanics; within its consciousness!

Again we repeat. You must come to know who you are! You must come to know that 'EVERYTHING' is exactly as it ought to be! Nothing ever needs to be Healed, Changed, Corrected, or Fixed!

There is only 'ONE' thing! And this 'ONE' is the 'ALL' and the all are 'THE ONE'! You are everything, and everything is 'YOU'! You are multi-dimensional; 'ALL THAT IS,' and all that there ever will be!

Of course, this is only my perspective; no thing more and no thing less!

09/08/2017
Dr. Ali

94
KEYS TO GREATER CONSCIOUS AWARENESS

You have weathered a great distance as you continue your forward motion into the fifth dimension. You have done a most beautiful job of letting go of old third-dimensional thoughts and assimilating newer and higher fifth-dimensional views. You have withstood many painful symptoms as a result of your progress and have received a significant degree of cellular and deoxyribonucleic Acid upgrades in return. We are the Sirians, Lyrans (Feline), Nommos, Blue Avians, Reptilians, Pleiadians, Orions, Arcturians, Adromedans, YahYel, Essassanians, only to name a few. We are all very proud and are sitting on the proverbial edge of our seats in anticipation of meeting you face to face!

What you are soon to accomplish has never been done before, not in all of creation! You are bringing along with you into the fifth dimension the physical body into which, at this moment, you incarnated in, while experiencing the third dimension. That body will not see death nor be resurrected. It will transcend, evolve, become more crystalline. Its ability to withstand the higher vibrations of the fifth dimension will be ascertained and achieved, oh, so gradually. And you thought that you were weak as babies.

You have traversed to the furthest outermost edges of creation, into the darkest of the dark, into the lowest vibrational resonance, and 'STILL' found your way back into the light! We have witnessed it all, and we stand in awe! We have yet to find a vibrational thought that would best fit your experience! We have yet to find a sound to describe such a feat of deliciousness adequately! There you are, at the leading edge of creative thought! So we decided to use the sound of your language, in your own vernacular.

'MASTERS OF LIMITATION'!

These following Keys will be of great empowerment to you now and in the coming moments.

1. All change comes from within.

2. Do not judge.

3. Your life is only a reflection, illusion/hologram; You are only passing through; Stay Detached!

4. There are no victims, only Creators.

5. View yourself, everyone, and everything as The ONE.

6. There are no Right, Wrong, Loses, or Mistakes.

7. What you put out is what you get back, so always identify with good feeling thoughts.

8. Nothing has to make 3rd–dimensional sense anymore.

9. Assimilate the 'Universal Law of Allowing.'

10. 'I AM' the 'I AM' that 'I AM'!

Of course, this is only my perspective; no thing more and no thing less!

11/27/2017
Dr. Ali

95
GLOBAL EARTH vs. FLAT EARTH

Many of you seem to have recently been struggling with the idea of Global earth or Flat earth. We think that all you need is a reminder for those who are genuinely consciously and Meta-Physically inclined. Pay close attention because many of you are allowing the illusion to once again bind you with cords of 3rd – dimensional glues, used to hold that construct together.

You are Multi-Dimensional Beings, Eternal in nature, and Infinite in power! You are a personification, a personality, or expression of your Higher Self. You are consciousness, telling yourself a story within your consciousness and are expressing only a portion of your nonphysical, conscious self, in an altered state; in an illusional – submersion duality, holographic matrix. You are on a journey, having a physical experience. Remember, it does not 'MATTER' whether your journey is experienced on global earth or Flat earth. Whatever you choose to **believe**, the **'YOU'-NI-VERSE** will **create** a self-perpetuating, systematic illusion of evidence to support that belief! *Did you get that?* It is not about what your physical reality is or is not. Your reality around you is, in your terminology, an oxymoron! IT IS NOT 'REAL'! It is all an illusion. The only thing real about this dream you are telling yourself is the **'EXPERIENCE'**!

For those of you that are 'Waking Up' and are consciously aware of your planet's progressive ascension further into the 5th - dimension, you must not allow 3rd – dimensional concepts nor circumstances around you to carry unjustifiable value. ONLY YOUR STATE OF BEING 'MATTERS' or possesses the most accurate value, and that is determined by what you learn and choose to believe from every experience. All is for your learning and growth as you increase your Vibrational Resonance! You are on an evolving journey. Stay on the path! If you stray off the aligned, in sync, or tuned path, you will be met with resistance. More karmatic experiences will be created, the cycle starts again, and you will have to re-incarnate to dissolve or overcome those new experiences!

It has never been about the props, stage, setting, or theme of your 'Reality'! It has always been about the experience obtained while in your 'Reality.' Let the Global or Flat earth concept go! **LET IT GO!** It is not important at all! It has become your anchor/distraction and will slow your journey as you choose to evolve.

Of course, this is only my perspective: no thing more and no thing less!

12/10/2017
Dr. ALi

96
REALITIES – SUPERIMPOSED

You are a multi-dimensional Being. Your mind is expanding exponentially. You are becoming more 'Aware' BUT! Are you 'Conscious' of it? You are shifting through billions of individual **reality frames** a second. These **reality frames** are perfect, exact, and synced in tone, to reflect your core 'Beliefs.' These realities are materialized/physicalized and warped to form your personal experience. It is all an illusion; A highly intricate, elaborate, and sophisticated hologram. BUT! Single **reality frames** none the less. They are expressions of each individual Being and are superimposed upon the collective throughout all dimensions, realities, dualities, trialities, universes, multiverses, domains, realms, planes, etc. Why? Because… 'Everything is Here and Now'!

You might now be able, if not momentarily ready, to cognize the different realities being played out all around you. As long as you do not consent and you hold your vibrational tone in constant sync to its highest pitch possible, nothing nor no one can possibly bring any harm to you! Now how does one give such consent?

That consent can be given by your 'Focused Attention' to the conditions that surround you, thus creating emotional pessimism, impatience, agitation, frustration, doubt, worry, anger, hatred, jealousy, guilt or FEAR, etc.

You are the Creator of your reality, as others are of theirs. You must let go of such third-dimensional concepts such as 'Life is ONE BIG reality experience.' It is not! Every reality that can be imagined exist. Everyone view's the world through their own 'Belief Lenses'! Global Earth; Hollow Earth; Flat Earth; Doomed Earth; Yes, even ONE BIG reality experience. Very paradoxical!

Whose truth is the true truth? No **one** - thought - is correct or true. It is not about right or wrong! It is not about this **OR** that. It is about this **AND** that! Every thought conceived after viewing through one's own 'Belief Lenses' is True, Right, and Correct! Every idea is Valid! Everything exists, here and now! But only if properly viewed through 5th-dimensional thinking or higher. According to every Being's individual 'BELIEFS,' the universe will create a 'Self-Sustaining, Self-Perpetuating system of Self-evidence to support ALL REALITY CREATORS.

Everything is possible, once placed in thought. One cannot think of anything that does not already exist, which is why everything is possible! There is not anything that cannot be created.

Though it may not be expedient, conducive, allowed within your reality parameter or beneficial for the present contracted reality theme experience. BUT! Everything is probable; everything is possible none the less! This is why 'ALL THAT IS,' is, all that is! Did you get that? Observe that which is around you while remaining detached, unengaged. Learn to focus on the world/reality you prefer. Learn to hold your emotions in high vibrational tones.

Example: Feeling Pity, Sorrow, Sadness, sympathy, or regret is to lower one's vibration. It does not matter how much 'Sorry' or 'Sympathy' you feel for someone sick; it will not heal them! While the feeling of understanding, omnistanding, acceptance, compassion, or unconditional love will have a truly healing effect. Omnistanding this thought is quite self-empowering! Do not allow another person's reality experience to dictate your vibrational tone. Hold your opinions true! Keep your cords sharp! Mind your thoughts and remember who you are!

You have played the most beautiful game of life. It has been played in the densest, darkest, and furthest crevasses at the most outer limits of created thought. You have wandered through and into the boundless depths of illusional yet believed separation. You have tip toed around in constant karmatic incarnations.

AND STILL! SLID YOUR WAY BACK TO THE LIGHT! The feat has been held as nothing short of... 'MAGNIFICENT'! You have brightened and made more famous the 'Marvel' in 'MARVELOUS'!

But now you are 'Waking Up.' Some of you are coming home. We all are waiting to hear your personal and enchanting testimony of how you did it! What more can be expressed in your limited language of spellings? You are the 'Masters of Limitation'! What you have demonstrated is simply...

'DELICIOUS'!

Of course, this is only our perspective; no thing more and no thing less!

01/02/2018
Dr. ALi

97
MENTAL BELIEF LENSES

Many of you are running around, telling others how wrong they are about their chosen beliefs. Some how, you have come to believe that you are the 'ONLY' one that has gotten it right. So, you think that everyone else is 'Wrong'! You think that you possess all of the proof, evidence, and examples necessary to settle such dispute once and for all. Now, we are not sharing that your belief is wrong. It is not. Such a position would only imply that we are in the same category as are you. All beliefs are True; all beliefs are Right!

Throughout your life, you have acquired from your parents, siblings, relatives, friends, school teachers, religious leaders, country's customs, etc.; various 'Mental Eye Glasses'. 'Mental Visual Eye Apparatuses' or 'Mental Belief Lenses'; 'THROUGH' which to view/filter your world/reality. Your core vibrational beliefs, which create your tone, frequency, or state of Being, were all formulated from a lifetime of learning. As you gazed through your particular standardized "Mental Belief Lenses', your personality, attitude, and disposition took on an equally – synced, vibrational reflection. You became an expression or reflection of your 'Mental Beliefs.' Yes!

You reflect/vibrate what you believe, as does your world/reality. This is how you all experience your world/reality; 'THROUGH' the 'Mental lenses' of your beliefs! It is also how your world/reality/life is vibrationally created and reflected in a materialized or physicalized form, right back at you, for your chosen dimensional experience. As the fourth Universal Law states, What you put out, *'through your vibrational core beliefs*,' is what you get back; *'in vibrational but physical form'!*

Ascension is a process of releasing and assimilating greater knowing; descension is a process of being blinded from that which was previously known. You are on a revolutionary journey. Some of your thoughts may lead more directly towards the light, and some ideas lead more away from the light. You are on an eternal **exploration**. You are infinite and thus have no time limit. So, when 'YOU' are ready, not when someone else thinks that you should be ready, you may begin to explore such thoughts that lead you more directly back towards the Light! Take that which is your time; No rush. Life is meant for your enjoyment. You forgot that during your journey. But! You must admit it has been quite an adventurous exploration none the less! Some of you are waking up more and more every moment of every day. Soon we will be communicating face to face. We are all very excited and are waiting for your arrival! 'Masters of Limitation'!

Of course, this is only our perspective; no thing more and no thing less!

https://www.youtube.com/watch?v=1DYmgoij4FQ

01/06/2018
By: Dr. ALi

98
THE LAW OF ATTRACTION & MANIFESTATION

The 'Law of Attraction' or 'Manifesting' has been on the lips of many for several years now. Everyone accepts this 'Universal Law' for whatever personal reason their inner desires demand. But we would like for everyone reading this missive to pay very close attention to what is about to be expressed. Are you paying attention? Well, here we go.

Often higher vibrational concepts have to be expressed to you in your 3rd-dimensional terminology, using your vocabulary for your optimal teach/learning. Usually, greater knowing has to be expressed on a very rudimentary level, mainly for clearer omnistanding. We do not intend to insult or belittle you by no means. But it is far time now for you to grow up in your thinking and start viewing through the lenses of your 5th-dimensional conscious awareness.

The 'Law of Attraction' could better be expressed as the 'Law of Possession by Experience.' You see, there is no 'Out There,' 'Over There,' or 'Under There'! There is only the 'HERE AND NOW'! Nothing is ever attracted from far out, over, under there or anywhere – to you. Also, nothing has to be 'Created'!

Only for your teach/learning experience is it expressed in such a manner. Everything already exists 'HERE AND NOW'! All you have to do is 'Match' the vibrational frequency tone of that which you so desire and you will **'LIVE THAT EXPERIENCE'** or **POSSESSING THAT DESIRED THING!**

Some of you, after **'LIVING THE EXPERIENCE,'** **'ATTRACTING'** or **'MANIFESTING'** that which you so desired; your dream home, car, or money; Will want to share your experience with others. "Would you like for me to tell you, *(some charge a fee),* how to 'Attract' your dream home, car or money," 'AS I DID'? Be very careful! Acts 8:18-21. Sorcery is real, even today. Low vibrational or negative 'Beings' are just waiting to 'ATTACH' to new but careless 'Glamour' minded creators. As your abilities begin to come online and your manifestation skills improve, remember who you are. Do not allow the 'Glamour' of things to take you down a path that leads away from the 'Light.' You are doing such a great job and awakening at such an astronomical speed. Manifesting 'Glamourous Things' does not entail 'Spiritual Enlightenment' nor greater 'Conscious Awareness.' We already hail you as 'Masters of Limitation'; soon, you will be deemed as 'Masters of Manifestation'!

Now again, we would like to be clear. This missive is not for everyone.

Remember: this is only our perspective; no thing more and no thing less!

01/11/2018
By: Dr. ALi

99
SELF EMPOWERMENT!

What can one do to bring on greater 'Self – Empowerment'? What can one do to raise their vibrational tone so more of their HigherSelf can be absorbed within their present state? We will answer the previous questions with certainty and clarity of thought. If you have chosen to continue moving with Mother Gaia on her ascension phase, these points should be recognized for their vital importance.

ATTENTION! ATTENTION! ATTENTION! You are 'Way-Showers'! Pathfinders for those to follow. Your responsibilities are increasing as you approach the widening or dividing of the dimensional rift of Mother Gaia. Your world is fluxing into a higher vibration. Only those attentive ones will visualize and be able to flux or merge along with her. This significant change is endemic to your world and mainly at this moment in time. You are approaching this crossover very rapidly. Now is the time to hold true! Keep your intent, Indomitable! Remain focused with no deviation from strict integrity!

1. **Surrender**, **let go** of whatever no longer serves you. If you continue to fight and resist those seeking to control you, you will continue to strengthen the ties that bind you together. You are not a race; Black, White, Hispanic, Mexican, Chinese, Negroid, Caucasoid, Mongoloid, etc.; You are 'Multi-Dimensional Beings, dreaming of a physical experience. Although none of the so-called unjust, oppressive, and evil forms of suppression heaved against you are real; nor what a parent, family member, friend, or associate has done to hurt you in any way, all must be 'FORGIVEN' and 'FORGOTTEN'! Admitting that you 'Forgive' someone but you will 'Not Forget', and if you are still holding on to Old Outdated Beliefs that no longer serve you but only continually cause you feelings of discomfort, uneasiness, disappointment, doubt, worry, blame, sadness, anger, revenge, jealousy, and FEAR, then these various states of being will not allow you to move smoothly with Mother Gaia into the 5th-Dimension! Your world/reality is dividing/separating. Soon, very soon, only those within your vibrational octave will exist within your world/reality! It is our hope that you have a genuine love for yourself. Because you are about to experience a world/reality of others basically 'JUST LIKE YOU'!

2. It is time to **'Cognize'** that Every Human, Mammal, Animal, Insect, Plant, Rock, or Thing is 'SORCE ENERGY'; 'PRIME-CREATOR'; 'MOTHER – FATHER GOD'; **'ALL THAT IS'**! Experiencing itself in all the ways that it can. And every Human, Mammal, Animal, Insect, Plant, Rock or Thing has 'Consciousness'! Because all are expressions, personifications of 'SORCE ENERGY'; 'PRIME-CREATOR'; 'MOTHER – FATHER GOD'! Which cannot be 'SEPARATED' from its original 'PRIME SORCE'!

3. Remember to stay in **'OBSERVATION MODE'**! You have become far too involved with the **Illusion** around you. Your photonic connection runs far too deep. There are far too many fibers of thought, holding you back—far too many cords of 3rd-dimensional sympathetic sorrows which are like glues that bind. You would be wise to remember Heb. 13:14. Many have identified themselves with this holographic realm, as with things; homes, cars, clothing, family, friends, etc. The forces of **Glamour** and **Maya** of your world has become your prana! You take your so-called human senses to be so real that they govern everything. When the only thing that is real in your subversion-illusion, holographic duality, is the experience itself! You are Creator Gods and are in the process of taking back your creative powers! Only when you are able to hold your thoughts and emotions in a balanced and harmonious manner will you be granted more access to those gifts *(Powers)* that await your rise through the ascension process.

4. There is no **'SEPERATION'**! You are your Higher Self! OverSoul! Monad! 'SORCE ENERGY'! YOU ARE 'ALL THAT IS'! Your awakening experience must come in steps—degree by degree. Proverbial, level by level. All you see and all that you experience is only a reflection as you learn more about Yourself. There is never a reason to fear anything that you learn about Yourself! You are everything, and everything is YOU! The purpose of the Ego has been fulfilled. The Rational Mind or Lower Mind is no longer needed. It is now time to live through the Heart Center. You are becoming more fully aware that you are the 'HIGHER SELF'!

Tears of rapturous joy are being shed for what you have accomplished! All are overwhelmed with amazement and formidable awesomeness! We all hold your accomplished feat in the most delicious regards. Unconditional Love has never been so expressed nor demonstrated in such a manner while yet, proverbially, so far out at the leading edge of seemingly created separated thought. We believe that this mantra would be of great assistance to you at this time.

I AM ADVENTUROUS; I AM AUDACIOUS; I AM AWESOME! I AM BEAUTIFUL; I AM BOLD; I AM BREATH-TAKING! I AM COURAGEOUS; I AM CLEVER; I AM COMPETENT; I AM DAUNTLESS; I AM HONORABLE; I AM MAGNIFICENT; I AM WONDROUS;

I AM THE I AM THAT I AM!

Of course, this is only our perspective; no thing more and no thing less!

By: Dr. Ali
01/18/2018

100
PAST – PRESENT – FUTURE

Date: /   /

By:

101
DISCONNECT... DETACH...
DISENTANGLE...

Your time is fast approaching as you phase-out of the vesica piscis of the 4th & 5th dimension and totally into the 5th density. You are approaching your complete dimensional shift. Soon only those that are within the same vibrational octave as your frequency will share the same reality. But! There is still a very considerable thought which meaning has been elusive for many. All would prove wise to pay attention and reflect on the following words.

Attention! Attention! Attention! Disconnect! Detach! Disentangle!

The third dimension is held together as a construct of many, many thoughts, concepts, and beliefs. These behave like 'Glues' that bind. Very, very sticky, and deceptive to all that are within. You cannot hold on to 3rd – dimensional habits, lifestyles, customs, enjoyments, friends, family, husbands, wives, boyfriends, or girlfriends and shift into 5D! You cannot continue your deep and convicted involvement with social clubs, associations, religions, politics, and efforts to save the world and shift into 5D! And yet, paradoxically, Disconnecting!, Detaching!, or Disentangling! is not necessary at all. And you will still, if your vibration is sufficient, shift or cross over.

BUT! You will not know that you have taken such a leap! Oh! There is so much you are yet to omnistand. And so the full 5th – Dimensional joys that could be yours to experience, will not be yours to experience. You will enjoy only that which you match in frequency.

The 5th – Dimension looks very much like 3D. You will even look somewhat the same as you do now, and your family, friends, and other associates will be recognizable as well. There are cities, towns, roads, transportation, libraries, schools, homes, and more, just as there is in 3D. The difference is in the nature or tone by which this municipality in this dimension is organized and operated.

The more you engage in the 3rd & 4th density reality affairs, through your hyper-superior emotions, the more you strengthen a 'Photonic' connection that binds you more and more in a physically solidified manner. You must stop taking one side of an issue and fighting against the other. Your fussing, debating, and arguing only strengthens the hold and sinks you like quicksand, slowly and more firmly in 3D.

You are doing much, unknowingly, to hold yourself from ascending. Are you paying attention? You are still far too involved with the affairs of 3D human life. You must continue waking yourself Up! Turn off your televisions; discontinue going to your seasonal sporting events;

Take more time out for 'Meditation'! Remember: You are 'Way Showers'! 'Observers'! Here only for the experience; you are only passing through! You are telling yourself a story! Your existence is 'NOT REAL'! You are all 'Channeled Beings'! On a quantum level, you are being held down/back with steel-like balls on a steel chain. Your hot air, helium balloon, cannot rise; there is far too much weight. You have got to release some ballasts such as right-wrong, good-bad, best – better; regrets of the past, fears of the future, make your present ability to shift more challenging; doubt, worry, blame, discouragement, anger, revenge, hatred, jealousy, guilt, **FEAR!** These thoughts will hold you captive like the **'Victim'**; they now have **some** of you thinking you are!

It is very evident to us that most are finding it quite a challenge continuing to believe that your world is only an 'Illusion,' and your life is only a 'Dream'! You solely accept this idea in thought, but you are yet to assimilate it within your frequency as a true conscious belief. You are falling back to sleep; Dozing off again into a drunken 3D stupor! You are once again placing far too much trust and value in your holographic creation! You are gradually re-identifying with your country's flag, patriotism, and your military. You are getting too overly attached to your sports teams, college fraternities, social clubs, family reunions, money, and even with the color of your skin!

Many are once again identifying far too intimately with the meat sacks through which you are living out your channeled experience, and some are identifying far too much with their automobiles and homes.

You are caught up with the 'Glamour' of your world and think that you will leave it and shift. You seem to be so caught up with manifesting or attracting material wealth as validation of being in the proverbial VORTEX! You are holding on to 3rd-dimensional thoughts that teach, 'I am Blessed because I just got the car, house, money, man, woman or job of my dream! Nothing could be further from greater knowing! **'ALL THAT IS' does not... 'BLESS'!** All persons, animals, mammals, places, things are all creations and are always blessed! If you have chosen to ascend, then it is time to disengage, detach yourself from your matrix. Now is the time to be in **'Observer Mode'!** Our intention is not to teach that a choice is Right or Wrong; only that your choice should be in sync with your higher self! And that whatever you choose, there are consequences and repercussions.

We do not share these sentiments with disdain in our heart nor with disappointment or scolding. We have only Unconditional Love for all of you. We are sharing with an earnest Unconditional Love for your greater enlightenment. We hope that you will heed our missive of compassion.

The fast-approaching days will usher in a new era, a new age! These times are very precious! These moments are very dear! **Some** of you are soon to be 'Welcomed Home'! And some of you~will not!

Of course, this is only our perspective; no thing more and no thing less!

02/07/2018
By: Dr. ALi

102
ALLOW... PERMIT... ACCEPT...

No more urgent of a message could we think of sharing, at this most exhilarating moment in Mother Gaia's history. All that you see happening around you and all that will soon break upon the world scene like an overwhelming surprise; we urge, insist, and downright plead with you to; 'ALLOW... PERMIT... ACCEPT...' This is not the time to be caught up with taking sides and expressing vehement personal thoughts on what you believe is Right or Wrong! (Such a 3rd – dimensional stand to make!) If you identify with the events taking place around you, you will match such vibrational tones with your own. One cannot slide further into the 5th – dimension while holding such low tones in frequency. You are only passing through, remember. Nothing, 'Out There,' is 'REAL'! To the degree that you become emotionally infected/affected, it is to that same degree you will become attached! It is all about energy! You are very powerful emotional Beings! Your DeoxyriboNucleic Acid is about to receive another very special Energy Boost in a spectacular Solar Event! It is our hope that you are all continuing your personal preparation!

These present moments in time are definitely not for impetuous decisions! You must stand firm as an 'Observer'! You must stand true as the 'Wayshower'!

You must remember that you are only telling yourself a story and having a very wonderful experience by personally witnessing every scene in its true-life panoramic realism!

There are no mistakes! As you focus your consciousness through your 'Mental Belief Lenses' while simultaneously focusing through each 'Static Frame Reality,' every dramatic scene is playing out exactly as it should! You see, if you believe you have to Change Fix or Correct any 'Static Frame Reality,' 'ALL THAT IS' would no longer be, 'All that is.' The reason is that the 'Static Frame Reality,' which you just changed, will no longer exist as it were, and so that expression of 'ALL THAT IS' would no longer exist as it was! Life around you is never Changed, Fixed, or Corrected. All change comes from 'WITHIN YOU.' As you alter your 'Belief System' in the slightest degree, so does your reality change. Life always reflects your 'Beliefs'; instantaneously! Always!

There is always an infinite number of Possible, Probable, and Presumable timelines or 'Static Frame Realities' from which you may choose to explore and journey through for an experience. And not one of them is in Error, Wrong, a Mistake, or by accident!

Every thought that has ever been thought still exists. Every 'Static Frame Reality' that has ever been experienced still exists! Everything is 'Energy'! Energy always has and always will exist!

Every experience, expression, and personification is only waves of energy, dancing forever and holding the essence of 'ALL THAT IS'! Though we may use your vernacular, 'Change,' we only do so to better teach/learn with you. More accurately, you are merely observing energy from a different **'Perspective,'** not from an actual 'Change of energy'! Remember: Nothing has to change **'into'** anything; 'Everything already Exists, and it exists Here and Now'! And yet the universal law states, "The only constant is 'CHANGE'! Very paradoxical!

All life is a beautiful flowing of musical highs and lows. They are inextricably bound like minors and majors, all contributing their harmonic tones to a perfectly orchestrated song that you refer to as… **'LIFE'!**

Of course, this is only our perspective; no thing more and no thing less!

02/14/2018
By: Dr. ALi

103
WHAT YOU BELIEVE
YOU FEEL

This missive may be used as a gage towards how much you are actually, 'Waking Up.' You do not have a consciousness, you are consciousness. You are only experiencing one of an infinite number of types, styles, kinds, forms, manners, and ways consciousness can be expressed. You, as consciousness is experiencing 'A' reality. Singular! Your reality is a 'Reflect – Ality'. Your 'Re – Ality' always 'Reflect precisely, exactly, and perfectly what is your core vibrational 'Belief'! Your 'Belief' is stronger than 'Graphene.' If there were a one-atom-thick sheet of carbon, it would be 200 times stronger than steel. When you more fully come to omnistand just how much 'BELIEF' plays in your 'Ality,' you will become far more particular about what you buy into and settle as a belief within your 'Mental Belief Lenses.'

'There are 'Re – Alities'; 'Bi – Alities'; 'Tri – Alities' etc. You are experiencing only 'ONE' of many single framed 'Alities' superimposed upon your planet's collective body. Continue to lift yourself out of your slumber. Use your cognitive abilities to trust your instincts, and as you do, your vibration will increase, and you will absorb more qualities that will reflect such recognition.

There is only 'ONE THING,' and you are that 'ONE THING'! Be the 'OBSERVER'! Learn/remember that you, as 'Consciousness,' exist within your physical body. YET! Paradoxically, your body exists within your 'Consciousness'! In time you will come to omnistand that,

'You cannot be affected by anyone's negative intention towards you unless you 'Believe' or 'Choose' to be!

It is the 'Ego' that must, once again, be placed back into its initially assigned role. And that place is as a 'Reminder Only'; that you are in a physical body having a human experience; within your consciousness. The 'Ego' uses 'FEAR' to remain in a usurped position over your 'Belief System'! There is never anything that you will discover, explore, learn or experience that needs to be feared! Continue enjoying your experience, but also remember that it is your time to 'Wake Up'! You cannot be forced! You cannot be pressured! Your free will cannot be violated. Feel your way into your next journey. Feel with your emotion, (energy-in-motion) what is 'YOU'! Excitement! Joy! Ecstasy! 'What you are Feeling proves what you are Believing!

Of course, this is only our perspective; no thing more and no thing less!

By: Dr. ALi
02/19/2018

104
A SINGLE REALITY

So much is happening around your world at this time. It would be wise for you to stay focused, as one only passing through. Keep in mind that your life is an individual/single re**ality**, as is the collective, and all are superimposed. You have been programmed to believe that your world is just one big re**ality**. When in actu**ality**, it is not. Each Being/Person creates and then perceives a 'Personal-**ality**' strictly based on their deepest and most core beliefs. This is why you should not argue, debate, or force anyone to believe as you. Remember, they are all perceiving what is **'TRUE'** in their own **personally** created **'Real – ality**.' But please do not think that all of this is just **'TRIVIALITY'**! *Pun intended!* You are now waking up and must keep up with present knowing. More is being revealed to you. More is expected of you. Do you expect it of yourself?

The superimposed realities of your world are becoming unmeshed. This is happening based on the vibratory energy of every single reality. You are shifting! Your new world will consist only of those individuals that are well within your single vibrational frequency octave! Do you omnistand? Well then; Do you love yourself?

Then be prepared because you are about to experience your new reality upon a terra, filled with Beings with a disposition, attitude, behavior, propensity, temperament, mood, tone, song, dance, etc., that is **'BASICALLY'** just like **'YOU'**! Though your vibrational frequency will always be different, the more you come in sync with your 'I AM,' the more all who may appear around you will **'SEEM'** to vibrate with basically the same frequency, rhythm, tune, song, and dance! **ALL AS ONE!**

You must begin to view what you think is **'Out There**,' more as the scene, stage, and prop that it is. Which means, your observance of what is going on **'Out There**,' is not any of your experience business, **'UNLESS'** – you make it so! With some and soon with some others, you will begin to reveal a type of **'Flux'** or **'Transparency'** in the eyes of those of a lower vibration, shifting out of your vibrational octave and into their own. As your vibratory energy increases, so will your frequency change/shift to match your new evolved state of being. Let go of the values placed so heavily on what you see **'Out There'**! By doing so, your world will more fully match the vibration of your heart. Many have not shifted into higher realms of frequency because they refuse, for whatever the reason, to let go of old, outdated beliefs, thoughts, and feelings; they remain unaware of the magnificence, majestic, deliciousness, and glory all around them; just waiting to be explored and enjoyed!

NO NEGATIVE INTENTION FOCUSED TOWARDS YOU CAN EFFECT YOU UNLESS 'YOU BELIEVE THAT IT CAN OR CHOOSE THAT IT CAN!

It is far time that you allow this statement to ring true within your consciousness. You are no more a part of another's reality experience than you choose to be. No chemical trail, storm, riot, starvation, drought, cold, heat, area catastrophe, or weapon aimed against you, that is perceived **'Out There'** can affect you unless you 'Choose or Fear' such experience. Many timelines exist! Many **'real-alities'** do too! Many earth's, Mother Gaia's, worlds as well. **Choose the one you prefer!** You are waking up to the knowing of your **'Multi-Dimensional Self'!** The more you believe this to be **'YOUR' – 'REAL' – 'PERSON' – 'ALITY,'** and the more you are able to hold your vibrational frequency in a consistent, steady, and balanced tone the sooner you will begin to display evidence of your rightfully inherited and natural abilities!

You are Multi-Dimensional, and you contain it all. Still, you are only able to view first-hand, upfront, and witness through experience, only **'ONE' 'REAL' – 'PERSON' – 'ALITY,'** at any present moment in your linear time continuum. This is your reason for coming into this dimensional realm of physicality. You came to experience this singular, physical, separate, dense yet intricate, miraculous, and awesomeness of **ALL THAT IS!**

Learn to start viewing everything as separate and not as 'ONE' whole thing. And yet everything is only **'ONE WHOLE THING'!** But this is what you came to experience. You may experience any frequency scene which matches your own or on a lower pitch. And maybe a few with a higher vibration, but that would involve a few limitations that we will not discuss at this time. Choose your involvement wisely. Choose which **'Real – Alities'** you wish to intermingle and merge with for your particular experiential pleasure. As far as the others are concerned, just be a bystander and remain the observer. Yes! You have these abilities! And many, many, many more extraordinarily unmentionable skills!

Of course, this is only our perspective; no thing more, and no thing less!

By: Dr. ALi
03/05/2018

105
U R CHANNELED BEINGS

Part A

By now, most of you omnistand what is meant by a 'Channeled' message. Once again, it is information that did not originate from the source expressing it. We are here to say that you are 'Channeled Beings'! By this, we simply mean that your Essence, Existence, or Beingness **IS NOT REAL!** This thought will surely take some pondering. While many will simply dismiss it through **'Cognitive Dissonance'** alone!

You are similar to an animation created or personified in your movie industry, only far more sophisticated. Whoever personifies the animated character is the **source**. That character on paper or film is as you are in your holographic, duality–submersion illusion! You are the **'Personification'** of another **source!** It does not make you beneath, insignificant, subordinate, or less important. You are simply a 'Channeled' Spark, Shard, Thought, Expression, Version, or Personification of a much Greater, Grander, or more evolved Consciousness of **'YOU'!**

Now that you know you are a 'Channeled Being,' you have obviously figured out that you are not in direct control of your life or reality.

Although it is 'YOU' in direct control of your life and reality, it is your **'HIGHER SELF'**; on a more evolved or ascended level. It is the **'Ego'** that has you believing that you are in charge! Your primary and only responsibility has always been 'Choosing' which thought in your brain you wish to identify as your own. As you choose more thoughts from your **'Higher Self'**; the more in sync, in tune, in the vortex, you become. This is when the magic starts, and things just seem always to work out. When that moment approaches, and you wake up entirely from your present level of stupor or sleep, you will recognize and acknowledge, "Wait a minute; that was not really me"; "This is who **'I Really AM'**! This is one of the most important areas of thought while on your hero's journey towards greater conscious awareness.

Remember if you are following any particular event around you with any degree of 'Emotion' – 'Energy in Motion'; to that same degree will you find yourself connected, involved, identified, and able to be affected! Keep in mind, though you get into your car, the car is **'NOT YOU'**! The vehicle and you are still having your experience inside of your consciousness. You are very powerful Beings.

You have created a world, unlike anything ever on the leading edge of creative thought. But the game has gone far enough now. All creation is on the 'In Breath.' It is time to 'Wake Up' and come home! She-Vi!

Of course, this is only our perspective; no thing more and no thing less!

By: Dr. ALi
03/04/2018

Part B

This missive is not meant for everyone. It depends very much on your TimeLine. If it vibrates with you, then assimilate and help others along their path. A Photonic Pleiadean Energy and New Photonic Era is enveloping Mother Gaia as she gently slides further into the Photon, Electromagnetic Energy Belt of Alcyon, your Central Sun. This new invigorating energy source is causing you to mutate. Your DeoxyriboNucleic Acid is increasing to twelve strands; you are physically becoming a semi-etheric, highly evolved species. Sit back and relax; How do you say it on your planet? **'THE BEST IS YET TO COME'!**

As 'Channeled Beings' your Higher Self 'CONCEIVES'; your lower/human 'BRAIN' receives; your lower/human 'MIND'... 'PERCEIVES'! You have never 'CONCEIVED' one thought in your entire life! Like a 'Play Station' Spark, Shard, Thought, Expression, Personification, or Character, your only role has always been to 'CHOOSE' with your mind, which thought, received by your brain, you wish to identify as 'YOUR'S'!

This is what all of your mantras, meditating, chanting, fasting, and reading was all about. It was all to assist you in aligning your present frequency more with your Guides or directly with your 'Higher Self's Frequency'; so that you could better recognize your grand, authentic, pure, and complete 'Self.'

There are many Species/Entities/Beings somewhat competing as they toy/play for you to choose their thoughts. They would love to have you as their private food source to **'Loosh/Feed** upon. You are always in control. **'CHOICE'** is the mechanism that represents that control.

But as we previously stated, you permit by **'Choosing,'** to seemingly, relinquish your control; by first choosing a lower negative thought over that of your Guides or your 'Higher Self.' Though you are never, 'not,' in complete control, you create the illusion of that state for the experience. This was a much less challenging task before your planet was taken over by some low energy negative Beings. Whose intention was not in your best interest. However, it was a part of the overall infinite plan. And they do help you by creating greater contrast.

The more you experience what you do not prefer, it strengthens your desire to choose that which you do. How does one know what they prefer if one does not know what they do not prefer? It is all a part of 'Free Will.'

You contain it all. Never this 'OR' that but always this 'AND' that! You may always freely choose to go into the darkness of lower vibratory energy. This is what creates true 'Self – Empowerment'!

This is 'Yourality'! You are in Complete Control! You are the ' Co–Creator'!

By: Dr. Ali
03/12/2018

Part C

ATTENTION! ATTENTION! ATTENTION! You are upon the most remarkable shift of the ages! Compared to that of the Myan's, ages before! Pay attention! Be alert! Be wise! Be vigilant! These are such exciting times! The multi-verse is on the, proverbially speaking, 'edge of their seats'; in anticipation, exuberance, and joy! Great photon light energy is penetrating the very core of your physical body, even as you read this missive. You are changing; Metamorphosing; Evolving! If you are unable to cognize the importance of this missive, then know this; you will not share in the most generous portion of this ongoing shift! Period! You are upon your final and greatest shifting moments!

Never has there been a more meaningful moment for you to be in 'Observer Mode'; than 'NOW'!

Never has there been a more earnest moment to remember all the tools from previous missives. You would be wise to go back and reread them!

If you raise your vibration high enough, you would not be so concerned about who is president; fake news; school shootings; wireless cell phone radiation; wireless wifi radiation; cell phone tower radiation; 4G – **5Gigahertz**; smart meters; electrical power grids; technology that you think threatens your freedom; Civil rights; Human rights; Black Lives Matter; White Lives Matter; Some Lives Matter; All Lives Matter: Fema Camps; etc.! If these and any other, 'OUT THERE' events have your deepest emotional attention, then you are far too involved with the illusion that surrounds you. You cannot shift to higher vibrational states of dimension; you must remain where the energy will support your deepest interest and concerns.

Are you paying attention? One secret of the universe is 'Minding your own business.' What is meant by this is, do not get so involved in daily events and life experiences, desires, and beliefs of others that you unknowingly cause incongruous, disharmonic, confusion, chatter, or wobbles in your vibrational frequency and compromise your true alignment. **Let nothing be more significant than your alignment with your Higher Self.**

If you apply this thought, the infinite flow of energy from the whole universe will be in concert with and for you! Now is the time to hold your vibration steady! The climax of the moment is fast approaching for why you originally came to Mother Gaia. You have done well. We are all proud!

"You are just gonna have to make up your own damn mind! CANDY?"

Of course, this is only our perspective; no thing more and no thing less!

By: Dr. ALi
03/25/2018

106
NEUTRINOS

I have no missives on Alcyon, our central sun. But allow us to share this info. It would be wiser to concern yourself less with categorizing, labeling, and dissecting into elements various particles of your reality. Naming Neutrinos into electron, muon, and tau only complicates your ascension experience. Neutrinos do not come from anywhere; they exist everywhere. Specific nuclear reactions only bring them more to a visible surface for those on your level of dimensional expression to physically see.

Depending on your vibrational frequency, neutrinos assist in the 'Crystallizing' of your human structure, as you are more prepared to cross further into the 5th dimension. Every vibration has its position within an 'Octave' of resonance. If your vibratory resonance is too low, this energy will have an opposite effect; your physicality cannot withstand such concentration of pure energy! All energy plays a part in the grand theme of life. Everything has a cause, and everything has an effect; everything is connected!

What is most important at this moment in your time is that your solar system is passing through the Photon Belt of Alcyon. This energy is also neutrinos in nature, differing only in degree.

It brings about a greater conscious awareness to all who have a high enough vibrational resonance. Your very 'DeoxyriboNucleic Acid' is changing, even as you read this email. Photon energy, neutrinos energy, and energy that has not yet been discovered and named are bathing Mother Gaia even now!

Focus on your 'Vibration' and keep it as high as possible. You are shifting, my friend. Your reality will moment to moment reflect your newest and most passionate beliefs! It is not about Neutrino, electron, muon, tau, neutron, proton, quat, etc. It has been stated in 3D, "You are asking the wrong questions"! But in actuality, there are no wrong questions. However, are you sure this is the area of thought that you wish to be informed?

Your shift is more about **'CONSCIOUS AWARENESS'**! And the omnistanding of who you are. Remember, you are even that of which you question and more! You contain it all! Although these subjects make for good conversation, do not get sidetracked and led down a timeline path you do not desire.

They are quite interesting, to say the least, but follow this path only if it is your **'GREATEST OF JOY'**! It is our hope that this has helped you while on your 'Hero's Journey' in such a realm of limitation.

You, Mr. Jackson, are much admired and graciously adored as a 'MASTER OF LIMITATION'!

Kun – Doo – Lock – Tar – Shoe, Boron – Tar – Za.
We love you, unconditionally, every moment.

04/15/2018
By: Dr. ALi

107
A WISE ADMONISHMENT
ATTENTION!   ATTENTION!
ATTENTION!

We are DraLi'! We offer this missive of caution in unconditional love. We speak mainly to those on your planet that find your dwelling in the land you refer to as The United of States,' Estados Unidos! All would be wise to follow our thoughtful offering. The drama being played out on your planet at this time is most intriguing and quite mesmerizing, to mention the least. But in keeping with your known true intention, we hesitate not in what we are about to share.

Far too many, who had initially awakened, have fallen and are falling back into a self - hypnotic stupor! You are creating parallel reality timelines that we know are not your true intent. You are being serenaded, charmed by a live dramatic play for divertimento. You are far too involved in your political games! Observe how much time you are spending on your electronic devices. Following those that have no desire to shift or ascend to the dimensional realms of your choice! Although some do and will!

Your incarnation is not about Politics! It is not about Religion! It is not about Party Affiliation! Evil/Negativity will always and has always existed!

Yet there are no lines to be drawn. There are no boundaries; there is no Good vs. Evil; only the paradox of Meta-Physical thought. You are genuinely at; how do you say it in your own vernacular? "THE CALM BEFORE THE STORM"! You are all deciding!

There are ascended Beings that have evolved to such levels, which you would consider as Masters but whose vibration is such that you are still far more powerful than they! Only, you are unaware! So they toy with you, as you continue to identify with thoughts that are of their personal vibrational tone. Like little birds, singing in your ear, or Mermaids, charming your soul with siren-like tones. They mock you as they lure you more as their looshing meal! Why are you behaving as though your eyes are wide shut?

Remember: it is all only a game! Everyone are actors, and you are the main character; you contain it all! What you 'BELIEVE,' you will experience; whether the proverbial 'Good Guys' are, so-called, winning or not! You should be enjoying the show but only as an observer! Your 3rd − dimensional low vibrational questions are clues revealing the direction of your shifting.

And yet still, some of you do not have a **Q!**

Where We Go 1, We Go All!   **'NAMESTE'**

Of course, this is only our perspective; Nothing more and nothing less!

By: Dr. ALi
05/10/2018

108
NOW IS THE TIME

We are not here to curse the darkness but to light a candle that can guide you through to a safe and sane future. Efforts and courage are not enough without purpose and direction. You must all work together. This present-day encounter for liberty is not only physical but a 'Spiritual' endeavor! Like lightning, which makes no sound until it strikes. Now is the time to strike!

The cost of freedom is always high, but Americans have always paid it. The one path that we shall never choose is the path of surrender or submission. Humankind must put an end to war before war puts an end to Humankind. By now, you should have all 'Had a Dream,' and at this time make that dream a reality. The time to repair the roof is when the sun is shining. The sun is now shining very bright, yet many do not have a **Q**!

Tolerance implies no lack of commitment to one's own beliefs. But there comes the moment when tolerance must evolve and the universal law of change implemented. Injustice anywhere is a threat to justice everywhere!

To continue allowing such mischief, immoral, and demonic behavior throughout our homeland and world governments; is to set an example before our children that is shameful, embarrassing, and downright disgusting! Geography has made us neighbors. History has made us friends. Economics has made us partners. Necessity has made us allies.

Let every thug, gang, dis-organization, alphabet regime or nation be fully aware, whether it wishes the 'NEW POWERS THAT IS' well or ill; what has begun cannot be stopped! We shall pay any price, bear any burden, meet any hardship, support any friend, oppose any foe to assure the survival and success of world liberty! Liberty for all nationalities, all religions, all creeds, all creative thoughts as long as they do not encroach, impinge, or usurp upon the liberties and rights of others!

We must all look forward to 'Making our planet 'Greater' and our future in which world governments will match their military strength with dignity, moral restraint, its collective wealth with wisdom, its power with honorable, righteous, and inalienable intent! We hold these truths to be self-evident that all men and women are created eQual!

All of this planet's disheartened and downtrodden are about to be exalted; every hill and mountain of dark, hideous governmental rule shall be made low; the rough, neglected places shall be made straight; the glory of Man & Womankind shall be revealed, and all the multi-verse shall see it together. ~ Silah!

WHERE WE GO 1 WE GO ALL~!

Quotes by: John F. Kennedy & Dr. Martin L. King Jr.;

Edited by: Dr. ALi
06/03/2018

109
I COULD CARE LESS!

As you move further into the many levels of 5th – Density, you must continually peel off old 4th – Dimensional habits and beliefs. One such habit and belief is your constant attempt to change what is 'OUT THERE' in your illusional – holographic – duality! The title does not imply that you should 'fly by the seat of your pants,' sorta speak; not having a reasonable concern or care in your reality. But instead, it merely means that you should incorporate the attitude of 'Allowing.' Allow or accept your reality just as it is reflecting. Real change has always come from within! That is a constant! So it is time to learn and start practicing looking within for the change we seek without!

For many years now, you have practiced the old ways of 4th – Dimensional energy. You have now crossed into a new, more powerfully pure and higher vibrational resonance of 5th – Density. This new photon light energy is from your central sun, Alcyon! This period is also referred to as the age of Aquarius! While you were in the 4th – Dimension and using lower vibrational energy, the 'Rational Mind or 'Ego' worked quite well. But now, all has changed; it is now time to start using your 'Heart Center'!

You must keep pace with your spiritual ascension growth. As you continue to evolve and learn how to hold your thoughts and emotions in a consistent, balanced, and harmonious tone, only then will you open the door to more superior forms of abilities, which are natural on your new higher level of evolved 'Conscious Awareness'!

'I COULD CARE LESS' is a beautiful attitude to cognize! Just remember to apply it correctly. If at any present moment you do begin to care so much that you desire to change what is 'OUT THERE,' stop for a moment and remember, 'GO WITHIN'! Do not attempt to change the image in the mirror. What you are seeing is only a reflection of your innermost 'Beliefs,' defined and accepted by you; it is all about your present moment duality; All coordinated to blend nicely with the collective screenplay in your current geographical sitting. You are very powerful and formidable Beings! You are about to discover just how powerful you are!

Of course, this is only our perspective! No thing more and no thing less!

06/18/2014
By: Dr. ALi

110
NO SUBSTANCE

What we are about to share with you is definitely not for everyone. The thought is on a level of cognitive dissonance that most will be determined to fight against. With that said, allow us to continue.

Your reality, duality, is as your motion picture in a movie theater. Your reality is no more 'REAL' and has no more **'SUBSTANCE'** than does the beam holding the images that is traversing through the air from the projector; which after slamming into the screen, reveals the images held in flight. What you see 'OUT THERE' is only a reflection of your innermost 'BELIEFS'! Strengthened by your thoughts as 'Energy in Motion.' This energy is solidified ever so consistently as your beliefs then settled chemically within. A highly sophisticated, majestic, and benevolently orchestrated matrix! A master illusion of vast quantum physical expression! Where only now have you reached a level, vibrationally, which will allow your cognitive abilities to at least get a more extended mental glimpse of a clearer omnistanding of how you are living out your experience.

Nothing is 'REAL' where you are! Neither are you! Only the experience is real! And yet everything is 'REAL,' as are you! Did you get that?

Open your mind and allow your thoughts to expand without the limitations of your Belief System's control. Just accept what is being stated and bath yourself for just a moment in its content. Detach yourself as much as possible from what is 'Out There' and feel your infiniteness! Remember who you are and all that you have learned. Apply it now! And realize that 'There is only 'ONE THING'! Experiencing itself in an infinite number of ways! You are only 'ONE' of those ways. This knowing, if assimilated, will be of great benefit!

As you continue to hold your vibration steady, consistent, and in a balanced tone, you will increase your frequency and tap into more extraordinary benevolent abilities grander than you have ever imagined. What you see 'OUT THERE' is actually 'WITHIN YOU'! You are the Co-Creator and Creator of all that you see.

Go ahead, pass your hand through the projector's beam. Cast a shadow on the movie screen. Only then will you know fully that your reality is no more 'REAL' and has no more **'SUBSTANCE'** than does the beam holding the images that is traversing through the air from the projector; which after slamming into the screen, reveals the images held in flight.

Of course, this is only our perspective: No thing more and no thing less!

07/05/2018
By: Dr. ALi

111
NO THING IS REALLY SOME THING
AND THEY BOTH EXIST

Part A

Some of you may be a little confused about 'No Thing,' which is really 'Some Thing.' Not to be confused with 'Nonexistence.' No Thing and Some Thing both exist. Some Thing is identifiable. Some Thing can be observed; it has character, quality, dimension, parameter, nature, and vibration. You can 'Behold' some thing. Although 'No Thing' has an identity; it cannot be observed; it has no character, dimension, parameter, nature, nor vibration.

Some thing occupies space and exists in a moment of time. No Thing, on the other hand, does not occupy space; it does not exist in any moment of what you know as time and has no vibrational frequency. Yet it is a 'Thing.' The physics behind 'No Thing' can neither be explained in your 3rd – dimensional terminology, omnistood, nor omnihended. 'No Thing' exists outside of your ability to wrap your mind around. If you are able to grasp that which has been expressed so far, then you are above the average in your world.

Often in your world, you speak of creating 'Some Thing' from 'No Thing.' Actually, that is 'Physically' impossible within the confines of your reality.

No Thing can never become Some Thing nor vice versa. Nor can No Thing or Some Thing become 'Non-Existent.' Non Existence is already filled up with all of that which does not exist, as is existence. No Thing, Some Thing, or Any Thing can never become that which it is presently not. All Things remain the same. And yet, 'Everything Changes'!

What about Ice and Water? They are opposites, you may say, and they can become the other. Well, let us see. Would you agree that Ice and Water are the same in element and nature? Both exist in two different states and at opposite ends of the very same spectrum; they differ only by degrees of vibrational resonance. Slow down your vibratory resonance, and you will behold the fluidity of ice; as you are able to witness the liquidity of water at your present rate of vibrational frequency. Every Thing is true from the perspective by which it is observed.

As you move further into the 5th – density, you must be willing to let go of what you think you may know. Remain open-minded and fluid in thought. Knowing is infinite! It is paradoxical, contradicting, inexplicable, and in some cases, unexplainable!

Of course, this is only our perspective; no thing more and no thing less!

By: Dr. ALi
12/29/2018

Part B

This missive has the intension of fun-ness. Although the principles are accurate and factual, do not get lost from its real purpose, which is for greater joy.

Often in your world, you speak of 'No Thing becoming Some Thing.' Well, we would have you to know that 'No Thing' is already Some Thing! So it cannot become that which it already is. You see, a 'Thing' as well as an 'It,' can be used to reference that which is known by some defined name, title, or identifiable designation, but a 'Thing' as well as an 'It' can also reference that which has no specified name, title or identifiable designation; It is 'Unknown'! 'No Thing' has 'No Identity.' It is not 'Non Existent.' It simply cannot be touched, seen, sensed, nor observed in any way. It is proving by definition its 'No-Thing-Ness'! BUT! 'No Thing' is 'Some Thing' because, by definition, it is a 'THING,' or should we say an 'IT'? Due to your limited communicative reality ability, you lack sufficient language to discuss this concept. This thought is lingering on your linguistics' border's edge and cognitive capacity. Yet we will continue to amuse you.

Continuing to refer to 'IT' by terms that 'IT' has already been proven not to be, is merely redundant. Now, 'IT' cannot be touched, seen, sensed, nor observed. So, since 'IT' is not a 'Thing' and it makes 'IT' a little clearer to refer to it as 'IT,' then it stands to reason that 'IT' which is 'Not' a 'Thing,' must hold a different identity from a 'Thing.' Yet, unidentified by you. Therefore, it is conclusive that 'It Is' but without a known expressed identity by you. And this, which is not a 'Thing,' does exist but without any known identity.

You see, 'No Thing' or 'It' is different from 'Non-Existence.' 'No Thing' or 'IT' cannot ever be 'Non-Existent'! By definition, Actually, 'No Thing' can be in 'Non-Existence,' Why? Because 'Non-Existence' **DOES NOT EXIST!** So, 'No thing' that Exist can be in that which does not Exist! This alone disqualifies 'No Thing' because 'No Thing' or 'IT' is 'Some Thing,' but it cannot be touched, seen, sensed, nor observed in any way. Does this make any kind of sense to you?

Of course, this is only our perspective; no thing more and no thing less!

04/21/2020
By: Dr. ALi

112
JUDGMENT!
(ANOTHER MOST POWERFUL OF KEYS!)

We share this point as one most powerful of all key thoughts! Some of you are very, very close to a rather startling, yet amazing and most joyous quantum shift! Be attentive, pay very close attention!

You have been experiencing the most beautiful and magnificent illusion. You have been in abeyance or sleep as you refer to it. But now, some of you are about to; how does one say it according to your dimensional - duality vernacular? 'WAKE THE HELL UP'! Pun intended!

When you watch someone or hear someone yawn, why is it that you seem to almost uncontrollably yawn? Yawning is only one of many examples that helps prove just how connected every one of you are. It is also performed to assist your body in the effort of 'Waking up.' The motion helps **stretch** the lungs and tissues, allowing the body to **flex** its muscles and joints. Now is the time for you to 'STRETCH' & 'FLEX' your thoughts like never before! There is only 'ONE CONSCIOUSNESS'! 'ONE ENERGY SOURCE'! 'ONE THOUGHT'! Experiencing itself in all of the ways that it can. But! You are experiencing an illusion.

And to 'WAKE THE HELL UP' from this illusion, you must; you have to, you need to 'SEPARATE' yourself from the fantasy! BUT HOW? By fully becoming the **'OBSERVER'**!

There have been layers and layers of **'BELIEFS'** sinking you deeper and deeper into this illusion of limitation. It took countless incarnations to get you to climb up or rather see through to this level of **'THOUGHT,'** where you can finally grasp the most enlightening omnistanding of the foundational glues that hold you within the 'FIRST of this TWO PART' illusion. Yes! There are two parts to this 'GAME'! Resistance and Non-Resistance!

You see, it has always been about **'BELIEF'**! What you choose to believe always leads you more into the illusion 'OR' it leads you more out. 'BELIEF' is that Photon and Neuron, hyper electromagnetic, etheric connection on a quantum level lost in translation. It is that which bonds you within the illusion and connects you to everything and everyone in it. Are you still with us? Alright, let us continue. This is going to get rather deep. Here we go.

If you are genuinely at the point of 'WAKEFULNESS,' then you will have very much limited your **'JUDGMENT'** of the illusion, if not totally! You would for the first time, be viewing things as they 'REA – ALI – TY' ARE! *(really are!)*

Everything is 'Perfect,' just the way it is. Nothing needs changing, improving, or correcting. Nothing or no one needs to be 'Saved' or 'Helped'! It is a 'GAME'! It is all one significant experience! Or many, if you prefer! You being Consciousness, are always shifting through billions of frame like realities from moment to moment to moment. One cannot change, improve, nor correct any structure. They are all eternal in their existence, as are you! Always there, somewhere *(everything is here and now)* to be experienced again, at will!

Then where does the change come from, you may ask? **YOU!** You are not even 'CONSCIOUSNESS'! But that which uses consciousness within this realm of thought for this experience. You are that which gazes through the eyes and feels through the heart of one having such experience; in the form of an expression or personified Consciousness. You are vastly far more than this limited form of communication can reveal in letters, words, and paragraphs. You are beyond that, which can even be expressed in thought! I AM OMNI!

We must close now. You have all you need for your final quantum leap. Just sit back and follow your joys, wherever they may lead you. Have no more 'OPINIONS,' 'JUDGMENTS,' or 'BELIEFS' about the illusion. OH! WE HAVE NOT WRITTEN ABOUT **'FEAR'!** Remember, Fear is also only a 'BELIEF' within the illusion.

There has never been anything to 'FEAR' and never will be! How will I know that I have finally 'AWAKEN'? You are probably asking, Well, this is how!

NOTHING AND OR NO ONE CAN EFFECT, TOUCH OR **'HURT'** YOU **'IF'** YOU DO NOT **'FEAR'**! **'IF'** YOU DO NOT **'RESIST'**! WHICH IS AN ILLUSIONAL BELIEF! **PERIOD!** WHAT YOU RESIST PERSIST! YOU HAVE RAISED IN FREQUENCY; FAZED OR FLUXED OUT OF THE VIBRATIONAL OCTAVE OF THOSE WITHIN YOUR SUPERIMPOSED REALITY AND THUS OUT OF REACH! YOU ARE MULTI-DIMENSIONAL! YOU ARE BECOMING MORE FULLY THAT OF YOUR 'HIGHER SELF' OR OF YOUR INFINITE 'I'! YOU ARE TRULY HONORABLE, BRAVE, GALLANT EXPLORERS! FAR WORTHY OF THE TITLE…

'MASTERS OF LIMITATION'!

P.S. Besides, being **'Hurt'** is also only a 'Belief'!

Of course, this is only our perspective; nothing more and nothing less!

By: Dr. ALi
08/13/2018

113
INFINITE THINKING

We are about to express 'INFINITENESS' in 3rd – Dimensional, limited vocabulary, limited word, limited thought. What is about to be done cannot be done, but if it could, it would be expressed in the following manner. Enjoy!

Your ability to think is limited. Your thinking is finite. Your reasoning, at its best, is only rudimentary, in its omnistanding of the infinite. There is a '**Source**,' a '**Thing**' that is Omni in Presents; Omni in Power; and Epic in Knowing! Whatever this '**One Thing**' is, '**IT**' is infinite in nature. Infiniteness cannot be omnistood from a limited, finite, or rudimentary state of mind. Every word you use as a label or title to describe '**The One**' is only an effort on your part to categorize, compartmentalize, synthesize, materialize, mold, subjugate, thus will stigmatize a construct, by way of thought, of infiniteness on your level of thinking in order to simplify for easier comprehension. It is an attempt to bring infiniteness down to your level to formulate a thought with concepts more easily conceivable; a more easily omnistood process by which 3rd – dimensional minds can hold in thought what this **'ONE THING IS.'** And by following the above process, distortion of '**THE ONE THING**' begins.

Even the term **'THE ONE'** or **'ONE THING'** belittles, degrades, and distorts! Yet, for the sake of conversation, you have to use some descriptive terminology. This, we are aware. But! You also must be mindful that you are not infinite in thought! Yet from your perspective, **'ONE THING'** must-have **'SOME THING'** to compare itself with in order to know of itself. Then how could you describe **'IT'** as Omni in Knowing? This **'ONE omniscient THING'** which we will from here forward refer to as, **'THE ONE,'** you now conceive as having to create a way to know itself.

Thus is the creation of the version you now know as **'ALL THAT IS'** or **'CONSCIOUSNESS'** by which you accept and consider as knowing itself! **'ALL THAT IS'** is a reflection of **'THE ONE.'** **'ALL THAT IS'** is one unbroken thing. Yet now, expressing itself as an infinite number of things. Everything that can be thought is expressed and in any way that it can be expressed. And every expression is conscious! No matter how inanimate a thing may appear, on some level, it has **'CONSCIOUSNESS'**! Why? Because everything is **'OF'** **'ALL THAT IS,'** which is **'CONSCIOUSNESS'**! You are as well, a version or expression of **'ALL THAT IS.'**

You are on a most delicious adventurous journey remembering who you are. Take your time. It does not exist anyway. You have an eternity to figure it all out and perceive 'Infinite Thinking'!

Of course, this is only our perspective; no thing more and no thing less!

11/17/2018
By: Dr. ALi

114
VICTIMHOOD

Of all of the identifying traits that you could claim, **'VICTIMHOOD'** is one of the stickiest of them all. You may recite your mantras, meditate, read, even listen to your favorite channel. But! If you are not mindful of your deepest thoughts and consider the definitions behind every word that you choose to express yourself, you are basically marching in place or standing still.

You must practice using 'EVERY TOOL/THOUGHT YOU HAVE BEEN GIVEN'! 'EVERY CONCEPT YOU HAVE LEARNED'! EVERY LAW/RULE/PRINCIPLE THAT APPLIES IN YOUR REALITY DOMAIN! You must learn and apply by letting go of old outdated 'BELIEFS' that no longer serve you.

There is no Past, Present, or Future! There is no linear time! There is no such moment as 'WAITING'! Everything exists here and now! You cannot blame another for anything without first believing that you are a **'VICTIM'**! Only 'VICTIMS' believe that something happens, **'TO THEM'**! Only 'VICTIMS' believe that life is happening around them! Only 'VICTIMS' can be victimized! You are 'THE **CO-CREATOR** OF YOUR REALITY'! Life happens; life is expressed. life is created. **'THROUGH YOU' and 'BY YOU'**;

FOR YOUR EXPERIENCE! Which is the 'ONLY' thing that is 'REAL'! You are an 'IMAGINATION'! An intricate, sophisticated, highly motivated personification of conscious awareness!

You cannot experience both at the same moment in time, 'VICTIM AND CO-CREATOR'! You must choose one or the other.

Now is the time for you to cease identifying yourself as a 3rd – dimensional human. You know far too much and have come far too far! We are not disturbed the least by your actions. You cannot make a wrong decision. As your guides and Higher Selves, we are only carrying out our responsibility to you as we Unconditionally Love! We are here to help you on your adventure as you journey your way back into greater harmony with 'ALL THAT IS'! If our roles were reversed, you would gladly do the same for us. Continue to 'WAKE YOURSELF, UP'! Do not allow yourself to 'DOSE' back off to sleep!

Of course, this is only our perspective; no thing more and no thing less!

12/09/2018
By: Dr. ALi

115
I AM RESPONSIBLE TO YOU
BUT NOT FOR YOU!

You are not responsible **'FOR'** another Being's happiness or joy! Now, this may sound to many as cold-hearted, but the raising of your vibrational frequency during these times is very momentous, and it depends tremendously on you omnistanding this concept! Many of you are still bound by past teachings. You are still caught up with family traditions and standards; social influences, customs, educational superiority, which, after obtaining, leads one to believe more in their abilities, savvy prowess, and often developed moxie arrogance! Our intention is not to belittle your educational system nor your level of academic achievements. Still, you must learn when to let go of childish and rudimentary information for greater knowing! This is one of those 'when's'!

Yes, according to your present customs, there are exceptions to this concept, such as caring for a child, an adult directly under your supervision or care, and your pets. We are not speaking about these situations. What we are referencing here are those capable Beings, with whom are of age and hold the personal aptitude to be fully responsible for their happiness and joy.

Many of you are still making decisions solely based on whether or not this or that person will be pleased. Will it 'Make' them happy? Will it 'Bring' them joy? Will they still like or love me? Yes, we do omnistand your reality; rules, laws, customs; Your relationships and acquaintances. Yet you have to remember; Following your greatest joy is a prerequisite to raising your vibratory frequency and staying aligned with your Higher Self! Joy and happiness are the keys to your shifting to higher plains of preferred reality experiences! Joy and happiness are characteristics of 'Unconditional Love'! There is nothing that should be allowed to stand in the way of becoming 'UNCONDITIONAL LOVE'! This is your destiny!

You are living in an illusion. You have been taught a distortion; this thought hinders you from purifying and fine-tuning your frequency. You must learn to let go of such distortions. Sticky, they are Yes? But! Your growth depends heavily on you grasping this one thought! YOU ARE **NOT** RESPONSIBLE **'FOR'** ANOTHER 'BEING'S' HAPPINESS OR JOY! **PERIOD!**

Of course, this is only our perspective: no thing more and no thing less!

By: Dr. ALi
12/17/2018

116
Life is a Version of
Your Created Beliefs

Meta – Physically speaking, you are not responsible for another's happiness and joy. Neither are they responsible for yours. You are not responsible for 'ANYTHING' that happens in another Being's life. Why? Because everyone is the 'CO-CREATOR' of their 'OWN' reality! Co-Creating with another is only an illusion based on 3rd – dimensional reasoning. There is only 'ONE THING,' expressing itself from various positions and angles of infinitely possible and probable perspectives. Everyone and everything you look out at and see is another a version of 'YOU'; of your own 'EXPRESSED BELIEFS,' based on a previously agreed theme you created. Every 'BELIEF' is expressed. On a quantum level, every thought speaks openly. Every 'PERCEPTION' vibrates a 'RESONANCE'! You are a Being of astonishingly prolific Expression! You are never silent! You are never 'Self Sealed'! You cannot ever– 'NOT EXPRESS'!

Whenever you point your finger at another and blame them about anything, remember, they are only an expression or version of 'YOU'; your 'Created Beliefs.' If you are unhappy with a friendship, marriage, or job, recognize, all experiences are created by 'YOU'!

You are the culprit! You are the prime and 'ONLY' suspect! Not believing this thought only reveals just how much you are still holding on to and even caught up in 3rd – dimensional beliefs. It shows just how much you are still illusional in 3rd – dimensional thought! It is time for you to take responsibility for your co-creation. Stop seeking and asking others to make changes. There is no **'OUT THERE'**! Everything is happening **'THROUGH YOU' not 'TO YOU'**! You are telling yourself a story and a compelling one if we may say so.

You are not a 'VICTIM'; you are a 'CO-CREATOR' of your reality. It is time to stop 'WAITING' for something to change 'OUT THERE.' **ALL CHANGE COMES FROM WITHIN YOU!** It is what you 'BELIEVE' that Creates/Actuates your reality. It is an illusion to believe in life-changing, linear, time, past, present, or future. You are waking up, dear one. Surely by now, you can grasp this thought? We would not have given it at this moment if you could not. Neither would **'YOU'** be reading it! This is your journey towards **'SELF – EMPOWERMENT'**! The universe does not make mistakes!

Of course, this is only our perspective; no thing more and no thing less!

12/25/2018
By: Dr. ALi

~ 322 ~

117
A GREATER OMNISTANDING
OF LOVE

Part A

We ask that you open your minds and hearts for just a moment; as we attempt to express to you a glimpse of 'A GREATER OMNISTANDING OF LOVE'! Although 'LOVE' is **eternal in nature and infinite in degrees of expression,** and one fails miserably even attempting to explain it in third – dimensional language; we will, however, make this attempt from our realm of sixth-dimensional density. It is within our hope that some of you may gleam... 'A GREATER OMNISTANDING OF LOVE'!

Most of you know of 'Love' from that which you were taught through your parents, siblings, family, friends, community, customs, religions, and cultural teachings. Those definitions reveal only a third-dimensional expression, level, or perspective of love. There is an infinite number of expressions, levels, degrees, and perspectives of which we will now refer to one as 'UNCONDITIONAL LOVE'!

In your dimension or reality, there are three basic types of love. 1. Phileo – love towards those, male or female, that you feel warm affection.

2. Eros – love towards those you feel sexual passion; usually, they are of the opposite sex. But! Need not necessarily be so. 3. Agape – love is shown on more of a divine or selfless level of sharing or giving. As you recognize, all of these expressions to be valid, yet they are all expressed by one common word in your realm of duality, and that is **AMOR, AMOUR, LOVE**. These three terms may be synonymous, but you never substitute their unique meanings. Your domain views them as distinct, separate, and individual. But! We tell you that on a higher evolved level of greater conscious awareness, they are not. You may express Unconditional Love by any term or word you choose. But remember, Unconditional Love cannot be separated; it is **'ONE THING'!**

Let us take, for example, the custom that you refer to as 'Marriage.' An oath-bearing, monogamous relationship between two people. This is where vows and promises are expressed to be loyal, trustworthy, and to keep one's fidelity through, better or worse, richer or poorer, in sickness or health; to love and to cherish until death due you part; so help you, GOD? You make promises from a religious belief that teaches of your own wretched and miserable state of Being. Rom. 7:24

You are taught that you are a sinner. Rom. 3:2 You are taught that you are not righteous. Rom. 3:10 And any righteousness that you may 'think' you have, even that, is as filthy rags. Isaiah 64:6

Now, since this is the flawed premise and unstable foundation for what you believe and teach as your spiritual state of being, how could you, before your marriage, promise to perform such perfect life? Can one promise a life of perfection from such a state of imperfection? So contradicting; would you agree?

Often you refer to animals mating for life and having only 'ONE' partner. Such as Pigeons, Barn Owls, Bald Eagles, but you mainly speak of Swans. Animals are on a lower level of conscious awareness than are you. Why would you compare your level of 'LOVE' to that which cannot reason as do you but instead rely on a more basic instinct? The universe does not expect such creatures to reason as do you! Yet you feel that their manner of expressing love for a partner warrants your respect, imitation, and admiration. As a mammal or Hue-man Being, you do not remain the same in natural instinctiveness as do animals. You change by intellectual growth to a different level, as do your mates or friends. Human relationships change!

The one whom you promised to love as a husband or wife and/or as your sexual partner, that relationship may one day change, and your love for them may be only as a sister, brother, or friend. They may become more of a mother or father figure rather than the mate they once were. Your sexual experience would no longer exist, nor continue to play the same role in your new love relationship.

Why? Because your love has evolved! It does not mean that your love has lessened or been withdrawn, which one should never do. You may even meet another whom you now feel sexual passion. It does not alter your current love affair. It only reveals the expanding and evolving nature of your love. Since you have limited, categorized, and subjugated your omnistanding of love, you have hindered yourself from growing and expanding consciously. Why do you not compare your love life to a Wolf, Coyote, or Condor? These animals mate for life as do the Swan. Why not a Gibbon Ape, Beaver, or Black Vulture? Is it because they do not meet your visual criteria as beautiful, pure, or majestic? You are unable to evolve when closed-minded, thus incapable of ascending to greater levels of vibrational frequency. Do you believe that Beings on a higher level of vibrational frequency view Unconditional Love the same as you do on your lower level of thought frequency?

At the beginning of a relationship, your frequencies are a match or at least within the same vibrational 'Octave.' But, as time passes by, each of your vibrations change because of your various life experiences! Some change to such an extent that your frequencies or 'Tones' no longer match, harmonize, or are within the same octave. You are now out of harmony with each other, yet forcing yourselves to stay together because of religiously founded oaths, vows, and promises. You are now resisting the natural flow to the expansion of life.

You are pushing against the natural laws of the universe and forcing a square peg into a round hole. You have outgrown the purpose of that relationship. Such relationships no longer serve or benefit the participants. Some of you may be asking, "Can one still learn from such a relationship?' The answer is 'Yes'! All relationships are teach/learn experiences. There is no right or wrong, but in the context from which we speak, expansion is hindered!

BUT! All relationships are not a spiritually vibrational match to each other's unique frequency! This is one reason why many relationships consist of so much tension, drama, and arguments. These types typically end in divorce, broken friendships and adversarial breakups, etc. One's spiritual growth becomes dwarfed, stagnated, and distorted when forced to relate to someone that does not possess the necessary awakening experience with which to relate.

So, following such beliefs and remaining together in a marriage or friendship, without reassessing and re-establishing updated and more appropriate agreements based on the growth of each partner, will only take the relationship beyond its time of fulfillment and create a timeline only to justify old, outdated beliefs. It would be as though you hit the snooze button on your alarm clock. You are now defeating the sole purpose for the Universal Laws set in motion within your density, which is for spiritual growth and greater conscious awareness!

On our world, we possess love on one accord, in total sync and vibrational harmony. We consider all as our mates, partners, and friends; Our relationships are not thought of in such a segmented manner. There are no seemingly distinct genders because energy has no gender. We live in a type of 'Flux' between physical and non-physical. Sexes are somewhat indistinguishable, yet still recognizable. Children are not birthed by physical therapy but created by thought through mental, energetic conjugation. An electromagnetic conscious portion of each participant, one, two, three, or more, offer to join their consciousness in the creation of a new living conscious Being. Every adult Being on our planet is now the parent of the new baby, and every new baby is the responsibility of every adult Being.

Unconditional Love is just that, 'UNCONDITIONAL.' This level of Love has no boundaries or borders. Love is forever expanding! Love is always clarifying and revealing a greater degree of itself. Every perspective of love is valid but within the parameter, realm, or density with which the perspective is subject. It is never this or that, but this and that! Be brave and allow yourselves to grow. Let go of old, outdated beliefs about 'LOVE' which only hold you in the lower realms of thought. You are shifting, ascending into higher levels of vibrational love. You cannot bring beliefs of animal behavior of love into the higher realms of thought, referencing it as an example of a purer and more elevated Love.

No matter how nice they may seem to appear. Those concepts of love serve their purpose perfectly, within and on the dimensional density level they were meant to serve. Every expression of love has its proper place, level, and degree of expression, as does Ice Skates. Ice Skates do not work well in a Roller Skating Rink! Yet both rinks use skates! One would find it most beneficial to use the proper skate at the appropriate rink!

These are challenging times for you; we know. Your customs, cultural habits, and religious beliefs hold a powerful resisting force on your hearts. Yet, you must choose to free yourself from your world of illusion. You are waking up. Do not hit the snooze button. Follow the existing laws for your density while allowing yourself to grow into greater dimensional frequency octaves. Do not be so stubborn and create a new timeline just to prove that you are right. Yet, in doing so, you would not be wrong!

Be brave and courageous! As you continue to Master your realm of 'LIMITATIONS'! Be wise and light-hearted. Do not take your experiences so seriously. Remember, **You are Co-Creator Beings, Eternal in nature, and Infinite in degrees of expression!**

Of course, this is only our perspective: No thing more and no thing less!

01/25/2019
By: Dr. ALi

PART B

You are Co-Creator Beings, Eternal in nature, and Infinite in degrees of expression! If you have read part 1 and are still stumbling over this expanded omnistanding of love, this example may be of great assistance. Love is ever-expanding, clarifying, revealing, and nurturing. The expression of love *(Jesus Christ)* is not the same Yesterday, today, and forever!

As we go into this very omniportant discussion, let us remember, **definition** is what creates your reality! It is momentous! Let us take, for example, a married couple and their newborn baby. From the day of its birth, that baby is loved and cherished. But! At some point in time, the parents will no longer love that 'Baby' but instead, love that 'Child'! Soon enough, the parents will no longer love that 'Child' but instead love that 'Teenager'! Soon enough, the parents will no longer love that 'Teenager' but instead love that 'Adult'!

Yes, we are well aware that in your society, it does not matter how old a son or daughter gets; they are still their parents **'Child'**. And they are free to love them accordingly BUT! If the parents attempted to continue loving their adult-child with **open expressions** as a teenager, that would incur some severe challenges and embarrassments.

~ 330 ~

Or their teenager with **open expressions** as a child or their child with **openly expressed displays** as a baby. Are you following along? Definition is the key here. The parents never stopped loving their child. But as the baby grows, so must one's **'OPEN'** expression or display of 'Unconditional Love' towards that baby. The baby must also grow, expand, and evolve. A parent has the responsibility for recognition and respect. The parent should not love their now fully adult son or daughter **'OPENLY,' 'PUBLICLY'** as a 'CHILD'! Nor should the parents, according to your definitions within your family, society, religions, and cultural beliefs, refer to their adult son or daughter as a **'CHILD'**!

Here lay an oxymoron! Why? Because the parents will always love their son or daughter as their 'Child,' and it is not wrong for them to do so within your society! What is being spoken of here is a most rudimentary first step into a 'Greater Omnistanding of Unconditional Love'! If you are able to wrap your minds around this thought, then you are well on your way towards much greater, divinely enlightened, consciously aware epiphanies!

 Of course, this is only our perspective; no thing more and no thing less!

02/052019
By: Dr. ALi

Part C

You exist! Everything is here and now! The One is All and the all are One! What you put out is what you get back! Everything changes, Except the first four Universal Laws!   EVERYTHING CHANGES!

As expressions, shards, personifications of I AM, THE ONE! SOURCE ENERGY! We all change! This duality and dimensional playground are built on change. But! not the construct; only the operating matrix system. There is no one right, moral path to follow in your life. A pet may change its behavior of domestication and become savage! A friend may change their views and opinions, which may lead to a new path of unfriendliness. A brother or sister may change their views and opinions, which may lead to a new path of family alienation. A wife or husband may change their views and opinions, which may lead to their new path as no longer fitting, matching, or being compatible with the one whom they vowed, promised and pledged to have and to hold; to honor and respect; from such a day forward, for better or worse, richer or poorer, in sickness or health; to love and to cherish till death do them part, so help them, God!

And if any of these mental, moods, or behavioral states change in any of these relationships, does the relationship remain just as it always was? The inevitable answer is indisputably, NO!

This is one of the leading causes of broken relationships today. Marriage or otherwise. It is caused mainly by a lack of allowing freedom for everyone to **'CHANGE'!** There is a universal law name, **'Allowing'!** It basically means, 'Allow everyone and everything to change.' It is the fundamental nature of your existence! Yet! There are some things that remain the same! And you must obtain the wisdom to learn the difference.

Just because a pet, friend, family member, husband, or wife is no longer fulfilling their role, the love frequency should not change to dislike or hate! Besides, love never changes to hate! You do not have to discard your pet, separate from your friends, family members, or spouse. BUT! The relationship has changed, and you must now make appropriate accommodations! This is the moment to open up your perspective and expand your conscious awareness. You should always continue to love but now from a different and more evolved state of Being! This is unconditional love! This is **Jupiter Ascending!**

Of course, this is only our perspective! No thing more and no thing less!

By: DR. ALi
06/06/2019

118
EVERYTHING STAYS AS IS
AND NOTHING EVER CHANGES!

It has taken much effort to get to this point of omnistanding on your journey. We are all very proud and joyful for your accomplishment. Allow us, for just a moment, to clarify a few key concepts.

You are a channeled Being, and your reality is only an immersion – dimensional densified – holographic – illusion! You are Consciousness! Everything that you think you see out there is not real; neither are YOU! Only your consciousness and your experience are absolute! Every split second of your life is like a still frame photo; Like on a film strip in a movie theater. You are **filtering, like light, through** trillions of these frames every second. This filtering or shifting creates a smooth continuous flow of continuity you call daily life. Time is a by-product, as is motion. These frames possess their very own particular and special frequency. They are all quite unique, as are you!

You cannot change any of these still frame like photos! You never could. BUT! What you have been changing is **'YOU,' the consciousness that is flowing through** these reality frames.

With the slightest change in frequency, 'YOU' change! **Literally! Completely! Totally!** The new frequency is a new 'YOU' which you have never been before! The previous person 'WERE YOU'! Notice we did not say 'YOU WERE'! BUT! The new 'YOU' was never that previous person! Did you get that?

Example: The sick will always be sick. Healing is a process of filtering through the different still frame like reality photos to reach the desired healed experience. As consciousness, you are changing your frequency and filtering through to the picture – still reality frame or 'SHIFTING' to the reality world that displays what you desire to experience! You are in control of 'EVERYTHING'! Everything, state of being, frequency, stays just as it is! Even your present state of Physical Frequency Being does not change. You leave that frequency state and move on to witness through the eyes, hands, ears, nose, and taste of the new 'FREQUENCY YOU'! The only change is of 'GREATER CONSCIOUS AWARENESS'! All states of Being exist. Always has and always will. BUT! They will forever remain as they are!

There will always be Parallel Realities! They will always exist. You can always re-experience any previous or, for the first time, experience any new parallel reality, by matching its exact frequency. If you can 'Think' of a scenario, imagine a scene, or dream of an idea, then that parallel reality exists! How is that?

You cannot think, imagine, or dream of anything that does not already exist! PERIOD! You are multi-dimensional in nature. You are everything, and everything is 'YOU'! You are presently only a portion, an expression or personification of your total Self. You are being absorbed more fully into your Greater, more expanded Higher Self; or it into your Lower Self. Either way, you both are merging! This thought will help you in becoming more consciously aware. This thought will help you evolve and raise your vibrational frequency to the next level. Bath your mind with these thoughts; become cognizant and steadfast concerning these vibrations! They are of such great omniportance!

This is 'MASTERING LIMITATION'! Did you get it?

Of course, this is only our perspective; no thing more and no thing less!

03/01/2019
By: Dr. ALi

119
THE DIVISIBILITY OF
ONE'S PHOTON SELF

You are multi-dimensional in nature. Your Self is Consciousness and is infinite in possibilities. You are seemingly separate and yet connected to all that you see. You are one limited thing and yet One Eternal Thing. You are no thing, and you are Everything! You, Self, Consciousness is 'ALL THAT IS', ALL THAT HAS EVER BEEN, ALL THAT THERE CAN EVER BE! If you cannot cognize this thought, then STOP~! Read no further; This missive is not for you at this moment on your journey!

When you get involved with any person, place, or thing, from that perspective, a photonic connection is formed. You create a melding on a subatomic, electromagnetic, quantum level. To the degree of your focused thought, intent, and desire, do you reconnect with that other portion of your original 'SELF'! You once knew that you had the ability to transform to any location at will; or become any other person, place, or thing at 'Will'! When you 'Day Dream', that is the memory of the ability to do just that! You become caught up, fixated for the moment, phased out of the present location, and totally absorbed and phased into a different geographical scene. On the top of a towering, wind blowing, blue sky mountain, in the middle of a lavishly lush, sweltering hot green jungle.

Or surrounded by the sounds of over a thousand insects, animals, mammals of all shapes and sizes! You are there, and you are here!

A fully contained, toned, and synced individual can control their personal consciousness transforming divisibility. This ability has been almost completely lost to your present species on earth. Your proverbial 'Falling in Love' so quickly! Your sexification of everyone that matches your criteria and your daydreaming leaves you scattered and confused. You have failed to omnistand that you are constantly giving away the very essence of your 'CONSCIOUSNESS'! Sending portions of your 'SELF' out, over and over, and in so many various directions. There is no more wondering why you feel so divided, alone, broken-hearted, weak, and lacking self-empowerment.

You are a stream of cosmic waves, electromagnetic, energetic possibilities! Your Conscious Self extends to wherever your thoughts may go. There are no limits except through your imagination! You are not just physical material Beings. That is just an expression of only one of your, now experiences. Self-Empowerment is the ability to cast one's essence out to the fullest of your imagination and pull your consciousness back at will, within your present hive. You are shifting with Mother Gaia, further into the fifth-dimension.
More of your Higher Self is being absorbed within your present vessel every day. More extraordinary abilities

will soon be yours to exercise as you become more aware of your 'HIGHER – SELF,' practice control! Believe, and you will be able to achieve! Identify yourself as such, and you will begin to act as such.

As you continue to increase your vibratory frequency, your physical body will begin to take on a more crystalline structure. You are approaching a type of quasi, less physically dense body. You will become lighter in weight; Healthier, and more self-assured in thought. You will become more of a true observer of all there is around you. Your knowing will increase, your wisdom and aptitude will heighten. You are no longer the so-called 'Human' you once thought were you. You are becoming your 'HIGHER – CONSCIOUS SELF'! One moment you will wake up and say,

'THAT WAS NOT REALLY ME; THIS IS WHO I really AM!

Of course, this is only our perspective; No thing more and no thing less!

03/10/2019
By: Dr. ALi

120
TRANSCENDENCE OF DUALITY

This transcendence starts with re-establishing dominance over one's 'EGO' and the 'DETACHMENT' from all things 3rd-dimensional. Because you 'Are All Things.' Belief in an attachment means that you do not believe you already 'Are' 'All Things.' Here lay the beginning to Mastering the Limitation of Duality and 'Transcending its illusion'! The idea is to remain in 'EQUANIMITY' whether one has, is, in profit or loss; pleasure or pain; sick or healthy; victory or defeat; winner or loser; criticized or praised; successful or failure, hot or cold, joy or sad; To do this one must moment by moment acknowledge that all is only a 'DREAM,' an 'ELABORATE SUBMERSION DUALITY – HOLOGRAPHIC ILLUSION!

There is only one Being in the infinite universe, and that is **'THE ONE,' 'SOURCE ENERGY,' 'I AM'**… **'YOU'**… **The Real Player One!** It is incarnate in every neutrino, electron, muon, tau, neutron, proton, cell, mineral, plant, animal, human, planet, star, solar system, galaxy, and multi-verse. No one is superior to a tree, bush, flower, mammal, cat, dog, insect, crystal, or rock!

Each is a specific personified incarnation of 'THE ONE,' 'SOURCE ENERGY,' 'I AM'! All with a particular purpose, mission, and attribute of The ETERNAL ONE's infinite nature, expressing itself and witnessing all the ways that it can experience.

Though this state of mind is quite challenging to obtain, it is still highly possible. Discipline, determination, and a focused will are the **'KEYS,'** and remembering the thoughts explained in this missive helps too. You must learn to hold your frequency in a consistent, balanced, and harmonious tone! This is the path of true 'Mastery'! Do not allow what you think you see out there to mislead you. Just knowing what you believe is not enough! You must 'Believe' what you know and demonstrate what you know by your actions. Many may view you as heartless and cold! Even out of touch with what they call 'Reality.' But always remember, **"NOTHING REAL CAN BE THREATENED, NOTHING UNREAL EXISTS! HERE IN LIES THE PEACE THAT IS 'YOU'!**

There are no 'Victims' in your duality; no, not one. And there are many of you that make this claim. Yet you live day by day in contradiction. You see, to still believe in dichotomies such as right & wrong; good & bad; success & failure: innocent & guilty; justice & injustice; fairness & unfairness; equity & inequity; domesticated & predator, etc., means you also still believe in 'VICTIMHOOD'!

Unfairness, inequity, injustice, and a predator all need one thing for them to have expression. A **'VICTIM'**! If one is considered victimized in any manner, it automatically makes them a **'VICTIM'**! One cannot believe in one without believing in the other. And to believe in either is **'JUDGMENT'**! A very 3rd – dimensional concept.

Allow life to flow freely. Learn to accept the duality experience presented to you. Remember that by your 'BELIEFS' 'YOU' created your reality! 'YOU' chose the reflected frames of reality, which perfectly matched your 'Belief frequency,' through which you shift your consciousness for the experience you are now witnessing. Resistance only creates more of that which is being resisted! Practice a life of **'NON – RESISTANCE'**! How? You may be asking. First, by 'Believing' that your reality/life is all just an elaborate submersion duality, holographic – illusional 'Dream'!

The **'UNIVERSAL LAW OF ALLOWING'** is a most wonderful and omnipotent concept; it would be wise to always keep this thought foremost in mind. Following this one universal law alone can heighten one's vibratory energy, strengthen one's frequency tone while helping to hold it at a consistently steady, balanced, and harmonious pitch! Being mindful of this one law, from moment to moment to moment, can help dissolve many sticky glues that seem to keep you attached to old, outdated beliefs, created by an overactive 'EGO'!

You see, the EGO's primary purpose was to **'HELP'** or **'ASSIST'** you, through 'UNCONDITIONAL LOVE,' to remain safe while experiencing this new limiting environment and **remind you**, through loving 'CAUTION,' by placing thoughts (electrical signals) in your brain, (which is only an energy signal receiver,) who you now are as a limited physical Being. Example: Do not jump off a three-story building because your new body is heavy and will not float. It will drop, hit the ground, and possibly release the energy life force, thus causing you to experience what is referred to as 'Death'!

BUT~! Something happened eons ago. Maybe it was when Adam and Steve, oops! We meant Eve. (*Pun intended);* ate the fruit and gained knowledge of Good and evil; Genesis 2:17; maybe it was not. *Now, pay close attention.*

WHAT IF? There was another more highly evolved benevolent Being, assigned by GOD, **'THE ONE'** – **'I AM'** – **'SOURCE ENERGY,'** with the sole purpose or role to watch over and protect you during your life as a human; to be a personal **'GUIDE'** or **'GUARDIAN ANGEL'** which you have been told all of your life that everyone has, but you refer to them/it, unknowingly as your **EGO!**

This highly evolved Guide or Guardian Being chose, at some point in time and for whatever the reason, to go rogue;

step out of harmony and peace with **'THE ONE'** – **'I AM'** – **'SOURCE ENERGY'** and caused a distortion in their frequency pattern. Now they are placing **'THEIR OWN'** narrative through electrical energy pattern signals or thoughts in your brain but from a leadership and controlling position. You, not knowing, continued to interpret or identify these thoughts as **'YOUR OWN.'**

Why? Because you previously only had **'THE ONE'** electrical energy signal to interpret from only **'ONE SOURCE'**! *Are you getting this?* But now, there are multiple more evolved Beings, on a separate timeline, with a lower negative vibration, fighting to control you. You are receiving 'THEIR' electromagnetic energy signal patterns within your brain. This is how some of you have developed multiple personalities or what you may refer to as having a Split Personality. Some of these low vibratory Beings are so powerful they have literally taken full control of their subject, which you refer to as **'Demon Possession'**! These Negative Beings have lowered their vibration, distorted their frequency tone, and separated themselves so far from **'THE ONE'** – **'I AM'** – **'SOURCE ENERGY,'** that they can no longer sustain their life force by receiving such a **HIGH** Vibrational, pure, harmonious supplemental energy frequency tone as nourishment.

Do you know where these Beings must now go to get such low vibrational energy for their life-sustaining nourishment? **FROM YOU!** But first, they must get you BORED, UNSATISFIED, PESSIMISTIC, AGGRAVATED, IRRITATED, FRUSTRATED, IMPATIENT, DISAPPOINTED, UPSET, WORRIED, DISCOURAGED, ANGRY, REVENGEFUL, HATEFUL, JEALOUS, INSECURE, FEARFUL, GRIEVING, DISTURBED, SAD, DEPRESSED, thus believing you are a **VICTIM!** This state of Being makes your energy so much more palatable for their **'LOOSHING'** or feeding experience! This reminds us of another very negative practice being carried out on your planet at this moment in your time, which produces a product and is feed upon by the wealthy, elite, and the famous of your society. You refer to this product as 'ADRENOCHROME'!

Having a choice from more than one source of electrical energy signals has developed you into a more evolved Being! One possessing, are you ready for this?

'Free Will'~!

Whatever happened eons ago gave this Guardian Being, whom you refer to now as your EGO, greater control over you. This Guide or EGO assumed control and started issuing its own narratives through **'FEAR,'** based on **'JUDGMENT,'** rather than through mindful **'CAUTION'** based on **Unconditional Love!**

Judgment based on **FEAR! FEAR** based **JUDGMENT!**

Now to him that overcometh; even as I overcame; Revelation 3:21; The most appropriate question to ask here is, **'OVERCOMETH? OVERCOMETH WHAT'?** And the answer must unequivocally be, **'JUDGMENT'!** FEAR based JUDGMENT!

When you **stop judging everything** and learn how to differentiate, distinguish the electromagnetic energy signals of your true Higher Self or newly assigned benevolent Guide or Guardian Angel from the electromagnetic energy signals of other low vibrational negative Beings, only then will you have **'OVERCOME'!** Because only then will you have eliminated 'JUDGMENT' from your life! This is a **KEY** concept! If you can wrap your mind around this thought and practice it in your daily life, then you may consider yourself, as we already do **'MASTERS OF LIMITATION'!**

You are far too overly concerned with changing what is going on **'OUT THERE' IN THE MATRIX! THERE IS NO 'OUT THERE ~ OUT THERE'!** You are telling yourself a story. Everything is happening within your mind and precisely the way it is supposed to happen! Sure, you may engage in everyday events just as much as you would like.

Just do not get so caught up that you lose yourself along the way and forget that it is only a game; only a highly sophisticated and elaborate submersion duality, holographic – illusional 'Dream.' **Stop judging everything! Get rid of your dichotomy mode of thinking!** View your daily life experiences as perfectly reflecting and matching your perception of life through your inner beliefs. Everything is fine, just as it is.

Just as Mr. Anderson/Neo had to overcome or defeat Mr. Smith/The Agent, in your movie named **'The Matrix**,' you must in your movie/dream overcome or defeat Mr. EGO or this Being gone malevolent.

You must be willing to **'BELIEVE'; lose your desire to cling to life; be willing to transcend or to say it more according to your colloquial manner of speaking, 'DIE'!**

Remember: 'You are only passing through' this unreal adventurous journey! Change always comes from **'Within'**! You are forever witnessing all the ways that you can experience! This is only one of them. You are everything! And everything is 'YOU'; You are Multi-Dimensional, infinite in nature, and eternal in consciousness!

Enjoy the ride. Stop and smell the roses as you journey. Take in the sights. Eat the fruit from all of the trees. Just keep in mind who you really are.

Enjoy such an ecstasy of exciting adventures in your very own **'VIRTUAL DUALITY'**!

WHERE WE GO 1 WE GO ALL!

Of course, this is only our perspective: no thing more and no thing less!

04/24/2019
By: Dr. ALi

121
~ DEFINITIONS ~
THE ULTIMATE RELEASE

We have been anxiously waiting for you to reach this very point in your vibrational frequency ascension process. Pay very close attention; you are going to love this.

It is very easy to make various claims: I am the Creator of my reality, I am not a victim, I am always in control, But, when it comes down to actually living, by vibrational frequency, the essence of each of these statements, you are yet to vibrate that cord – so sweet, so melodious and so precise in pitch.

You are continually being hurt, offended, and frustrated over being taken advantage of, used, misunderstood, and here is the best one, treated unfairly! These are all frequency experiences of individuals that still believe in **'VICTIMHOOD'**! Deep down inside, you are still holding on to the belief that what is going on 'Out There' is real! You are still holding on to the idea that you and others are **'VICTIMS'**! You must focus more specifically on how you are defining your experiences. Are things happening 'TO' you or 'THROUGH' you? Are you going through or ascending through experiences?

In other words, nothing can happen 'TO' you as a Creator! NOTHING! **"Nothing real can be threatened; Nothing unreal exists'**! Nothing 'Out There' is real! Wake up! It has been said that only the experience is real! But that too is an illusion; only the learning from that active physical experience is actually ~ real!

There is no right or wrong process. There is no fast or slow pace. It is all just an elaborate, most sophisticated holographic, submersion duality illusion. You are a Devine Eternal Being. You have an eternity to learn, remember, grow, and ascend in frequency. So, relax; breathe. It is all for your enjoyment!

You have reached your most **challenging ascension point yet**! You cannot witness any higher frequency experiences until you let go of those old, outdated beliefs. The more challenging, troubling, and demanding the release, the more heightened and elevated in pitch is your new tone.

Allow us to be redundant. You cannot shift to a higher, more melodious tone until first letting go of the old and outdated! There is no need to ever **'JUDGE'**! You are accepting more full-heartedly, completely, and totally, that you are an **expression** of **'I AM'**; a **personification** of **'THE ONE,'** a note from the **'CREATOR'S** song; a **pitch** within the melody of **'ALL THAT IS'**!

Of course, this is only our perspective: No thing more and no thing less!

10/12/2019
By: Dr. ALi

122
CONTROL YOUR ANGER

All of your human life, you have been taught to control your anger. You have been taught that anger out of control is like that of a drunk; thus, the term, 'Drunk with Anger'! Some even go so far as to attempt the perceived final step, freeing themselves from, eradicating, or getting rid of their anger once and for all! Some have become very good at **'Controlling'** their anger even to the point where they are admired and exalted for having achieved such a degree of self-discipline. And there are others that show no sign of anger whatsoever! BUT! These acts or performances are very self-hypnotizing, misleading, and deceptive. Although one action may appear to be proving higher in vibration than another and 3rd – dimensionally speaking, they are; the end result is a mixture of deeply covered low vibrational tones held within, which in the 'long run' can prove to be very disheartening to your ascension process. We are here to inform you that though all of the above are roads to a higher vibratory state of Being, none are the ultimate answer to the issue dealing with 'Anger'!

First, let us correctly identify 'Anger' for what it is 'NOT'! Anger is not an original foundation, root, or self-perpetuating state of Being. Anger is an emotion, and no emotion is a foundation, root, or state of Being.

Anger is a created match to an already existing particular frequency. Yes, anger is a low vibration that has a distinct negative frequency, BUT it originates, grows, or is derived from a parent source! Anger is only one vibration, note/cord/pitch, emotion or key amongst thousands within your overall Frequency Tone, and that is your State of Being! So, do you know what your next question should be?

Yes! Very good! That parent source is your **'BELIEFS'**! Your Beliefs are as graphene, which is the strongest element known to man at this moment in your time. All emotions come from an original belief. It is impossible to even have an emotion or feeling about anything without first believing something about that person, place, or thing. Everything in your life is pure unadulterated, unconditional Love energy! Take that energy you imagine, hear, touch, feel, taste, or see and filter it through your life's accumulated belief system. What emerges on the other side from that process becomes your 'Vibrational Frequency'! And from that process, beliefs are updated, eradicated, formed, or sustained and strengthened! Your beliefs have always been and will always be the **'CAUSE'**!

Now, let us get back to our original thought! **ANGER!** Actually, Anger has never been the matter or issue. Anger is only a byproduct, a result, or symptom. Focusing on Anger to find the solution to a negative issue is like focusing on the head aching because you have a headache.

What is the best way to eradicate anger? Here it is, clear and simple! Well, at least to us, it is. Ask yourself this one question. **'WHAT DO I BELIEVE AT THIS MOMENT FOR ME TO BE ANGRY'?** You see, your beliefs are what creates your duality, and determines all of your life's experiences, responses, and actions. Belief is the very foundation of the Verse (uni), with which you exist. Thus the reason for the 4th Universal Law,

'WHAT YOU PUT OUT IS WHAT YOU GET BACK'!

Of course, this is only our perspective! No thing more and no thing less!

12/22/2019
By: Dr. ALi

123
LOOKING BACK

Thoughts of the past and fears for the future will create a (Gift) for yourself most undesirable. You have a custom within your society where you take photos to preserve and remember your past experiences. That still frame remembrance of that which once was. Those frames take on mostly positive vibrations— wonderful and joyous times when you experienced pleasurable moments worthy of eternal keep. Thus the primary purpose for such desire is to once again, at a future moment in time, revisit what once was an incredible ecstasy in your life.

But for some less practical purpose, you find it also necessary to capture frames of remembrances that are quite emotionally negative in frequency. Experiences that once lowered your vibratory frequency to that of regret, sadness, and even anger! This state of being is used by more evolved Beings to 'Loosh' or feed energy off of you! Unknown to you, such Beings keep you mentally trapped in a deceived hypnotic karmatic cycle of emotional satisfaction for the previously stated sole purpose.

Often an entire society will create framed photos, joyful or sad, of past events and memorialize them.

They do this in historical writings preserved by designating a geographical location and by erecting statues, all in the attempt to remember a particular experience forever! You must break this self-sabotaging habit!

Dear ones, having a memory of a past account or re-experiencing an old traveled path just for 'good old time sake' sounds nice. Reuniting with some old friends or connecting up once again with an old fling. WOW! Sounds exciting, huh? This may seem to be all well and good. But! One must be careful not to become inundated with past thoughts of trails already walked, whether of a high or low vibratory energy! Those old and past sad moments, tragic ordeals, loss of life, kinships, friendships, or flingships are now outside your present frequency octave. Making such reconnections will be stepping into a lower reality frequency timeline. If you are sensitive enough, you can feel the difference in its vibrational tone. If not, and you become so delighted by the experience, you can become far too distracted! Such an experience has happened to many in your past, and some were more evolved than you.

They became far too caught up in the sadness of the illusion, captivated by the thrills, emotionally and mentally mesmerized by the satisfaction once felt while intimately raptured in physical therapy! Like a reality glue, many became stuck and lost sight of their true identity! What was, has served its purpose.

Your present frequency is of a different pitch now. *That person of the past use to be* **'YOU,'** *But!* **'YOU'** *were never that person! Did you get that?*

First, you must remember what 'Past' experiences are. They are your spiritual paths of growth, during a particular frequency moment; while vibrating at a particular energy frequency tone, and it was all for a particular purpose. Once those paths have been walked, metaphysically speaking, that particular energy frequency tone's usefulness has been fulfilled! You have eternally captured all that was needed. Some of you may be questioning, but what if I did not learn what I needed from that experience?

Our answer would be, then, another 'New' reality path, timeline, using updated, newly established vibrational energy, matching your now elevated frequency tone will be constructed (already exist) for your further spiritual growth experience. **You do not control this! This is not your responsibility, nor ever will be!** Your responsibility is to stay in the updated **'PRESENT NOW MOMENT'!** Everything is experienced, created, and known from the **'PRESENT'!** Attempting to create past, outdated, old energy which has already served its purpose is like being all stinky and sweaty after a wonderful and most enjoyable workout; taking a nice soapy cleansing shower but putting the same stanken, *(pun intended)* and sweaty clothes back on, all to help recapture how much you enjoyed that workout; then going out to eat dinner!

Remember: The 'Higher Self/Mind' 'Conceives'! The human brain 'Receives'! The human mind, 'Perceives'!

It is because you have forgotten who you are that you have lost yourself in multiple timelines, creating a self-sustaining, self-supporting system of beliefs that fulfills such a created reality experience! Did you get that? This is why it all seems so rational, reasonable, and logical! You are responsible for peeling away those distorted beliefs. Merging out of those karma created timelines and stepping back in sync, harmony, alignment with your Higher Self! Raising your frequency, being in sync, harmonizing, and becoming more aligned with your 'Higher Self' is referred to as **'Spiritual Growth'**!

It is time for you to start creating a present (Gift) for yourself that is much more desirable!

Of course, this is only our perspective; no thing more and no thing less!

03/03/2020
By: Dr. ALi

124
INSTRUCTION MANUAL

In our evolutionary path, we simply have discovered and experienced the ability to actually see the nature and structure of existence. In this instruction manual, we express a basic, simple, and clear manner, a practical, fast, and most pleasurable path that you can follow! If! You choose to do so. We are not forcing or insisting that you follow this path.

We have distilled down for you, in an Instruction Manual, the essence of how 'EXISTENCE' is structured, what it's nature is, and how it best works to your advantage! We have distilled it down into the simplest possible form of understanding, in your language, in order for it to be the most efficient and practical methodology. Still, you do not have to believe that! For many years, we have gone to great depths of explanation and detail about the instructions in the manual, but there are no more instructions.

1. Acting on your greatest passion from moment to moment to moment, to the best of your ability, with no insistence or assumptions of the outcome.
2. Remaining in a positive state of mind, no matter the experience.

UNLOCKS! THE DRIVING ENGINE OF YOUR LIFE!

A – the organizing principle of synchronicity;
B – the path of least resistance;
C – the path of connection to all expressions of excitement in your life;
D – the idea of being supported in whatever form or abundance you need to be supported, to continue to act on your excitement;
E – the reflective mirror that reveals to you anything that is out of alignment to that excitement, so that you can bring that belief to your consciousness and let it go.

This is the entire instruction manual. There are no more instructions! This is the concept that will accelerate you the most. We have talked about all sorts of ways of understanding the Instruction Manual; all sorts of permission slip ideas that go hand and hand with how to use the manual to get you into a more proper space to use it most efficiently,

BUT!

There are no more instructions!

04/14/2020
By: Bashar
Transcribed By: Dr. ALi

125
ABOUT THE AUTHOR

I was born November 5th, 1954, on a Tuesday or Thursday at or around 2:10 am. I can still remember my very first medical shot. It was done while I was sleeping in my crib. I was awakened from my peaceful slumber just in time to catch a glimpse of the corporate who administered such a sinister and sneaky attack against an innocent, defenseless sleeping, loving, sweet, and handsome baby. It was my Aunt Bertha!

I started school in 1959, when I was five years old. My mother could not take another year of me being at home twenty-four hours a day! It is 1962, and I am in the third-grade being taught by a very mean teacher! She called me a 'Dunce' and labeled me, **'Doctor Professor Stupid'**! By the forth-grade, I had met my best friend, Shelby Leon Porter. I use to copy off of his paper. Shelby was an 'A' honor roll student. That boy was smart! I was copying off of Shelby's paper one day, and so not to miss anything important, I copied everything. Right down to his name. LOL! No, wait, stop laughing for a moment! How was I supposed to know? I could not reed or spill! I must admit, I was one ignorant child. I got that from my father. Bless his heart! Do you believe me?

No, not that, the ignorant child part! Alright! Check this story out. I made myself a peanut butter and jelly sandwich one day and proceeded to leave with only the sandwich in my hands. I went out of the back door, and while going down the steps, I stumbled. Catching my balance was what I thought was most important, but I forgot that I was holding my sandwich and dropped it on the ground. I quickly picked it up and noticed the dirt on the underside. Now how was I to get that dirt off of my fresh peanut butter and jelly sandwich? When I saw only four feet from me was the faucet. I immediately had an idea. So, I went over to the faucet, stuck my peanut butter and jelly sandwich under it, and turned the faucet on. That peanut butter and jelly sandwich melted, no wait, disintegrated, and dripped all through my fingers! Do you believe me now?

It is 1965. My very first job was that of the neighborhood Paper Boy. I picked up my Charlotte News Paper bundle from in front of a designated house on Moretz Ave., and delivered them, seven days a week, to about sixty-four homes. I was so proud of my job. I had a little red wagon in which I placed all of my sixty-four papers. This made it easier than carrying them in the sack or bag that Charlotte News supplied.

I was so happy and joyful. I had a job! I can remember the Charlotte News at that time could be delivered to your home for about $.45 a week.

WOW! But help me figure this out. I could go to a house to collect, and still, the homeowner would say to me, "Can you come back?" Well, in time, I advanced enough mentally to figure out that I was making less than $4.00 a week! And that, to me, was not enough based on the hours of work being performed.

In the summer of 1967, at twelve completed years of age, but living in my thirteenth year, my mother introduced me to a gentleman named Mr. Odell Fisher. He was an excellent carpenter. Through my mother's request, Mr. Fisher hired me as his apprentice. So, while other children chose to play outside in the street or go to the playgrounds, I decided to work with Mr. Odell Fisher and learn all I could about carpentry. Of course, the money had a little to do with my decision as well. I went with Mr. Fisher to do all sorts of carpentry work. I went throughout the week during summer months and on the weekends when in school. We laid tile, put up paneling, designed cabinets, framed houses, built decks, laid shingles, fixed leaks, etc. If you needed work done to or in your home, Mr. Odell Fisher was the man! It was from this man that I learned the foundation for my building, fixing and repairing skills. I can still remember helping Mr. Fisher, all day, for three days, while doing work at Friendship College in Rock Hill, S.C.

Another friend, Don Taylor, from down the street helped as well. But he asks to go back home the very first day. Anyway, I got paid $65.00! I was so ecstatic that I had to be rushed to the emergency room! I could not get my breath! I am rich! Help me, I am dying! LOL!

I was raised going to church, so religion became the foundation for my belief system. For some reason, I felt at an early age that there must be more to this religious stuff than that which I had been taught. The contradictions were quite obvious when I compared my religious teachings to my father's behavior during my life. So, around 1969 I set out to discover greater knowledge or greater truth. I visited the Catholic Church on Statesville Ave. It was right around the corner from my home; the Muslim Mosque on Beatties Ford Rd.; the Jehovah's Witness, Kingdom Hall on Newland Rd. Now, this was the first time that I thought I had found greater truth, and I immediately wanted to share this great discovery with the ones I loved. So I started by inviting my sister, Estella, to attend one Sunday morning service along with me. Estella was a rather timid and caring sister. But, with her, that first visit was all it took. She in time joined, became a member, and has remained a faithful Jehovah's Witness to this very day. I, on the other hand, had second thoughts and continued my quest.

It was during these times that I met a friend in junior high school name Johnny Gray. His family was 7th Day Adventist. Johnny invited me to attend his church, introduced me to his family and one particular sister. WOW! This young lady was the most beautiful creature I had ever laid my eyes upon! I was spellbound, mesmerized, infatuated, and hypnotized! This was my very first romantic love affair. I had never felt like this towards any young girl. But not only that, she was smart. I was amazed that she was interested in someone like me. How is that for self-esteem? Remember now; I was young. Say what? Did I join? Do I really need to answer that question? This was my junior high school sweetheart. We boarded a ship that sailed until about the year of 1974.

When it came time to graduate high school, I begged my British Literature teacher to give me a passing grade. I wanted to graduate with my class. I guess she felt sorrow for me because she changed my 'F' to a 'D.' By the way, please tell me how in heaven or in hell, British Literature was going to help me in my life! When I graduated high school, I was reading on a fifth-grade level. All through school I was in group three and always made 'D's and 'F's. Consistency!

I had already joined the United States Marine Corps before graduating. So about ten days after graduation, I left for Paris Island, S.C. It is 1972. When I took my Skill Level Qualification test, I qualified for the MOS – 6113; the air wing! I became a crew chief on the Marine Corps CH-53D model helicopter. Now how in the world did I pull that off?

I loved me some boot camp! The physical training, (PT), the marching, the drilling! And then there was the beating by the Drill Instructors (DI). WOW! How pleasurable! I can still remember, on one warm sunny day, my Senior DI striking me in the abdomen and nearly knocking my breath out! I bent over in pain! "Are you going to get it together, Ms. Owens?" Obviously, I had made some careless mistake. I would then reply, "Sir, Yes, Sir!" And my Senior DI would say, "OH! Now ya lying to me! And he would strike me again! I would bend over again, only this time further. Are you lying to me, Ms. Owens?

I would then reply, "Sir, No, Sir BUT! No matter what I say sir, The Senior Drill Instructor is gonna hit me again," Sir! And my Senior DI would say, "Shut up Ms. Owens! You are lying to me!" And my Senior DI would hit me in the abdomen again. Now, I am completely down on my knees. I am struggling to stand up at attention. Waiting and wondering how I should answer the next question. Again I am struck! Down I go. Now I am hurting like @%&$; And earnestly struggling to get up. My Senior DI would then say to me, "Ms. Owens? Are you crazy? What the hell is wrong with you? Just stay down!" The other recruits are now yelling up and down the squad bay, "Stay down! Stay down!" But noooo!, not me, I just got to get back up! And I DO! It was not long, and I earned the name, 'Mouth Almighty'! I guess that is better than 'Bruce'! Goosh, I loved boot camp!

After graduation, I returned home on my thirty-day leave and wore my Dress Blues to church on the first coming Sabbath. WOW! I WAS SO PROUD OF MYSELF! I stayed after church for what we referred to as 'Potluck.' There I saw and was introduced to the second most beautiful creature I ever laid my eyes upon. I was spellbound, mesmerized, infatuated, and hypnotized! But there was something very strange about the way this most charming lady moved and behaved. I could not quite wrap my mind around it. Down through the years, and to this very day, we remained close friends.

Yes, years later, I did finally figure out what it was that had left me so puzzled about this lady's behavior. The ship we boarded sailed for the rest of our life. Our relating to each other continued and became quite romantic. Let us call her Martha!

My first assigned duty was in Jacksonville, N.C., at New River Air Station. At this time in my life, I considered myself a devout Seventh-Day Adventist. But being a devout Adventist, I should have joined as a 'Conscientious Objector'! That title came about two years later after the Marine Corps spent thousands training me as a helicopter mechanic. Once arriving at my duty station and getting settled in, I went out into town, searching for my church of worship. I found a small group of Adventists, mostly women, and children, renting a Baptist Church to worship. I could see right away that my help was needed. But if I chose to offer my support, sooner or later, I would find myself standing up front with a Bible in my hand and still unable to read.

So, I did what any other red-blooded American would do. I bought my first book and taught myself how to read; out loud and in front of an audience. Of course, this also meant me studying more. And I studied deep too. I bought all types of reference materials. Greek and Hebrew dictionaries, concordances; every Ellen G. White book I could get my hands on. Oh! She is the prophetess of the Adventist Church. The more I read and studied, the more I questioned. And the more my questions were not answered. This led me to seek answers outside of my home church. My thirst for greater knowledge grew precipitously. It is June 1976; I am now discharged from the United States Marine Corps with Honors. Stay with me now; this is going to be good.

Around 1977 I met and boarded a ship with a pretty little Adventist that was rather popular in the church. We soon got married because she was found begotten with child, by none other than 'Moi'! Now how could that happen to such a loyal and devout Christian like me? I would rather not print her name. I might get sued. We got married and the voyage lasted for about (30) thirty days! WOW! We conceived a child from that marriage. I still have an original copy of my daughter's certificate of live birth. Her name is Faith Nichole Owens. I never got the chance to raise Faith. While Faith was still young, around seven or eight, we spent a couple of visits together, along with her younger sister. Years later, Faith went to work with me while hanging wallpaper. Her mother later moved away, and we lost contact. Years passed, and one-day, Faith decided to contact me. I think it was by letter. We arranged a day and time for her to come to visit. She brought with her Amirah, her daughter, my first and only granddaughter. This was around 2007 – 2011. Now, let us get back to 1977.

I hesitated one day, standing motionless at the back door. I was about to leave for church. My mother noticed me and spoke up, "Don't stop going," she said, encouraging me to keep attending. My mother was a great encouragement and example to me in my life. So, I did keep going. But I felt empty inside. It was almost like something within me had been broken! My façade had been torn down. My hypocrisy had been uncovered for all to see. It was during these times that I contemplated suicide.

My self-righteous, Christ-Like, Christian life was now seen for what it was. A FAKE! A HYPOCRITE! Oh! But I could always ask for 'FORGIVENESS.' That, too, would have been hypocritical. Why? Because I knew I was going to continue having 'Physical Therapy'! Attempting to live this biblical 'Perfect and Righteous' life was frustrating, to say the least. Here I am being told by those same biblical scriptures just how much of a wretched sinner I am; that I am unclean and if I have any amount of righteousness at all, even that is as filthy rags. Isaiah 64:6 But! Through this particular Being, Man, I could take on his 'Perfection' and 'Righteousness'! BUT! I, myself, personally, could never achieve such a state of glory. I felt trapped with no known options! Knowing this left me very, very disgruntled! That belief was never favored.

Hold on; it gets even more absorbing yet!

It has got to be about 1980. I signed up and got accepted at the 7th-Day Adventist college name Oakwood. WOW! What a marvelous time in my life. I lectured/preached both on campus and out in town. And I was pretty good at it if I have to say so myself. This was when I met the most intelligent, smart, ingenious, and astute Jamaican man named Conrad McKnight. You thought that I was about to mention another lady, didn't you? We became best friends and still are to this day.

A few months past and I choose to become a Student Missionary.

So, I signed up. Next thing I know, I am landing on one of the Marshall Islands, in the south pacific name, Majuro! Check this out. I am there to teach sixth graders—math, spelling, English, etc. at the Adventist Church Academy. I do not understand their language, and half of them cannot even understand English! But! We made it work. I was known as 'Brother.' I did not want my students addressing me as 'Mr. Owens'. I became rather popular with the youth across this small thirty-mile long island. Being the type person I am caused me a little trouble. I just found it so challenging to follow all those stupid religious school rules. On clear sunny days, I would take my students out to a grassy field, and we had class outside. The students LOVED ME FOR THAT! I loved me too! We played games most of the time that we were out there, but I made my students also dig into their books a little bit. Of course, it was not long before the principal finally put a stop to all of that. "Oh, mean thang"! Needless to write, but I am going to write it anyway, it got so tense between the principal and I that the church ended up giving me about $300.00 and sending me back to the states. I did not go back to college. Instead, I started another adventure. Bar lo koh!

I am back in the states now, and it is 1982. I met and married another Adventist. No, this one was not pregnant! My thirst for greater knowledge continued. By this time, my studies caused my new wife and I to leave the established church on a more profound spiritual quest. We joined others and formed a small group of offshoot reformers, as we were referred to by the established church. This wife was also a very pretty young lady. We were both, astrologically speaking, Scorpios! Do you know anything about Scorpios? If so, then yes! You guessed it. It was a marriage with many fireworks! The sea that this boat sailed on was very stormy. Talk about tidal waves! We argued every day! Scorpios are known for their angry temper, and we were no exception. Especially me! We never put our hands on each other, but words can leave bruises, scars, cuts, and broken bones. One day while the sun was setting in the distant sky, living in the hills of Tennessee, in a single-wide mobile home, with no running water, telephone, or electricity; My wife turned to me and stated, "William, guess what," What? I replied. "We did not argue today!" About a year or two later, after getting laid off from my job at Suburban Propane, where I drove a gas truck, we moved back to Charlotte, N.C. and lived with our parents.

The mobile home dealership had someone to burn that trailer because they did not want to repossess it, and after they got their portion of the insurance money, we also received a check. No! I did not burn that trailer!

With that check, we made a down payment on six acres of land in York, South Carolina. This ship/marriage voyage lasted four long argumentative, fusing, fighting but with some pleasant times, years. We traveled, talked, and studied the scriptures together. I learned so much on this ship. This was a great 'Ship' to be on! We related to each other in ways that helped us both see ourselves for who we were; that is, if we choose to see it.

This is what relating to people, animals, plants, and your total environment is all about. It is all for your spiritual growth. It is all for your teach/learn spiritual experience. There are no good or bad ships, just experiences. You, define each 'relation' you encounter on each ship. This wife decided to move out and back to Charlotte, N.C. one day. We later devoiced, and I remained in York, S.C. living in another trailer; out in the country; on a dead-end street; The Last House On The Right! Do you remember that movie? This time I had electricity and running water. We are still friends to this day. It is now at or around 1983, and I am emotionally broken—two failed marriages, ending in divorce.

At or around this time, I started my own business in the field of 'Interior Decorating' or, more specifically, Wallpaper Hanging. I hung both commercial and residential. I went everywhere, installing wallpaper. Some may refer to it as Wall Dressing.

Anyway, I hung wallpaper in dentist, chiropractor, and real estate offices; hospitals, banks, restaurants, churches, and once at the Marine Corps Exchange in Virginia.

It is now around 1984, and I had an opportunity to hang some wallpaper at a new club in Charlotte, N.C. It was named the Pink Peacock! The wallpaper was stunning! It was custom-designed, and I was told by the owner, very, very expensive! Remember now; I had only been hanging wallpaper for about a year. So, I still had so much more to learn.

Alright, I got set up, measured my wall, and cut my first roll. I rolled the paste on my first sheet, and the side edges of that paper rolled up like a scroll! Those edges would not lay down flat at all. Even after putting the paper on the wall, the paste could not hold the edges down. Over an hour went by, and I found myself sitting on my piano bench, which I used as my step stool, crying like a baby! But without allowing any of the other workers seeing me, of course.

I did not know what else to do. I had exhausted my knowledge and could not get that paper to stay on the wall. I had almost given up. When someone walked through the entrance door and gracefully made their way across the room, over to me; It was my youngest sister, Joyce! "What's wrong, William," she asked. I answered while still crying, "I can't figure out how to get this paper to stay on the wall!"

"I have done everything that I can think of"! Joyce walked over and glanced at the paper on my table; then, over to the wall, looked at the paper up and down, then gracefully walked back over to me. She then laid her hands on my shoulder and said, **"You can do it!"** Joyce then turned and walked out. Even now, as I am writing this, my eyes are leaking! I had an awful temper and anger issues, and Joyce was the one sister who was always 'PUSHING MY BUTTONS'! She loved it! I mean, the sista jump up and down on every one of my secret/private/personal buttons! She even found a few levers that she could also pull, and she did not mind pulling them either! I fought with Joyce the most in my life growing up. Joyce was the one sister that I disliked, argued with, and just could not get along with, 'So help me God!

Yet this one sister gave me such encouragement at the moment in my life when I needed it the most! It was a significant turning point! With that, **"You can do it!"** I took and constructed a new and greater **'Belief' in myself**! I figured out a better paste to use, with the proper mixture. And I hung that beautifully, hand-printed, pink peacock wallpaper. I also hung some very deliciously cut, Purple Suede fabric in the foyer! Now that was some dope wallpaper! As the years past and my wallpapering skills were perfected, I earned the title, **South Carolina's First and Only, 'Master Wall Paper Hanger'!**

It has got to be about 1985 now. I decided to attend the New Home Methodist church around the corner from my mobile home. This is where I met this sweet little, Whitney Huston looking, 110lb, graceful, and charming lady; Julaine (Judy) Hemphill. We boarded a ship and spent over ten years together, off and on. Now that was the most wonderful ship to be on! We learned marvelous things about our characters. We related mutually in so many ways, and we got along very nicely. But my temper was still a huge problem. Also, I was still too young and immature to understand how to remain on that ship with such a charming and pretty lady.

It is 1995 or thereabout. I am single again. I joined a 7th-Day Adventist dating site and became acquainted with a gorgeous Jamaican Queen, living in London. We will call her LaLee! It was a loving and excellent match from the start.

She was quite beautiful and delightful for the eye to behold. Lalee was very intelligent, smart, and mature. Qualities that were not quite the norm for me. I believe the only reason we did not get married is that neither of us was willing to leave our present country. Our ship was very promising. We visited each other, but we did not spend enough time together to build a more promising and lasting voyage. I believe that LaLee was either a Twin Flame or a Soul Mate. We have remained friends and are still in contact with each other to this day. I became a much more balanced and mature man after having met LaLee. Finally, I have reached a frequency level of relating with greater reasonable competency.

In 1998, through a dating service named V–Singles Connection, V101.9, on your radio dial. I met Cynthia Jeweline Johnson. Even though neither of us were the other's type, we dated anyway. We did not talk about if we loved each other. There was not much romance or affection on this ship. Nor did it seem to be the main reason why we were on this ship in the first place. Why were we together? Something on a cosmic level of supernatural guidance had brought us together.

I had shifted to a higher level of vibrational frequency. It was almost like we knew that we were meant to be together. Some of our family members had already met. Of course, we did not know this at the time. It was as though there was some unseen universal force causing a powerful attraction between the two of us. Within months I knew that Cynthia was the 'ONE'! I hired a lawyer and added her name to my house and six acres of land. How did I know that Cynthia was the one for sure? Mama Cora told me! Wrap your mind around that! About one year passed, and we got married. Weird huh?

We were married by the Humble & Honorable Papa Seydou Ndiaye, of Senegal Africa! Pap, as most people address him; is the owner of The House of Africa, located at 1215 Thomas Ave. in Charlotte, N.C. Pap is also the Founder and President of the Juneteenth Festival of the Carolinas, originating in 1997. This gentleman can speak seven different languages, fluently!

Cynthia had previously dated a guy for over ten years. So, I told Cynthia to contact him and invite him to the wedding. She did, but he could not believe that Cynthia's fiancée would be inviting him to our wedding. So, she put me on the phone. Carter McClain agreed to be one of my five Best Men at the wedding! The marriage was not traditional nor legal. SO? I do declare that lady reminded me so much of my mother.

As the years passed, I stopped hanging wallpaper and we got into a Multi-Level Marketing business selling health products. I must have passed out thousands of fliers and hundreds of business cards. I also started working as a Security Officer during this time. Cynthia and I noticed that we were becoming more & more like siblings than husband and wife. We were metamorphosing!

The physical and emotional affection thing was not working very well for us, if ever at all. What were we to do? The Christian church does not give a married couple any options. They must have and hold from that day forward, for better or worse, for richer or poorer, in sickness and in health, they must love and cherish each other, 'til death do them part', so help them, God! BUT! We are not Christians anymore!

By this time, we were introduced to Meta-Physics. By none other than, you guessed it, my youngest sister, Joyce. It was another positive turning point in my life. Joyce had a very close male friend who had given her a CD. She watched it and thought it was what I had been looking for all of my life. So, Joyce called and asked me to come over to the family home. We watched it together. When it ended, I cried like a baby!

THIS IS IT! THIS IS WHAT I HAD BEEN SEARCHING FOR! MY QUEST FOR GREATER KNOWLEDGE HAS FINALLY BEEN FULFILLED!

Do you know the name of that CD? It was 'The Secret'! By: Rhonda Byrne. But still, I did not take this new information to heart for another year or two. A couple of years later, I pulled the CD out again; Cynthia & I watched and listened to it very carefully. We did this more than once.

After watching and listening to 'The Secret' several times, I suggested that we desire something specific. The main point of focus in this CD was 'The Law of Attraction.' So, I suggested that we should put our entire heart, mind, and soul into this so-called 'Law of Attraction,' and focus on asking for something so big, so out of the ordinary, so totally unlikely and nearly impossible, based on the odds, So that 'IF' it materialized and became 'TRUE' within a reasonable time in our life, we would never need to doubt nor question this new 'Belief' ever again! So we ask for One-Million Dollars! Soon, our solar system would be entering the photon belt of Alcyon, our central sun. A higher and more powerful energy will be flooding mother Gaia/earth. The world was about to make a quantum shift.

Around 2007 I was at a store in York S.C. when I noticed a young lady standing in line with tears rolling down her cheeks. It touched my heart. Not able to just let it go, I paid for my items and waited outside for the young lady to exit. When she did, I walked up, introduced myself and ask if she needed help.

Me, being a stranger, of course the young lady was hesitant. She looked around, then down and this is when I met the Carroll family. This young lady's name was Andrenna Carroll; spelled with two 'R's and two 'L's. More about this family later.

It is now 2012! Oh! The answer is YES! Multi!
We will soon be purchasing a home in the Caribbean Islands, where we will be living out the remainder of our life! How it happened will be explained during my future lectures. I cannot tell everything right now!

Knowing that we no longer needed to follow a Christian standard by which we were both raised. (Like we ever did!) So, we mutually decided to change our ship to one quite exceptional. We did this by getting a devoice but remaining together. I know, really, really weird! You see, Cynthia & I decided to create our category and new ship rules. Rather than board another already established ship, with its rules, labels, titles; one considered as normal by society; We decided to remain on our already established ship and simply redefine, re-categorize, relabel and retitle our Relations on our Ship based on how it best fits our new code of beliefs and feelings. It did not matter to us what others thought about our decisions based on our new found beliefs. What mattered to us is that we were satisfied, at peace, and happy. Our 'Relation' – 'Ship' was purely filtered through a much higher level of thought, from a greater omnistanding of 'Unconditional Love'!

This is why so many ships with family, friends, marriages, etc. are not as beneficial to the participants. They are afraid to think outside of the box. People are so scared to reach for a higher or different approach. Most are afraid to create their personal rules and thus create new ships and live by their new codes of conduct.

They think that they must board already existing ships and follow established rules, laws, codes, and beliefs! Most believe that their ship must match some title, label, or category. Believing this way can become a great hindrance to one's advancement while on their spiritual journey. It leaves one feeling that there are no alternative actions. But there are!

To this day, Cynthia and I were not quite sure exactly what was going on during that time in our life. Still, we remained open-minded and concluded that a platonic relationship might work better than marriage or breaking up and getting off our ship. No one and no religion was going to dictate how we should or should not live our lives. We decided to think outside of the proverbial box and create our version of the type ship we wish to sail on for the rest of our life. Unconditional Love has no conditions with which to Love. Unconditional Love is not something that one turns on and off. Unconditional Love is not something that you possess! Unconditional Love is that which you already are! You only need to remember. It is the essence of 'ALL THAT IS'! This type of Unconditional Love is revealed more prevalently as one becomes more consciously aware.

Slowly, and with much deep-hearted, emotionally painful effort, we began to accept each other more as family members, brother & sister.

Yes, I still carried a temper, but even that emotion was slowly being raised in vibratory frequency. We melded more than ever before as one and truly created a deeper, richer, and more meaningful relation-ship with which to sail.

I put Cynthia through so much mental and emotional hell! I vented on and at her with such vehement anger down through the years! My demons ripped at her delicate feelings with such relentlessness, which no lady deserves. Even now, as I write this in remembrance, I find my eyes leaking again with drips of heartfelt pain! I can only imagine how she must have felt! Yet she took it all, many times just standing there in silence, with tears in her eyes, slowly dripping down her cheeks. Listen, let's move on, I can't take any more of this~.

Today, I consider Cynthia the youngest of my now four sisters, my Soul Mate, and bestest friend in all the whole multiverse! She is beautiful, caring, compassionate, kind, and the most unconditionally loving friend, companion, and Soul Mate, anyone, could have by their side. It has been said, "If you have not found something worth dying for, you are not fit to live!" I found mine! Have you? We have remained together as friends, companions, Soul Mates, family members, and business partners to this day.

Where We Go 1, We Go All! Hachiko!

I am still working in Security but now I am an Armed Officer. While out on a Security Escort Call, I received an inference or notion. That day I recognized my 'Higher Self,' whom I named 'Ephraim'! Non-corporeal Beings do not identify themselves by names, nor do they possess any particular gender. They are telepathic with no specific gender! Naming my Higher Self makes it a bit easier for personal reasons. He/we/I have taught our lower self about health, biology, epigenetics, banking procedures, taxes, law-101, legal documents, Espanol, and now meta-physics!

We even got the opportunity to defend ourselves in court—Eso fue bastante interesante. We won our first trial but lost our second, which got us three years in school. You call it 'Jail' or 'prison'! But, we only had to do one. 06/04/2014 through 06/29/2015. That one year in school was fantastic! I had the time of my life. I mean, well, after I stopped crying of course.

I gave personal names to every facility where I was incarcerated. In Columbia it was, Kirkland Theme Park. And when I was shipped to Rock Hill, it was Catawba Men's Club. I wrote a poem about Cataba Men's Club. Would you like to read it? No, maybe another time.

One day while in school I got the idea to experience a seventy-two-hour food and reticent fast. This is something you may like to experience yourself. It consists of not eating or speaking for 72 hours or three days! WOW! I do not have the words to express what I felt nor what it was like. There was one very critical, most mind blowing lesson that I learned at the end of those seventy-two-hours.

"I TALK TOO MUCH"!

Cynthia went to live with her sister in Charlotte while I was away. The banksters took our home, six acres of land, and car. But! Not my 'Will'! Hey! Guess who was the only person that wrote me letters and even put funds on my account while away in school? I was able to purchase much-needed shoes. And when I got out of school two people gave $500.00 each to help me get my life started again?

One was my Aunt Janice Witherspoon Hoover. She is a very loving and kind hearted aunt. Janice's father was the radio hit Disc Jockey name Joy Boy!; On WGIV out of Charlotte, N.C.! Of course that was many years ago! And the other person was my youngest sister, Joyce!

Years have passed; Cynthia and I are making the best of our new relation-ship. It continues to sail the high seas. We were stumbling around in the dark for a while, still living together but somewhat individual lives. We did what we could to make sense of everything without going our separate ways. It was challenging. But we hung in there. You see, some relation-ships do not have to make 3rd-dimensional sense. All that is needed is joy, happiness, and peace of mind! Oh! Guess which one of my five best men called the other day? Carter McClain!

Alright now, it is June of 2015 and I have graduated from school. With those funds that I had received, I bought a 1997 Chevy Pickup truck, and started a business recycling pallets. When the timing chain broke in February 2016, I got a job driving a forklift at Black & Decker. Seven months later I got fired, purchased a car and moved us out within the first year. In September 2016 I got a job as a Material Handler with Safe Fleet. We rented single rooms and slept on the floor until April 2017, when we rented a one-bedroom apartment in Mt. Holly N.C.

While driving home one afternoon from Safe Fleet, I passed a lady walking down Hyw-49, a country road, coming out of South Carolina. I turned around, stopped and offered her a ride. The lady looked rather tired from walking, hot, and quite sweaty! She stood for a moment staring at me, and proceeded to accept my offer. This is how I met the soft spoken, witty, and quite visually inspiring, Adrienne Turner.

I quit Safe Fleet around May 2017, and cried all the way back to where Cynthia and I were living, and still sleeping on the floor. In May I started driving for UBER! They let me go in December after finalizing my background check and realizing that I had been labeled a felon, by America's corrupt federal government. I had a 4.6 Star rating. Weeks later I got a job washing dishes at Famous Toastery. This is where I met Professor Lucas Giglio. The reincarnation of my childhood best friend, Shelby Leon Porter. In January 2018 I left Famous Toastery and on Febuary 4th, 2018 I started driving a 26ft. box truck for Global Logistics. This is when I met Gregory & Eric Foushee, the owners. I am still a driver for Global Logistics today, September 2020.

One day at or around August of 2017, through a dating service called Match.com, I met my Twin Flame, the lovely, considerate, kind-hearted, and beautiful Carole, spelled with an 'E,' D. Rose. LOL! Carole re-introduced to me that which had been lost from my life for over fifty years. A true child-like 'Romance'! She rekindled a flame within me that made my life appear magical.

An emotion fired up in my heart that I had not felt since being introduced to my junior high school sweetheart. Do you remember who that was? I was mesmerized, infatuated, and hypnotized once again! We have been the closes of friends now for over three years. And the odds are, we will be for the rest of our life!

It was not long and Cynthia & I moved into a two-bedroom; May of 2019 and paid off the car in Feb. of 2020. We finally purchased a bed.

I consider myself an advancing man! Conscious and a multi-dimensional Being; in a hue-man body, having a hue-man experience.

Since I am playing my role in this particular body, I realized that the name of its earthly race had been stripped or lost. So I decided that I had the right to identify with whatever race I want, of course, without being stupid about it. I mean, come on, I am not Japanese! Or am I? I decided to study Black History to determine what this body's most recent racial origin could have been. Since African American, Coon, Colored, Abeed, Black, Nigger, Negro, are 'NOT' races, I approached the study of blackamoor or the Moor. Did you know that the Moorish Empire fought their way into Spain and ruled for over eight-hundred years? The Moor's advances in mathematics, astronomy, art, and agriculture helped propel Europe out of the Dark Ages and into the Renaissance.

Education was universal in Moorish Spain, while at that same time in other areas of Christian Europe, 99 percent of the population was illiterate, and even some Kings could neither read nor write.

This information caught my attention. So, I decided from that day forward, my race will be Moor, and my nationality, American! I am a Moorish-American! Tell me something. Have you ever wondered why people from Europe are not, European-American? Since the original Moors spoke Arabic, I thought having an Arabic name would be nice. So I looked at some Arabic names and settled with Quadama Fareed Azzam ALi. I like that vibrational tone! As 'MORE' time passed, get it? *(Pun intended!)* I created and filed at the court house, a certificate of live birth in my new Moorish name.

Not long after, I came to think, since I had acquired so much information on so many different subjects in my life, I began to see myself as a qualified teacher. Who says that one must attend some university; acquire a piece of paper from some recognized academic facility before esteeming themselves worthy of the title 'Maestro,' 'Teacher'! The word "doctor" is the agentive noun of the Latin verb docere (do-ke-re), which means TO TEACH or EL MAESTRO. Thus how I acquired the nickname Doctor ALi.

In life, you never know who you are going to meet or why you met them. This is why we should always apply positive meanings to every encounter.

We should always be willing to learn and teach, be helped, and help; to receive and give! In this brief introduction, I could not possibly share with you all of the people that have meant so much to me in my entire life. Friends like David McNealy and Billy Morris – my childhood bullies; Don Taylor, Stanley Westmorland & Bobby Ray – we all grew up living on Jefferson Davis St. in Charlotte, N.C. Mia and Renata Freeman; the Hemphill, Presley, and Robichaud families. Lucas Giglio; the reincarnation of my best friend, Shelby Leon Porter; Zackuary Gehring, one of many red-headed, Scorpio males that have play interesting roles at various times in my life; Rodney Lytle (Bubba), a man that if I did not know better, I would believe that we were best friends in another life; And finally but not the least or last, GrandMaster Wayne Lewis – my martial arts instructor! A knowledgeable, friendly, and the most kind-hearted man anyone could ever meet! Oh yea! Master Lewis use to be one of Chuck Norris's body guards.

Hey, wait a minute! Remember, I told you that I passed out many fliers and business cards while pushing my MLM business? Well, one of the many places I worked as an Armed Security Officer was Clinton College in Rock Hill, S.C. That was around 2010. I made sure every student knew about my health products. Well, one of those students held on to my business card? Her name is SeQuenn Fitzgerald! SeQuenna had been through much h and pain during her life experience. And the follov years did not offer her much to brag about either.

I know all of this because SeQuenna contacted me and shared much of her life's story. I learned that SeQuenna's dream had been cut short because she never had the money to attend a Cosmetology School; but this lady is an excellent beautician! I have seen a few magnificent pictures of her creative and professional hairstyling skills! One day, very soon, I see SeQueena's life dream coming true!

Now, back to the Carroll family and Anndreena. You thought that I had forgotten, didn't you? Well, down through the years I stayed in touch with the entire Carroll family; helping whenever I could and learning from the experience. Ms. Della the mother; Dartanian & Arron, the brothers. The family is now very much indoctrinated with life benefiting health principles and spiritually enlightening Meta-Physics. And Anndreena has adopted the nick-name, QueenDreena! Alright! This is the big one. Guess who I met by chance while at Catawba Men's Club. Dartanian's father, Mr. Mason Mackins! Now, what are the odds of that?

Some people are ripples in your life and some people are waves. Only a few are Tidal-Waves! We are all energy and are all connected in this big adventurous journey called, LIFE!

Now, just as soon as I receive my 'Law of Attraction' 'unds, I plan to help as many young people fulfill their 's dream as possible, and I intend to assist them in 'izing whether this life is real or just a ride!

One of the great challenges in life is having enough information about a subject to think that you are right but not enough knowledge about a subject to know that you are wrong!

By: Neil deGrasse Tyson
Edited By: Dr. ALi

P.S. Do you remember the witty lady that I picked up, walking down Hyw-49, out of South Carolina? What I did not tell you is that she is... 'alto, encantador, e impresionante en apariencia! Because of her love for her religious beliefs, there was a respectful border kept between us. She helped Cynthia and I move into our first one-bedroom apartment. A few months past and Ms. Adrienne Turner moved away!

Through the Exoteric Order of Melchizedek, a Comic Priesthood, Dr. ALi is an Initiate in this ancient mystical mystery school of enlightenment!

04/09/2020 – 09/14/2020
Written By: Dr. ALi

126

ABOUT THE AUTHOR'S FAMILY LIFE

My familyship was one of extraordinarily personal discovery! We all agreed to sail together on this ship before we crossed over the veil of forgetfulness and into this realm of density. Most do not accept this perspective about life's journey, and that is alright. But they can still rise in frequency tone. There are many paths back into greater light. My story is just one of many family adventures.

My mother was my very first girlfriend. During her incarnation, she played her role very, very well. She got angry, revealed a mean side, showed selfishness, was shy and was imbued with a few insecurities. Yet Mama Cora, (as the grandchildren called her), was loving, nurturing, caring, compassionate, bold, brave, and even daring. Hitting a lady was learned from my father's example. No, I did not grow up hitting ladies. Well, maybe just one. You can guess who that might have been as you continue reading. My father played the role of a mean, unreasonable, illogical, angry, sickly, wife-beating, and emotionally confused, smoker. We did not get along very well. Actually, he did not get along with anyone well. I am the youngest of six children. Yes, that is right! The youngest, not the baby! From oldest to youngest, my two brothers, Richard and Howard-*(Adlee-Akbar), and* three sisters, Delores, Estella, and Joyce. I do not believe in using the term 'Half.' Whoever started that term should be slapped!

You should be quite familiar with Joyce already. Joyce and I were always fussing, arguing, and physically fighting. My three oldest siblings were from my mother's first marriage to Richard Perry Sr. He transitioned early in their life, leaving them without a father and their mother without a husband. Our mother was frightened, alone, and with three children to house, clothe, and feed at that time. The next two youngest siblings, and I, were from our mother's second marriage to William Douglas Owens Sr. We three grew up in the same household.

Richard, Howard-*(Adlee-Akbar)*, and I were never close because they were much older, and by the time I was born, they were married, with children of their own. My oldest brother Richard was always happy. He gave me counsel on integrity, which I still remember and follow to this very day. I have never in my life seen Richard upset, angry or in an argument with anyone. When I was very young, Howard-*(Adlee-Akbar)* took me to Washington, D.C. I remember having a wonderful time. For Adlee-Akbar, to take me with him on a trip meant the world to me! That was a very kind and thoughtful gesture towards his youngest brother. My oldest sister Delores, for some odd reason, I always viewed her as my aunt or cousin. I never understood why. As we were talking one day, I referred to our mother as 'My Mother'! Ouch! That must have hurt. When I later realized my careless mistake of reference, I apologized.

I learned from Delores that I could study, educate myself, increase my intelligence, and become what some consider as smart.

From my sister Estella, remember her? I learned that I do not need to give my earned income in a tithe or offering to any organized religion, just for some preacher, evangelist, elder, bishop, guru, sage, or swami, to tell me what I can or cannot do nor what type of life I can or cannot live! And finally, from my sister Joyce. She taught me that I am not always 'RIGHT'! ~ LIAR, I AM! (Just joking!) How right she was. And that, no matter how tripolar one may be or how much you may be at odds with someone, that same individual can still show you kindness, compassion, and love. Are we still talking about Joyce?

And when everyone else has turned their backs on you, the one individual that is the most unlikely may prove to be your closes friend. Especially when you need someone the most!

Wait, let us go back for a moment to 'THE REVEREND WILLIAM DOUGLAS OWENS SR.'! Please do not feel antagonistic toward 'THE REVEREND WILLIAM DOUGLAS OWENS SR.'! Why? Because he played one of the most challenging, heart-wrenching, and humiliating roles. He did a spectacular job, earning him, at least I think, the award of 'Best Actor'! What I am saying is that because of 'THE REVEREND WILLIAM DOUGLAS OWENS SR.'! I developed into 'THE MAN THAT I AM TODAY'! LOL! I know your laughing! So am I!

I saw my mother show favoritism towards her children, and I could sometimes see in the eyes and feel the hurt in some of my siblings' hearts. I am sure there festered much anger and resentment down through the years. Which I think some never got over. For this type of treatment, I do apologize to all of my siblings. Our mother performed her role the best that she could. Well played, Mama Cora! We must remember that she was only playing the character that we all ask of her before we crossed over the veil of forgetfulness; into this third density, immersion, holographic, illusion, we call Gaia or Earth. My mother worked at Jack's Cookies, located on Louise Ave. in Charlotte, N.C.! Should I be saying 'OUR'?

Mama Cora received an Achilles Tendon injury one night at work. She never went to the doctor. A few days later, I witnessed my mother crawl on her hands and knees from her bedroom to the bathroom. She did this to wash and get ready for work! Now that was determination! She could have chosen to stay at home! But Nooooo! Not Mama Cora!

To this very day, I go in to work whether I want to or not; for better or worse, rich or poor, sick or healthy, until death. Wait a minute! My mother taught me that, "The only legitimate reason to stay out of work is if you are DEAD!" That's right; even death is no excuse to stay out of work! You can die on the job!

At least you will be earning some money until you finally 'Kick the Bucket'! I have always wondered why everyone kick buckets when they die? But all in all, my mother taught me to have a 'STRONG WILL'; WISDOM; A 'DETERMINED MIND'; A 'LOVING & CARING HEART'!

THE REVEREND WILLIAM DOUGLAS OWENS SR.! I get such a kick out of saying that! Can I repeat it? With emphasis?

THE REVEREND WILLIAM DOUGLAS OWENS SR.! @&*$#@ THAT FELT SO GOOD! Now, the role of THE REVEREND WILLIAM… alright, enough! Now, the role that my father took on was more humiliating, shameful, and demeaning than any other family member's role.

From the title, you already know that he was a preacher. Baptist, if you please. This man played a very unreasonable, illogical, mean, angry, violent, and mentally disturbed husband and father. Girlfriend! I mean, the man played his role like a champ! He had to have played this role many times before in other incarnations to be that good!

He was very much tripolar, as was my youngest sister. I have been told that he was just like his father. Really? I sure hope I am not!

Talking about a split personality. I never knew which father was coming out of the bedroom. All three of my fathers were on many prescribed psychotropic drugs. No, not Joyce. She was/is strong as a bull, as our mother used to say. Maybe this could have been the cause of our father's weird and strange behavior? Really? NOOOOO! That man was 'Simplemente loco'! Wait a minute now! Hold on! Remember, it took one of strong will, exceptional character, and extraordinary strength of mind to handle such an important, responsible, and challenging role!

From 'THE REVEREND WILLIAM DOUGLAS OWENS SR.,' I sequestered the art of 'Public Speaking'! Now I am telling you that man could preach a sermon! He did not say much of anything in his sermons, But! The performance was very exciting and invigorating! I also learned about the power behind 'Self-Expression'~! Oh! And I learned not to ever, never, physically, hit a girl, lady, or woman! Even if she is beating the #@&% out of you! (Run Forrest Run!)

The entire family and I all agreed on the roles we played during this incarnation. There are no victims here. Only highly evolved eternal beings playing particular roles in such an elaborate, mind-boggling, and sophisticated game! Of course, this is only my perspective, nothing more, and nothing less!

Congratulations to everyone on such a marvelous performance! We successfully developed the most pretentious, unloving, cruel, jealous, resentful, vengeful, angry, emotionally disturbed, and mean spirited dysfunctional family ever! I am forever grateful to have been allowed participation in such a challenging, creative, and adventurous clan, presenting the ultimate opportunity for a tremendous advancement in spiritual growth.

Remember, this adventure made us all the wonderful, loving, caring, and successful adults we are today! LOL!

I LOVE YOU ALL!

I AM, Dr. ALi, and I create my own destiny! ~*Selah!*

Made in the USA
Middletown, DE
27 May 2021

40484913R10225